Overcoming the Neutral Zone Trap

OVERCOMING
THE NEUTRAL ZONE

TRAP

HOCKEY'S AGENTS OF CHANGE

UNIVERSITY *of* **ALBERTA** PRESS

Cheryl A. MacDonald &
Jonathon R.J. Edwards
Editors

Published by

University of Alberta Press
1–16 Rutherford Library South
11204 89 Avenue NW
Edmonton, Alberta, Canada T6G 2J4
Amiskwacîwâskahican | Treaty 6 | Métis Territory
uap.ualberta.ca

LIBRARY AND ARCHIVES CANADA
CATALOGUING IN PUBLICATION

Title: Overcoming the neutral zone trap : hockey's
   agents of change / Cheryl A. MacDonald and
   Jonathon R.J. Edwards, editors
Names: MacDonald, Cheryl A., editor. | Edwards,
   Jonathon R. J., editor.
Description: Includes bibliographical references.
Identifiers: Canadiana (print) 20210201738 |
   Canadiana (ebook) 20210201746 |
   ISBN 9781772125795 (softcover) |
   ISBN 9781772125887 (EPUB) |
   ISBN 9781772125894 (PDF)
Subjects: LCSH: Hockey—Social aspects—Canada. |
   LCSH: Hockey—Social aspects—United States.
Classification: LCC GV848.4.C3 094 2021 |
   DDC 796.9620971—dc23

First edition, first printing, 2021.
First printed and bound in Canada by Houghton
Boston Printers, Saskatoon, Saskatchewan.
Copyediting by Kirsten Craven.
Proofreading by Mary Lou Roy.

University of Alberta Press is committed to
protecting our natural environment. As part of
our efforts, this book is printed on Enviro Paper: it
contains 100% post-consumer recycled fibres and is
acid- and chlorine-free.

University of Alberta Press gratefully acknowledges
the support received for its publishing program from
the Government of Canada, the Canada Council for
the Arts, and the Government of Alberta through
the Alberta Media Fund.

This book has been published with the help of
a grant from the Canadian Federation for the
Humanities and Social Sciences, through the Awards
to Scholarly Publications Program, using funds
provided by the Social Sciences and Humanities
Research Council of Canada.

We dedicate this book to Dr. Colin D. Howell of Saint Mary's University in Halifax, Nova Scotia. In 2001, Dr. Howell established the Hockey Conference, one of the inspirations for this book. As he retires from his role in academia, this dedication is a token of our gratitude for his service to the hockey scholar community.

Contents

Preface

CHERYL A. MACDONALD & JONATHON R.J. EDWARDS

ACTORS (e.g., players, administrators, parents, coaches, stakeholders, and officials) within a sporting environment attempt to control situations by establishing and implementing policies, procedures, and rules that implicitly and explicitly create norms that ultimately legitimize the sport. For example, ice hockey (henceforth identified as hockey) in North America is predominately played by white masculine hockey players, or the two most legitimate ways to get to the National Hockey League (NHL) are through the Canadian Hockey League (CHL) and the National Collegiate Athletics Association (NCAA), as indicated by Edwards and Washington (2015). These norms create a closed system where external forces (e.g., social, political, economic, technological, and legal) are shielded from the actors within the internal environment, which restricts these actors from adapting and changing (DiMaggio & Powell, 1983; Edwards, Mason, & Washington, 2009). Specifically, hockey in North America operates as an institutionalized sporting environment where inclusionary and exclusionary norms are created. This specific type of sport system can be understood through the analogy of the neutral zone trap.

The *neutral zone trap* is an on-ice defensive tactic that is employed as a means of preventing the offensive team (i.e., the team with the puck)

Figure P.1: The Neutral Zone Trap

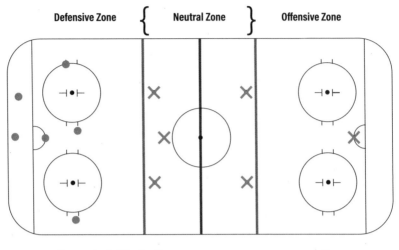

from entering into the defensive team's end to score a goal. The defensive players position themselves in the neutral zone in a manner that inhibits the offensive team from gathering speed and then disarms the player in possession of the puck (see Figure P.I). Put differently, the central area of the ice surface is closed off to the opposing team and a boundary is created.

Within the context of this book, the neutral zone trap comprises the defensive institutional norms (i.e., the players labelled *X* in Figure P.I) that restrict the marginalized offence (i.e., the players labelled with a shaded O in Figure P.I) from succeeding. The boundaries established in the neutral zone trap can be penetrated or overcome when the offensive players, which we call *agents of change*, are able to mobilize up the middle of the ice and disrupt the trap, which is interpreted metaphorically as institutional norms.

Evidence of attempts to overcome barriers in hockey exist in the development and growth of organizations such as the You Can Play Project and Black Girl Hockey Club, which seek to normalize the participation of racial, sexual, and gender minority groups that have typically been misunderstood and excluded in the community. One complete example of how institutional norms are created and overcome can be understood through the lengthy career and eventual firing of hockey media pundit Don Cherry. Cherry was a divisive voice in Canadian hockey culture on the television program *Hockey Night in Canada*, where he would make inflammatory comments about women, concussions, and violence, among others. Allain (2015) argues that, since 1982, Cherry used his platform to "valorize the experiences of white working-class men—men that he...feels are at risk from new social forces (for example, feminism, immigration, and the movement away from physical labour) that look to devalue their cultural positions" (pp. 109–110). In short, Don Cherry helped to establish a neutral zone trap that normalized beliefs about who has value in the hockey community.

Despite still having a tenable cult following, Cherry was swiftly removed from his position in late 2019. Although Cherry has perhaps always made contentious comments on television about subjects like race and gender, the one that led to his termination was an accusation that recent immigrants to Canada allegedly ignore Remembrance Day and the symbolic meaning of the poppy. His employer, Sportsnet (a division of Rogers Communications), issued an apology for the remarks, noting that Cherry's comments were not in keeping with the network's philosophy that sport should bring people together (Sportsnet, 2019). In this instance, Sportsnet acted as an agent of change that opened up a laneway for the inclusion of the individuals that Cherry, a gatekeeper, had previously disparaged.

This book is a collection of essays that sheds light on agents of change in hockey who are confronting or have overcome the neutral zone trap. In other words, the essays address the pursuit of inclusion and acceptance for those typically excluded (Allain, 2008, 2012; Robidoux, 2001; Szto, 2016). The book grapples with the established norms that create and reinforce stigmas in hockey and the broader society. The combination of stories and research illustrates how different empirical settings disrupt the institutional arrangements (or "break down the trap") as a means of implementing change within hockey. It is through these uncommon voices that the barriers begin to come down. In the broader societal context, similar institutional barriers relate to challenges faced by Indigenous communities in Canada and the Truth and Reconciliation Commission (TRC), shortcomings in gender equity and equality, and equality for individuals with disabilities. These issues are not new to society, yet they continue to be perpetuated. Nonetheless, many of these minority groups and individuals have increasingly begun to speak out, which is disrupting restrictive norms.

The inspiration for this book came from two sources. First, the theme of the ninth International Hockey Conference—a biennial academic forum—was diversity and inclusion. The event successfully brought together guest speakers who identified as women, as ethnic minorities, as openly gay, and as having experienced disability—all agents of change who have had to confront the neutral zone trap. The conference took place after the NHL reimagined its Hockey Is for Everyone initiative, which seeks to make hockey a "safe, positive and inclusive environment for players and families regardless of race, color, religion, national origin, gender identity or expression, disability, sexual orientation and socio-economic status" (NHL, 2019, para. 1). In our capacities as both hockey scholars and fans, we share this commitment to legitimizing hockey in all its forms. As such, we were motivated to contribute to broader social context through the lens of hockey, and to continue ongoing conversations about diversity.

Our second source of inspiration was the writing of Stevens and Holman (2013), who noted that, although hockey has increasingly been taken up as an academic subject of study since the 1990s, there is a dearth of what they call "rinkside" scholarship. In their words:

The bulk of the scholarly attention to ice hockey has come from historians and literary scholars whose interests focus on the lost or misunderstood meanings of signal past events in the sport. They have been concerned chiefly with the ways that hockey represents symbolically and figuratively—the identities of the communities that sponsor the game. This literature is rich and growing and intellectually profound...The field of hockey studies would benefit from getting closer to the game, from making connections with those who experience the sport daily or weekly at rinkside. (pp. 251–252)

We have partly answered their call for further research in this volume by assembling an eclectic patchwork of scholarly endeavours and critical autobiographical pieces, some empirical and some symbolic, that we hope will satisfy readers in both the sporting and academic communities, including those who occupy the space in which the two overlap.

There is a wide variety of subject matter in this book, including the various struggles of minority hockey players, the organizational legitimacy of teams and leagues, matters of gender and sexuality, mental health, and identity construction. The book does not need to be read in any particular order, although we have attempted to organize it into a sequence of chapters that supports a cohesive set of stories about how hockey's agents of change have taken charge of their offensive roles and broken through, or at least challenged, the neutral zone trap. As such, we have divided twelve individual essays into sections of four that respectively examine gaining access to participation and support, challenging norms and assumptions, and pushing boundaries within the context of hockey in North America.

The first four chapters in the volume showcase the disruption of norms and values in the hockey community. Professional athlete Cameron Braes and sport management scholar Jonathon Edwards lead off in Chapter 1 with a focus on the viability of U SPORTS men's hockey as a pathway to professional hockey. Braes and Edwards contend that, despite the popular belief that major junior and American collegiate hockey are the only ways to move to the professional level, men's university hockey in Canada is proving itself as a legitimate route that increasingly sees its graduates sign professional contracts. In keeping with the idea of alternative approaches, author Angie Abdou shares her experience in Chapter 2 as an offbeat hockey parent who has met resistance when she is critical of the potentially harmful aspects of hockey culture on her son. Abdou describes some of the pushback she has received for going against the grain and also divulges that she has found an unlikely collaborator in Karl Subban, who has three sons in professional hockey.

Chapter 3 bridges Abdou's line of thought by further demonstrating the opposition that can present itself in response to alternative discourse in the hockey community. Written by sport scholars Catherine Houston, Kyle Rich, Tavis Smith, and Ann Pegoraro, this chapter investigates the public reception of two viral exchanges on Twitter: Nora Loreto's critique of the crowdfunding campaign in response to the Humboldt Broncos bus crash in Saskatchewan, and Daniel Carcillo's commentary on his negative experiences with hazing and violence in junior hockey. Carcillo also makes an appearance in Chapter 4, authored by media scholar Brett Pardy, on mental health in hockey. Pardy wraps up the section on challenging hockey's norms by highlighting the ways in which NHL players publicly endorse solutions to mental health issues, without necessarily practising these solutions themselves.

The next four chapters in the volume centralize opportunities to participate in ice hockey and the challenges associated with obtaining various kinds of support. In Chapter 5, human kinetics scholar Chelsey Leahy discusses the subject of access to participation and support in her piece on the limited availability of competition, funding, and other resources in Canadian university women's hockey. Leahy posits that the gendered structure of Canadian university (U SPORTS) ice hockey contributes to the athletes' understandings of the amount of support they receive and to what they are entitled. In keeping with support for women's hockey, in Chapter 6, sport sociologists Noah Underwood and Judy Davidson examine the US Women's National Team's threatened boycott of the World Championships in 2017. Underwood and Davidson unpack how the team's use of labour tactics, including a vigorous social media campaign, ultimately created an unconventional pathway to increased funding for the development of girls' and women's hockey from USA Hockey.

Paralympic athlete Kieran Block picks up the concept of access in Chapter 7 and pivots to the ways in which official definitions of disability complicate an athlete's qualification for the Canadian para hockey (sledge hockey) team. An alumnus of the Canadian Hockey League's major junior system, Block shares the story of how a near-fatal cliff diving accident led him to sledge hockey and how his options for participation were limited, given both the availability of elite competition and the nature of his (dis)ability. Vicky Paraschak, a sport management scholar, maintains the theme of access to participation in Chapter 8 with a discussion of hockey's role in Canada's Truth and Reconciliation Commission. Specifically, one of the TRC's Calls to Action suggests drawing more attention to Indigenous participation in sports and Paraschak has produced a chapter that highlights that community's participation in hockey and the barriers that prevent them from taking part.

The last section of four chapters in the volume features a contemporary subject of enquiry in hockey—masculinity and sexual orientation. Sport sociologist Roger LeBlanc leads the section in Chapter 9 with a contextualization of the silence around homosexuality in the NHL. He uses existing research on masculinity and sport to construct an interview with a fictional closeted athlete in an attempt to give voice to what potential closeted athletes may think and feel. In light of the silences surrounding the NHL, Cheryl MacDonald—also a sport sociologist—seeks to shed light in Chapter 10 on openly gay athlete Brock McGillis, who played professional hockey outside of the NHL. In this collaborative chapter, MacDonald reports on an in-depth interview with McGillis during which they review his career and analyze how his experiences might provide insight on the reasons that a closeted elite-level men's hockey player may not feel safe coming out.

In Chapter 11, sport sociologist William Bridel flips the topic of masculinity and sexuality in hockey on its head with a personal account of life as a non-hockey player. Bridel explains that his identity as a figure skater and young gay man growing up in Canada frequently existed in opposition to masculine heterosexual norms, which had significant implications for his sense of self and belonging in a culture so focused on hockey. In the final essay, Chapter 12, socio-historical sport scholar Fred Mason takes up portrayals of men's hockey players as manly and aggressive in his treatment of two novels that feature the sport's "enforcers." By dissecting the identity of the enforcers in Lynn Coady's *The Antagonist* (2011) and Jeff Lemire's *Roughneck* (2017), Mason unpacks both the stereotypical and humanizing aspects of each character, suggesting that the construction of such an identity runs deeper than its surface suggests.

References

Allain, K.A. (2008). "Real fast and tough": The construction of Canadian hockey masculinity. *Sociology of Sport Journal, 25*(4), 462–481.

Allain, K.A. (2012). *"The way we play": An examination of men's elite-level hockey, masculinity and Canadian national identity* (Unpublished doctoral dissertation). Trent University, Peterborough, ON.

Allain, K.A. (2015). "A good Canadian boy": Crisis masculinity, Canadian national identity, and nostalgic longings in Don Cherry's *Coach's Corner. International Journal of Canadian Studies, 52,* 107–132.

Coady, L. (2011). *The antagonist.* New York: Vintage.

DiMaggio, P.J., & Powell, W.W. (1983). The iron cage revisited: Institutional isomorphism and collective rationality in organizational fields. *American Sociological Review, 48*(2), 147–160.

Edwards, J.R., Mason, D.S., & Washington, M. (2009). Institutional mechanisms, government funding, and provincial sport organizations. *International Journal of Sport Management and Marketing, 6*(2), 128–149.

Edwards, J.R., & Washington, M. (2015). Establishing a "safety net": Exploring the emergence and maintenance of College Hockey Inc. and the legitimizing strategies of NCAA Division I universities and colleges. *Journal of Sport Management, 29*(3), 291–304.

Lemire, J. (2017). *Roughneck*. Toronto: Simon & Schuster.

NHL. (2019). Hockey is for everyone. http://www.nhl.com/community/hockey-is-for-everyone

Robidoux, M.A. (2001). *Men at play: A working understanding of professional hockey*. Montreal: McGill-Queen's University Press.

Sportsnet. (2019). Sportsnet announces Don Cherry to immediately step down from HNIC. https://www.sportsnet.ca/hockey/nhl/don-cherry-immediately-step-hockey-night-canada/

Stevens, J., & Holman, A.C. (2013). Rinkside: New scholarly studies on ice hockey and society. *Sport in Society: Cultures, Commerce, Media, Politics, 16*(3), 251–253.

Szto, C. (2016). #LOL at multiculturalism: Reactions to Hockey Night in Canada Punjabi from the Twitterverse. *Sociology of Sport Journal, 33*(3), 208–218.

Acknowledgements

WE WOULD LIKE TO TAKE THE TIME TO THANK certain individuals, without whom this book would only have been a daydream. First, we give thanks to our contributors, without whom there would be no book at all. It has been a pleasure watching each chapter come together, and it was touching to see the authors reference one another in their chapters—this is true collaboration. Second, we express our gratitude to our colleagues, near and far, for their valuable input on the manuscript: Kristi Allain, Jason Blake, Ryan Hamilton, Cory Kulczycki, Fred Mason, Bryan Mortensen, Erin Morris, Ann Pegoraro, and Charlene Weaving. We would also like to thank Mat Buntin at University of Alberta Press for his guidance throughout the publication process. Cheryl would like to acknowledge her doctoral supervisor, Dr. Marc Lafrance, for his ongoing mentorship and friendship. Lastly, our most heartfelt thanks go out to our families and friends who have supported us in this endeavour and in our careers more broadly.

I

Challenging Hockey's Norms

1

The Forgotten Canadian League

The Voices of U SPORTS Men's Hockey Players and the Legitimacy of University Hockey in Canada

CAMERON BRAES & JONATHON R.J. EDWARDS

TWO HOCKEY ORGANIZATIONS that are recognized as affecting a sixteen-to-twenty-one-year-old hockey player's pathway to a professional level of competition are the National Collegiate Athletic Association (NCAA), and the Canadian Hockey League (CHL or major junior). Edwards and Washington (2015) identified NCAA Division I and the CHL as two equally legitimate pathways to playing professional hockey. The term *legitimacy* (also identified as legitimate) is defined as "a generalized perception or assumption that the actions of an entity are desirable, proper, or appropriate within some socially constructed system of norms, values, beliefs, and definitions" (Suchman, 1995, p. 574). Absent from Edwards and Washington's (2015) identification of two legitimate pathways to professional hockey is a discussion around the legitimacy of U SPORTS as a pathway to a professional hockey career, which is the focus of this chapter. U SPORTS men's hockey has been identified as the place where a "player's career goes to die" (Chard, 2013).

The most talented Canadian players that continue with hockey will reach a key transition point typically around the age of twelve, where they need to choose between the CHL or NCAA Division I route (Edwards & Washington, 2015). This is a critical decision for elite Canadian hockey players as, generally, players are not able to do both routes. On rare occasions a player may decide to leave the NCAA Division I pathway and pursue the CHL pathway; however, this decision cannot be made in reverse order. For those players who choose the CHL pathway, there comes a second transition point where an elite CHL player has to decide between turning professional or playing U SPORTS men's hockey. Subsequently, the third transition point at this time would be retirement from competitive hockey.

Commonly, U SPORTS men's hockey has been viewed negatively among junior hockey players (aged 16–21). A study conducted by Chard (2013) explained that U SPORTS is "perceived as a league for relative failures, confirming its status as an inferior brand. Perhaps this perception of inferior quality is related to the lack of promotion of the successes of [U SPORTS] athletes" (p. 336). Furthermore, Chard (2013) found that the consensus among major junior hockey players was that playing in U SPORTS was not viewed as a way to advance their careers toward professional hockey. Similar sentiments were expressed by Edwards (2012), who stated that U SPORTS is not a legitimate pathway to the National Hockey League (NHL), "[as U SPORTS players are] more likely to play in European professional leagues or to get a career outside of hockey" (p. 11). Chard (2013) concluded that the current view of U SPORTS is that "the relevance of [U SPORTS] is greatly affected by the perception that players' hockey dreams are over once they are playing in the Canadian university league" (p. 335). Therefore, the purpose of this chapter is to explore current and former hockey players' perceptions of U SPORTS men's hockey as a means of gaining insight into how legitimacy is maintained by the member schools as it pertains to a pathway to professional hockey.

One of the challenges facing U SPORTS men's hockey is the perception that, if any player had interest in post-secondary education and hockey advancement, they would have chosen the NCAA Division I pathway (Chard, 2013; Edwards & Washingon, 2015; Gruneau & Whitson, 1993). As it is explained by College Hockey Inc. (2017a), "College hockey, in short, is the fastest growing development path for the NHL" (para. 4). While Chard, Hyatt, and Foster (2013) explained that within Canada "an argument can be made that despite the significance of the sport to its citizenry, almost the entire country ignores intercollegiate men's hockey" (p. 246). This is an interesting concept, because the CHL and its players are held in such high regard as the best development league in the world (CHL, 2018), while U SPORTS, which is predominately made up of CHL players, is seen as an inferior brand of hockey (Chard, 2013).

The Key Organizations

Canadian Hockey League

The CHL is widely considered the premiere hockey league in the world for junior-aged players; indeed, the league produces more NHL players than any other development league (Hockey Canada, 2011). Since 1969, the CHL has produced over 50 per cent of the players that played in the NHL (Ontario Hockey League [OHL], 2010). As a developmental league, the CHL resembles the NHL in terms of policies and actions (i.e., number of games, travel, policies, draft), and professional approach to the treatment of players (Edwards, 2012). Academically, the CHL offers a scholarship package that covers tuition and books at a Canadian educational institution for every year a player plays in the CHL. It is important to note that the CHL scholarship is administered at the university level and does not require that the player continue to play hockey in order to receive the scholarship (Edwards, 2012). This means once a player has played a season in the CHL, they have earned one year of paid tuition and books without the ability for the CHL to rescind the scholarship due to player performance, injury, or lack of community involvement.

NCAA Division I Men's Hockey

The equivalent to U SPORTS and the direct competitor of the CHL is the NCAA Division I men's hockey league. The NCAA is a multi-billion-dollar institution that is the governing body of university and college athletics in the US (Edwards & Washington, 2015) and men's ice hockey is one of the sports the NCAA oversees. Collegiate athletics in the US are divided into three competitive levels, Divisions I, II, and III (College Hockey Inc., 2017b). For the purpose of this chapter, Division I of the NCAA will be referenced. This is due to the fact that typically players that are competing in Division III do not get the opportunity to make it to a professional level, as the competition level is limited.

The NCAA Division I men's hockey provides a platform for Canadian players to pursue a professional hockey career, including the NHL, while receiving a world-class education (College Hockey Inc., 2017b). In the 2016–2017 NHL season, 32 per cent of the players were former NCAA Division I hockey players (College Hockey Inc., 2017a). A study done by Krukowska et al. (2007) projected that the average cost of a four-year education at an NCAA Division I university or college without scholarship would be an estimated $187,936 USD. The thought of earning a "full ride" scholarship while playing NCAA hockey at the same time is incredibly attractive from a financial point of view. The NCAA classifies a "full ride" scholarship as covering the costs of tuition, books, fees, and residence (NCAA, 2016).

U SPORTS

U SPORTS is the governing body of university sport in Canada. Ice hockey is one sport that falls under the U SPORTS umbrella. U SPORTS men's hockey consists of thirty-three universities across three regions that compete for the U SPORTS championship, the David Johnston

University Cup. The three regions involved in men's hockey include Atlantic University Sport (AUS), Ontario University Athletics (OUA), and Canada West (U SPORTS, 2018). The CHL is a feeder system for U SPORTS due largely to the CHL scholarship package. Krukowska et al. (2007) reported the projected cost (e.g., tuition, books, residence, and travel) of a four-year education at a U SPORTS university would amount to $53,610 CAD. Fortunately, for U SPORTS men's hockey players who previously played in the CHL, tuition and books are covered as part of the CHL scholarship.

The CHL scholarship is flexible in terms of allowing players to try professional hockey (e.g., American Hockey League [AHL], or the East Coast Hockey League [ECHL]) before accessing their scholarship (Western Hockey League [WHL], 2016) prior to a specific date in the U SPORTS men's hockey schedule. Unless a player has signed an NHL contract, or in some cases, with a top-level European club, a CHL player can try professional hockey for a full year without any repercussions in the form of being ineligible for competing for a U SPORTS school (WHL, 2016). If a player decides to continue playing professional hockey past that first year, they will forfeit their CHL scholarship package. U SPORTS is also flexible in terms of allowing players the opportunity to come back from professional hockey and pursue an education.

Theoretical Framework

To understand the opinions and perceptions of former and current U SPORTS players, organizational legitimacy was explored. Organizations can achieve legitimacy through the perceptions of observers and stakeholders. As such, "Legitimacy emerges when organizational activities align with constituent expectations" (Lock, Filo, Kunkel, & Skinner, 2015, p. 362). Although legitimacy of an organization is produced internally, the perceptions and assumptions of the observers to the organization will regulate legitimacy (Suchman, 1995). There are various reasons why an organization would strive for legitimacy. For one, "obtaining legitimacy is important for sport organizations as it leads to the accrual of constituent support (e.g., participants, consumers, coaches, volunteers, parents)" (Lock et al., 2015, p. 362). Suchman (1995) expressed two reasons in particular that were important to address: "(a) the distinction between pursuing continuity and pursuing credibility and (b) the distinction between seeking passive support and seeking active support" (p. 574). It is important to note that legitimacy affects both how people act toward and interpret an organization (Suchman, 1995).

Types of Organizational Legitimacy

There are three different types of organizational legitimacy: pragmatic, moral, and cognitive. Suchman (1995) expressed "all three types involve a generalized perception or assumption that organizational activities are desirable, proper, or appropriate within some socially constructed system of norms, values, beliefs, and definitions" (p. 577). The first type of organizational legitimacy is pragmatic. Pragmatic legitimacy "rests on the self-interested calculations of an organization's most immediate audiences" (Suchman, 1995, p. 577). Often, this immediacy involves direct exchange between organization and audience (Suchman, 1995). The second type of organizational legitimacy is moral. Moral legitimacy "reflects a positive normative evaluation of the organization and its activities" (Suchman, 1995, p. 577). The final type of legitimacy is cognitive. Cognitive legitimacy "may involve either affirmative backing for an organization or mere acceptance of the organization as necessary or inevitable based on some taken-for-granted cultural account" (Suchman, 1995, p. 582). As such, cognitive legitimacy does not deal with an evaluation, as society accepts an organization as necessary. It is created when organizations pursue goals that society accepts as proper and desirable (Suchman, 1995). When an organization has reached "taken-for-granted status," an organization is beyond dissent (Suchman, 1995, p. 582). The three types of organizational legitimacy are defined in Table 1.1.

Table 1.1: Legitimacy Types and Definitions

Types of Legitimacy	Definition
Pragmatic Legitimacy	
Exchange	Support for organizational policies due to the policy's expected value benefit to the constituents.
Influence	Constituents support the organization not only because they believe it provides favourable exchanges, but also it is responsive to their larger interests.
Disposition	Support for an organization due to the good attributes (e.g., motives, values) constituents believe the organization has that are compatible with their own.
Moral Legitimacy	
Consequential	Relates to what an organization has accomplished based on criteria that is specific to that organization.
Procedural	Can be obtained by an organization adhering to socially formalized and accepted procedures.
Structural	People view an organization as legitimate because its structural characteristics allow it to do specific kinds of work.
Personal	Derives from the charisma of an individual leader.
Cognitive Legitimacy	
Comprehensibility	Generally, a view of the world as a messy cognitive environment, where participants struggle to organize their experiences into clear understandable thoughts.
Taken-for-Grantedness	Organizations transform disorder into a set of intersubjective givens that submerge the possibility of dissent.

Source: Suchman (1995).

Methodology

The philosophical underpinnings of qualitative inquiry are an attempt to construct an understanding of a phenomenon. One of the main focuses in qualitative research is to explore and understand the experiences and perceptions of a group of people (Kumar, 2014). Accessing potential respondents with extensive knowledge about U SPORTS was achieved through purposive sampling. The premise of purposive sampling is using a wide range of methods to find participants from a highly specific and difficult-to-reach population (Neuman, 2000).

Semi-structured phone interviews were conducted with former players who played professional hockey following their U SPORTS career and players who finished their competitive hockey careers at the U SPORTS level. Representation of the participants was focused on those players who were among the schools that had the highest number of players that have transitioned to the professional levels of competition throughout Canada. The universities with the highest number of professional athletes since 2005 were selected for this study: the University of New Brunswick (UNB; $n=32$ players), St. Francis Xavier University (ST. FX; $n=32$ players), University of Alberta (U OF A; $n=30$ players), and University of Calgary (U OF C; $n=26$ players). Open-ended and probing questions were used within the context of semi-structured interviews (Creswell, 2003; Edwards & Skinner, 2009; Patton, 2002). Interviews consisted of twenty to thirty questions, allowing flexibility for the researcher to probe further as the interview naturally transpired. The duration of the interviews ranged between twenty and forty minutes, depending on the participant's openness and responses. All interviews were audio recorded and transcribed. Ethical privacy was maintained through a coding system (e.g., Participant 1 [P1] through Participant 12 [P12]). Data saturation was achieved after twelve interviews were conducted.

Data Analysis

Data analysis for the primary and secondary data sources for this chapter consisted of a three-step process, a modified version of Miles and Huberman's (1994) five-step process. A three-step process allowed for steps two, three, and four from the Miles and Huberman (1994) process to be combined into one step. The stages used for this chapter were:

1. Familiarization
2. Thematic framework, coding, and charting
3. Interpreting

The first stage of data analysis for this research was familiarization. In this stage, the researcher became familiar with the data by means of reviewing the interview process, the transcribed data, the primary and secondary sources, and notes related to the study (Edwards & Washington, 2015).

The second stage began with developing a thematic framework that involved the researcher reviewing the transcripts from the interviews for recognizable emerging concepts. Themes arose from real-world examples participants provided during the interview process (Ryan & Bernard, 2000). Themes were also supported by secondary sources through content analysis of U SPORTS social media and websites. The researcher charted and categorized the data into coded themes. The researcher used the computer program QSR NVivo 10, which allowed for a place to organize, store, and retrieve data more efficiently (QSR International, 2018).

The third stage of data analysis for this research was interpretation. As a researcher, data interpretation was displayed by charting the results. In an effort to understand the data, an interpretivist approach was applied to the research. Creswell (2003) and Smith, Evans, and Westerbeek (2005) described interpretivism as a means of examining social actions and the true meanings behind the actions in an effort to understand

and explain the behaviours of the study participants and the meaning the behaviors hold for them. Within interpretivism, a researcher looks to "explain the reasons for intentional action in relation to the whole set of concepts and practices in which they are embedded" (King, Keohane, & Verba, 1994, p. 37). A matrix display was implemented as a means of interpreting the data. Matrix display is an effective strategy for presenting interpreted data clustered together by themes (Riddick & Russell, 2008).

Findings

The findings revealed the following themes to be influential for member schools in the maintenance of legitimacy as a pathway to professional hockey: athlete development, education/scholarship opportunities, professional career opportunities, and reputation. Each theme came from data retrieved from the interviews and secondary data. The subthemes are discussed within the context of the corresponding main themes.

Athlete Development

Athlete development (also identified as development) was a theme that was identified as how the players were trained to develop their skills and how they progressed through their hockey careers. Athlete development in this context refers to the growth and evolution of an individual player's personal game during their U SPORTS career. An underlying concept that was evident among the interviews was based on the participants developing their "games" or enhancing their talents against "men," as opposed to competing against "kids" in the CHL, where players range in age from sixteen to twenty-one years. P1 explained their experience:

> Right away from the second you step into the U SPORTS hockey league every guy on the team is already bigger, faster, and stronger. They were all 20-year olds in the CHL and are smart hockey

players, so right away you're adjusting to a bigger faster game. In U SPORTS you practice four times a week with two intense games on the weekend, so it really pushes you to get better.

P1 further explains,

I think just the fact that they're all coming from the Canadian Hockey League, which is a great feeder to professional hockey. Everyone comes into U SPORTS hockey league as big strong men. Playing at that pace with the physicality, and how big everyone is I think it prepares you quite well for pro.

Additionally, P8 said, "I think U SPORTS is definitely a good stepping stone for professional hockey to develop players into not only professional players, but people that can have an impact on the professional level."

Building off the previous statement, P10 expanded on the theme of athlete development by explaining,

I've been able to round out and mature my game. Understanding that if I am going to play at the next level, I need to be good in all areas and not just one. But it definitely opened my eyes that I am going to be more ready to make the step to pro.

P2 described being skeptical at first of the quality of hockey; however, his perceptions changed when he started playing: "I think it's made me a better player and it's developed me a lot. I think it's a great league and although, maybe I didn't think that before, I definitely do now."

The theme of athlete development within the context of these findings would indicate that the participants perceived U SPORTS as a "stepping stone"; a way to prepare for a second attempt to play at a professional level of competition. Being considered a stepping stone has only been a recent development for U SPORTS men's hockey. As P11 explained,

> I think it's a growing league, it's a development league; I think over these past five to ten years, I think it's been a legitimate development program for players that maybe needed a year or two, or four years, to continue to grow as a player.

The understanding that U SPORTS can be a development league was expressed by P12, who stated, "I could have went and played in the East Coast [i.e., ECHL], but I decided to come to school for a few years and see if I could develop any more and maybe get a different contract."

The ECHL is not publicly viewed on the same tier as the AHL, and the NHL; however, it is still a legitimate professional league. Firstly, the ECHL is part of an affiliate system for the NHL, as NHL teams use the AHL to call players up, and the AHL uses the ECHL for the same purpose. An example of the affiliate system between the three leagues is the New York Islanders (NHL), Bridgeport Sound Tigers (AHL), and Worcester Railers (ECHL). Furthermore, the ECHL has had 641 graduates play in the NHL (ECHL, 2018). This speaks to the quality of players coming into U SPORTS who turned down professional opportunities to further develop as a hockey player while earning a degree.

All the participants discussed the importance of developing as a player at an individual member school in U SPORTS and giving themselves an opportunity to play professionally following their U SPORTS career. For example,

> For me, once I got here I wanted to one and done [leave after one season] and go play pro. But it shocked me how good the quality of hockey was and I realized that a couple more years of playing, and obviously the benefits of getting my degree, it really helped

me and now that I have my degree I am looking forward to playing professionally. (P10)

In the above quote, what was apparent for P10 was that because of the quality of play there was an opportunity to play professional hockey. The overall discussion that was generated by 90 per cent of the study participants was that U SPORTS men's hockey was an opportunity to develop against bigger and stronger players, which in turn enabled the players to prepare for the transition, and it provided them with a better opportunity as opposed to coming out of the CHL.

The Importance of Education/Scholarship Opportunities

The importance of education/scholarship opportunities refers to the CHL scholarship and the scholarships that U SPORTS teams offer to players in order for them to receive a free education. Education refers to the degree these players are working toward while playing U SPORTS hockey. Both education and scholarships were themes that emerged naturally from the interview process. Education was discussed by all twelve study participants, while scholarship was discussed by eleven participants. All the participants valued education and it was one of the major reasons why they chose U SPORTS. P2 explained that U SPORTS was a backup plan:

I think the big thing for me was that I was done playing hockey and I either had to choose between going pro or getting a degree and having a little bit of the backup plan, so for me the choice came to go to [U SPORTS], get a degree and then pursue pro afterwards. That's the goal at least.

Another example regarding the decision-making process for playing for a U SPORTS school was further explained by P1, who said,

After playing a few years in junior I was speaking to current team-mates and former teammates about the routes they took and a few of them had gone to the U SPORTS hockey league. I decided that it was in my best interest to try and go get an education first before I turned professional.

P11 explained his situation by stating,

Originally, I thought I was just going to postpone and grow my game and try for a better contract. But the longer I was here the more I started to realize schooling was something that was important in life.

Similarly, P6 explained, "I knew going to school I can still play at a really high level of hockey while not delaying my life at all."

Receiving a scholarship was highly valued among participants as all twelve referenced this theme. These players identified the importance of the scholarship and how it influenced their decision to attend university. The study participants felt the value of the scholarship outweighed their professional hockey ambitions coming right out of the CHL. One of the study participants put numbers toward the value of the scholarship by stating, "I can say with a lot of confidence, maybe 95–100 per cent, that if I did not have that scholarship from junior that I would have not gone to university" (P7).

The selection of what school a player will attend was found to have an influence on the player's life decision pertaining to a hockey career. An example of why P4 selected his university was, "I just wanted a school that was giving me an opportunity to do well academically. For me that was a bigger school. Also to go to a team that was sending players to pro after they're done university." Education/scholarship opportunities were financially important for P11, who said,

The scholarship allows you to get a free education. You start to realize how much that stuff actually costs and how much time goes into it, so originally it was a one, two year plan max, but when I got here I realized that I was going to stick it out and get my degree and that was something that was important to me.

A subtheme for the importance of education/scholarship opportunities in the context of this research was university life. The participants indicated the expected university life experiences were perceived comparable to the importance of receiving an education and scholarship. P11 explained the connection between university life and education as he became "mentally more mature, and developed an understanding of how the world works." University life is understood as everything associated with the university experience and the benefits that go beyond playing hockey and getting a degree. The study participants discussed university life as an area where they matured as a person both on and off the ice. Off the ice, P4 explained, "I think coming to university, playing hockey you make a lot of relationships and connections that you're going to use later down in your life." On the ice, P9 felt that,

The university program in general and getting through your undergrad is something that can really prepare you for your life and instill values in you. When hockey becomes a profession as a career you have the knowledge and know-how to really pursue it as a career instead of just a sport.

Furthermore, participants talked about transferable skills and situations they experienced in university that helped them mature as people. Time management was a concept that all of the participants stressed as important to succeed at the U SPORTS level. Other experiences that were mentioned that helped players mature as people involved living on their own for the first time and everything that goes into being away from home (i.e., laundry, cooking, groceries, and paying bills). These life experiences acquired at university can translate to the real world. P9 explained how university helped his life in the professional setting by stating,

> I think I got really good at being able to time manage and prioritize. Just having to balance a full course load with hockey and making sure you're studying and giving yourself ample time to work on projects and term papers. I think that has already translated into my professional life after school.

Attending university is a general transition and maturity phase for most undergraduate students. It could be argued most students have to learn aspects of time management and how to prioritize life events, as some may even work while attending university. The study participants felt the demands and commitment that came with juggling a full course load and playing a full hockey season were challenging. Committing most of their weekends to playing games, and practising every day while staying on top of their studies and enjoying university life, were challenges that better prepared them for the rigours of professional hockey or joining the workforce.

Professional Career Opportunities

The theme of professional career opportunities was understood as playing in a professional hockey league. All participants had different interests and experiences involving their views on professional sports; however, over 90 per cent of the study participants felt they could play professional hockey following their U SPORTS career. One participant felt strongly that his U SPORTS teammates could all be professional hockey players if they desired:

> When I look at the calibre of players I played against in pro hockey and I look back to my teammates, I don't see why all of them

couldn't play professional hockey given different roles. But I think they could definitely all play. (P7)

P8 expanded on this statement, saying,

I can't speak for other conferences, but I know in my conference there were many players who left their U SPORTS teams after their season last year and went on to play professional hockey and had significant roles on their professional teams after playing a full season in U SPORTS.

Although P7 and P8 both played in different conferences, both felt strongly that teammates and players in their conference had the ability to play professional hockey. The high level of play and competition has allowed for a number of players to not only move on to professional hockey but, as P8 said, play significant roles on their professional teams.

A subtheme for professional career opportunities in this context is level of play. Using the level of play in U SPORTS as a benchmark to the CHL, NCAA and professional hockey helped shape participants' perceptions of the ability of players to move on to professional hockey. Research participants felt that U SPORTS was a better league than they had anticipated, and the level of competition made the league "very strong." P9 believed that "every player that plays U SPORTS is a legitimate hockey player and that makes the games really structured, fast paced, and there's not a whole lot of mistakes." P3 added, "The quality of hockey is high enough that it could probably allow guys to develop and be contributors at the pro hockey level."

Using the CHL as the gold standard, all participants felt that U SPORTS was a higher level of hockey. For example, P10 stated, "The majority, if not all, the U SPORTS teams would be able to beat the CHL teams." At the same time, the NCAA was viewed as an equal or comparable level of play to U SPORTS. The study participants had a good understanding of the level of play, as most U SPORTS teams play exhibition games against the NCAA every year. P2 drew on his experience and described the level of play between the two leagues:

> I think if you throw us [his member school] into an NCAA conference we'd be right there at the top. I think it is really comparable to an NCAA conference; whether we are a little bit better or a little worse, I'm not sure.

Reputation

Reputation was a theme that was identified as how U SPORTS hockey is perceived and viewed by its players; however, in this context, following Fombrun (1996), organizational reputation is an understanding of the organization as it exists in the minds of the stakeholders. The stakeholders for U SPORTS hockey are parents, players (past and current), coaches, managers, administrators, and fans. The perception displayed by athletes retrieved from the interviews can impact organizational reputation.

The study participants, while playing in the CHL, did not initially know or think highly of U SPORTS's reputation. An understanding of this perception was well articulated by P9, who felt,

> When I was that age being really trained towards just playing in the NHL obviously it really discounted the legitimacy in my eyes of U SPORTS, but I think that was more a lack of information and understanding.

If the players' perception of U SPORTS is not taken into account, the participants felt the hockey community's perception is also affected. P1 explained this perception by saying,

> I think a lot of people are misled in the hockey community. I think most people would understand that it's a step up from the

Canadian Hockey League because these are graduating players, but to the untrained eye I would think that they perceive the league as fairly weak, which is due to lack of knowledge and not seeing any games.

The reputation of U SPORTS has been negatively viewed, in the opinion of some participants, due to a lack of marketing and understanding. P10 indicated, "I know the general population around Canada, it's not viewed as good or not as comparable to other leagues, which is not the case whatsoever." The fact that U SPORTS is not viewed as comparable to other leagues, especially the NCAA, is an obstacle for U SPORTS being seen as a legitimate pathway to professional hockey. Subthemes for reputation in this setting are the comparison to NCAA hockey and perception.

NCAA Division I male hockey is considered to be one of the top amateur leagues at producing NHL talent. As an example, 32 per cent or 314 former NCAA players played in the NHL during the 2016–2017 season (College Hockey Inc., 2017a). U SPORTS struggles relative to the NCAA Division I men's hockey, when comparing the number of players being drafted and playing in the NHL or other professional leagues. This is evident in the opportunity players received in the 2016–2017 season, as no free agent U SPORTS player signed an NHL deal during that time, while three of the top four NCAA Division I scorers (i.e., Zach Aston-Reece, Mike Vecchione, and Spencer Foo) who were undrafted free agents signed NHL deals (College Hockey Inc., 2017c). This can be frustrating for U SPORTS players, as professional opportunities tend not to present themselves as often as they do to NCAA Division I players. P10 shared his frustration by stating,

The thing that's really tough for players in U SPORTS is when we play these teams and at the end of the year, you see some of these kids in the NHL. These players are getting an opportunity and you kind of question, how can we beat these teams badly or have good success and how is this player getting more of an opportunity? And that kind of goes back to why [U SPORTS is] the best-hidden secret in hockey.

The idea of a brighter spotlight on U SPORTS hockey is something P2 discussed: "It's definitely something that I hope will change. I hope U SPORTS will receive more exposure to pro teams because I do think it's a really good league and comparable to the NCAA." Furthermore, P2 continued to say,

> If you look at US (NCAA) schools and the Canadian (U SPORTS) schools, you see that there is a difference perception-wise. When a player is going to [the] NCAA, people in the hockey world kind of perceive that differently than if a player is going to [U SPORTS].

A subtheme for reputation in this context is perception. The participants viewed perception as their initial impression of U SPORTS and also how the general population views the legitimacy of the league. Participants felt past teammates influenced their perceptions of U SPORTS, although they recognized the perception alters as players age in the CHL. P8 summarized by saying,

> When you talk to a 16-year-old they may have a very different opinion than a 20-year old on a junior team. The older guys on my team had a different perception and maybe they realized how good U SPORTS actually is.

By determining the type of legitimacy that exists, it can be explained how U SPORTS and its individual member schools maintain legitimacy and are perceived as a legitimate pathway to professional hockey.

Discussion

The findings revealed that the legitimacy indicators in U SPORTS men's hockey are athlete development, the importance of education/ scholarship opportunities, professional career opportunities, and reputation. The above themes were similar to the findings of Edwards and Washington (2015), who focused on NCAA Division I male hockey legitimacy in the US. Thus, pragmatic legitimacy was determined as the type of legitimacy that was found within the context of U SPORTS men's hockey in a Canadian context. Pragmatic legitimacy was found to align with this study's findings, as it involves the judgment and an evaluation of organizational behaviour that results in determining consequences for any given decision or activity by the organization. Drawing on the work of Bitektine (2011), pragmatic legitimacy is judged through the overall value that is assessed by an evaluator. In this chapter, the evaluators were former and current players. The participants felt that, as a governing body, U SPORTS did not share their values and have their best interests at heart.

Pragmatic Legitimacy and U SPORTS Men's Hockey

To repeat, pragmatic legitimacy is judged through the overall value that is assessed by an evaluator, as indicated by Bitektine (2011). Bitektine (2011) also suggested that within organizational theory, legitimacy, reputation, and status are key theoretical concepts. Since legitimacy is not on a continuum, meaning an organization either has legitimacy or not, maintaining legitimacy is a fundamental aspect to ensuring the success or nonsuccess of an organization's survival and its ability to compete with other competitive organizations (Bitektine, 2011; Edwards & Washington, 2015; Fombrum, 1996; Podolny, 2005). Drawing on the work of Edwards (2012), credibility, sustainability, and social judgment were used to discuss the impact that pragmatic legitimacy has on this current research.

Organizations that have credibility, or are seen as credible, have positive associations related to their actions and policies (Guido, Pino, & Frangipane, 2011). These terms are often associated with a favourable evaluation of a certain entity, U SPORTS men's hockey and its member schools in this context. Guido et al. (2011) indicated, "Credible sources are accepted as truthful and are likely to exert a more persuasive effect on receivers' opinions" (p. 210). Persuading an organization's policies and actions toward a receiver (i.e., stakeholders or constituents) is increasingly impactful from a credible source (Engel, Blackwell, & Miniard, 2000). Credibility represents an organization's ability to communicate policies and actions positively, thus affecting "receivers'" beliefs about the validity of their assertions (Ohanian, 1990). Guido et al. (2011) drew on the work of Ohanian (1991) and explained that there are three main dimensions of credibility that are all present in the current research: "1) trustworthiness, which is the level of liability perceived in the source; 2) expertise, which is the receivers' beliefs about the communicator's knowledge of a particular subject; and 3) attractiveness, which is the extent to which the source is judged to be pleasant or familiar" (p. 210).

Credibility is understood as policies and actions of an organization that are perceived by an external actor (e.g., stakeholder, or athlete/player) as trustworthy and reliable (Suchman, 1995). Evidently, the findings demonstrated that the research participants felt that credibility was established in U SPORTS through the themes of athlete development, the importance of education/scholarship opportunities, and professional career opportunities. In contrast to the work of Edwards (2012), these findings were found at an institutional level (i.e., member schools) and not at a governing body level. The member schools used in this study are establishing credibility and trustworthiness for potential recruits and players through exchange and influential legitimacy.

Suchman (1995) describes credibility as constituents' support of policies and actions of an organization. This leads to favourable social judgment and the organization being seen as trustworthy and reliable.

If an organization is deemed credible, and exhibits elements of being stable, which match the organization's policies and actions, then favourable social judgment will be reflected. The participants in this study perceived, at a member school level, a trend toward credibility improvement. The trend toward improved credibility was understood through positive social judgment through the four main themes. Scholarship acquisition, development expectation, and professional advancement opportunity have led to this perception. Member schools are relying on these actions to develop credibility and to establish trustworthiness to potential recruits and players in part with past actions (i.e., championships, programs reputation, and culture).

Potential recruits and players are also influenced by member schools' former players' testimonies highlighting actions and policies that helped them advance to professional hockey. Hodson (2004) indicated, "Organizational trustworthiness is a precondition for productivity and meaning in work" (p. 433); thus, by establishing trustworthiness, players will be seemingly more productive and value the opportunity for playing U SPORTS men's hockey. Support of policies and actions from constituents establishes credibility, making the member university trustworthy and reliable (Suchman, 1995). Jepperson and Meyer (1991) suggest that credibility recognizes or explains what an organization is doing and why and consequently builds toward sustainability.

Although there is no widely accepted definition of sustainability, Ciletti, Lanasa, Luchs, and Lou (2010) described sustainability as presently sufficing current needs without obstructing future needs being met. An organization that is stable has the aptitude to connect a community, broaden a customer base, lower operating costs, and benefit society (Ciletti et al., 2010). Based on Ciletti et al. (2010), the definition of sustainability within the context of this research is understood as an organization's current policies and actions that are not obstructing growth and the progression of evolving policies and actions of future constituents. Communication is an important aspect of sustainability in providing an organization competitive advantage (Doorley & Garcia, 2007; Ioakimidis, 2007; von Kutzschenbach & Brønn, 2006). Ensuring the stability of an organization creates the perception of less uncertainty for the organization and its operation within the environment, which allows for the organization to sustain its operations. Furthermore, an organization that values sustainability and communicates its policy and actions clearly can increase the value of its image and brand, providing a competitive advantage (Ioakimidis, 2007). The sustainability of U SPORTS member schools' ability to maintain their legitimacy requires effective communication tactics.

Furthermore, the sustainability of U SPORTS as a governing body to meet the needs of the participants of this study and future recruits of U SPORTS is inadequate because of the poor communication to potential male hockey players. To reiterate, effectively communicating an organization's message can increase its brand and image (Ioakimidis, 2007), which is essentially what management has looked to do through rebranding from Canadian Interuniversity Sport (CIS) to U SPORTS. On the rebranding effort, U SPORTS CEO Graham Brown said,

> I felt that we were doing such a good job of branding and marketing from a school perspective. Some of the schools were very good at representing their institution on campus, and at the national level we were letting them down a little bit. (Bennett, 2016, para. 5)

The shortcomings of U SPORTS as a governing body relate back to communication, an essential part of credibility and sustainability.

The communication of credible sources accompanying the perception of a stable organization influences the social judgment of that organization. Bitektine (2011) defined social judgment as an evaluator's perception and decision about the policies and actions of an organization. Once an action is witnessed or experienced, constituents form their social judgments based on their expectations of suitable practice (Lock et al., 2015). As previously discussed, the research participants had their social judgment influenced by former teammates in the CHL prior to playing in U SPORTS hockey. The research participants' perceptions and evaluation of U SPORTS changed as they aged and experienced, first-hand, the policies and actions of individual member schools and the league as a whole.

At best, the general population's social judgment is rendered through spectatorship, not on a day-to-day evaluation of policies and actions of the organization. The general population's social judgment can be understood as "outsiders'" perceptions about what distinguishes an organization and establishes the image of the organization (Dutton, Dukerich, & Harquail, 1994). Social judgment impacts the credibility and sustainability of an organization moving forward. Furthermore, social judgment can be understood as the appropriateness, acceptance, and desirability of an organization (Zimmerman & Zeitz, 2002), which is a similar understanding to Suchman's (1995) definition of legitimacy. Essentially, the players' decision to attend a Canadian university and play hockey was often evaluated based on the opportunities that these institutions can provide.

Based on the findings, the member schools used in the study were perceived as a viable option for developing players into professional hockey; thus, reducing the uncertainty that exists for players making the decision to play U SPORTS and continuing their hockey careers. The participants felt the communication of U SPORTS through the marketing and promotion of the league has ultimately affected its reputation. Since the policies and actions of U SPORTS sustainability are not aligned with the larger interests of the players and member schools, social judgment remains a concern. The social judgment of U SPORTS as a step backwards and not a means of advancement to professional hockey discredits its reputation in the university hockey landscape.

Conclusion

This chapter sought to explore current and former hockey players' perceptions of U SPORTS men's hockey as a means of gaining insight into how legitimacy is maintained by the member schools as it pertains to a pathway to professional hockey. Through qualitative research methods, data were collected through the voices of current and former U SPORTS men's hockey players that provided the perceptions of competing for certain teams in Canadian university hockey. Based on data collected from the interviews and secondary sources, four main factors were found to contribute toward legitimacy maintenance in U SPORTS member schools: athlete development, the importance of education/scholarship opportunities, professional career opportunities, and reputation.

Through Suchman's (1995) categories of legitimacy, these factors can be categorized within the context of pragmatic legitimacy. In Chard's (2013) study, U SPORTS as a league was positioned as the place where "careers go to die"; thus, this reputation makes it challenging for U SPORTS to attract the most talented hockey players. However, the findings from this research present an alternative view as there has been an evolution where male hockey players have competed in the various leagues throughout Canada (e.g., AUS, OUA, and Canada West) and then transitioned to professional levels of competition. This is an indication of the legitimacy of the league by providing credibility and sustainability. Participants from this research suggested they or their teammates personally turned down professional offers in order to play U SPORTS hockey. This research demonstrated that although U SPORTS is not the most direct path to professional hockey, research participants did not view it as a step backwards but as an alternative pathway to professional hockey while also gaining an education.

References

Bennett, D. (2016). Q&A: U SPORTS CEO Graham Brown talks re-brand, next steps. *Sportsnet*. https://www.sportsnet.ca/usports/qa-u-sports-ceo-graham-brown-talks-re-brand-next-steps/

Bitektine, A. (2011). Toward a theory of social judgments of organizations: The case of legitimacy, reputation, and status. *Academy of Management Review, 36*(1), 151–179.

Chard, C. (2013). Understanding the brand meaning of Canadian Interuniversity Sport hockey league: An insurance policy if all else fails! *Sport in Society: Cultures, Commerce, Media, Politics, 16*(3), 327–339.

Chard, C., Hyatt, C., & Foster, W. (2013). Assets and obstacles: An analysis of OUA hockey from the coaches' perspective. *Sport, Business and Management: An International Journal, 3*(3), 246–259.

CHL. (2018). WHL education. http://chl.ca/whlinfo

Ciletti, D., Lanasa, J., Luchs, R., & Lou, J. (2010). Sustainability communication in North American professional sport leagues: Insights from website self-presentations. *International Journal of Sport Communication, 3*(1), 64–91.

College Hockey Inc. (2017a). In the NHL. http://collegehockeyinc.com/in-the-nhl.php

College Hockey Inc. (2017b). About NCAA hockey. http://collegehockeyinc.com/about-ncaa-hockey.php

College Hockey Inc. (2017c). Pro signings, 2016–2017. http://collegehockeyinc.com/pro-signings-2016-17-nhl-college-ncaa-free-agent.php

Creswell, J. (2003). *Research design: Qualitative, quantitative, and mixed methods approaches* (2nd ed.). Thousand Oaks, CA: Sage.

Doorley, J., & Garcia, F.G. (2007). Rumor has it: Understanding and managing rumors. *The Public Relations Strategist, 13*(3), 27–31.

Dutton, J.E., Dukerich, J.M., & Harquail, C.V. (1994). Organizational images and member identification. *Administrative Science Quarterly, 39*(2), 239–263.

ECHL. (2018). ECHL alumni. https://www.echl.com/alumni

Edwards, A., & Skinner, J. (2009). *Qualitative research in sport management*. Oxford, UK: Butterworth-Heinemann.

Edwards, J.R. (2012). *Recruiting and retaining Canadian minor hockey players by local youth club hockey organizations, Canada's governing hockey organizations, major junior, and intercollegiate hockey organizations: Exploring Canada's elite level hockey development system*. (Doctoral dissertation). University of Alberta, Edmonton, AB.

Edwards, J.R., & Washington, M. (2015). Establishing a "safety net": Exploring the emergence and maintenance of College Hockey Inc. and NCAA Division I Hockey. *Journal of Sport Management, 29*(3), 291–304.

Engel, J.F., Blackwell, R.D., & Miniard, P.W. (2000). *Consumer behavior* (9th ed.). Fort Worth, TX: The Dryden Press.

Fombrun, C. (1996). *Reputation: Realizing value from the corporate image.* Boston: Harvard Business School Press.

Gruneau, R., & Whitson, D. (1993). *Hockey Night in Canada: Sports, identities, and cultural politics.* Toronto: Garamond Press.

Guido, G., Pino, G., & Frangipane, D. (2011). The role of credibility and perceived image of supermarket stores as valuable providers of over-the-counter drugs. *Journal of Marketing Management, 27*(3–4), 207–224.

Hockey Canada. (2011). *Canadian development model—Parent information handbook.* http://www.hockeycanada.ca/index.php/ci_id/22107/la_id/1.htm

Hodson, R. (2004). Organizational trustworthiness: Findings from the population of organizational ethnographies. *Organization Science, 15*(4), 432–445.

Ioakimidis, M. (2007). Green sport: A game everyone wins. *The Sport Journal, 10*(2), 27.

Jepperson, R.L., & Meyer, J.W. (1991). The public order and the construction of formal organizations. In W.W. Powell & P.J. DiMaggio (Eds.), *The new institutionalism in organizational analysis* (pp. 204–231). Chicago: University of Chicago Press.

King, G., Keohane, R., & Verba, S. (1994). *Designing social inquiry.* Princeton, NJ: Princeton University Press.

Krukowska, L., Christie, M., Akinwekomi, T., Muruganathan, M., Huang, X., & Song, H. (2007). *Canada vs. U.S.A: The financial implications of the choice.* http://english.cis sic.ca/information/members_info/pdfs/pdf_research_and_stats/july2007CanadavsUSAresearchfinal.pdf

Kumar, R. (2014). *Research methodology: A step-by-step guide for beginners* (4th ed.). Thousand Oaks, CA: Sage.

Lock, D., Filo, K., Kunkel, T., & Skinner, J. (2015). The development of a framework to capture perceptions of sport organization's legitimacy. *Journal of Sport Management, 29*(1), 362–379.

Miles, M., & Huberman, M. (1994). *Qualitative data analysis.* London, UK: Sage.

NCAA. (2016). Scholarships. http://www.ncaa.org/student-athletes/future/scholarships

Neuman, W.L. (2000). *Social research methods: Qualitative and quantitative approaches* (4th ed.). Boston, MA: Allyn & Bacon.

Ohanian, R. (1990). Construction and validation of a scale to measure celebrity endorsers' perceived expertise, trustworthiness, and attractiveness. *Journal of Advertising, 19*(3), 39–52.

Ohanian, R. (1991). The impact of celebrity spokespersons' perceived image on consumers' intention to purchase. *Journal of Advertising Research, 31*(1), 46–54.

OHL. (2010). The best of both worlds [PowerPoint presentation]. http://www. omhavideos.com/Initial%20Content/Education%20Page/OHL%20Education/ MMidget%20CND.pdf

Patton, M. (2002). *Qualitative research and evaluation methods* (3rd ed.). Thousand Oaks, CA: Sage.

Podolny, J.M. (2005). *Status signals: A sociological study of market competition.* Princeton, NJ: Princeton University Press.

QSR International. (2018). What is NVivo. http://www.qsrinternational.com/nvivo/ what-is-nvivo

Riddick, C., & Russell, R. (2008). *Research in recreation, parks, sports, and tourism* (2nd ed.). Champaign, IL: Sagamore.

Ryan, W.G., & Bernard, H.R. (2000). Data management and analysis methods. In N.K. Denzin & Y.S. Lincoln (Eds.), *Handbook of qualitative research* (pp. 769–802). London, UK: Sage.

Smith, A., Evans, D., & Westerbeek, H. (2005). The examination of change management using qualitative methods: A case industry approach. *The Qualitative Report, 10*(1), 96–121.

Suchman, M. (1995). Managing legitimacy: Strategic and institutional approaches. *Academy of Management Review, 20*(3), 571–610.

U SPORTS. (2018). Standings. http://presto-en.usports.ca/sports/mice/2017-18/ standings-conf

von Kutzschenbach, M., & Brønn, C. (2006). Communicating sustainable development initiatives: Applying co-orientation to forest management certification. *Journal of Communication Management, 10*(3), 304–322.

WHL. (2016). WHL Scholarship. http://whl.ca/whlscholarship

Zimmerman, M.A., & Zeitz, G.J. (2002). Beyond survival: Achieving new venture growth by building legitimacy. *Academy of Management Review, 27*(3), 414–431.

2

Karl Subban & Me

The Parents Take on Hockey Culture

ANGIE ABDOU

IN JUNE OF 2018, I attended the Hockey Conference at the University
of Alberta with the intention of finding readers for my forthcoming
memoir, *Home Ice: Reflections of a Reluctant Hockey Mom* (2018). I also
wanted to meet keynote speaker, and famous hockey dad, Karl Subban.
Karl and I were scheduled to speak together at a Saskatchewan literary
festival in Moose Jaw later in July. I doubted I would find much overlap
in our attitudes toward amateur hockey. I wrote *Home Ice* because,
despite coming from a family with a history in elite sports, and despite
wanting to encourage my children's passion for any sport, I found myself
very troubled by hockey culture and compelled to address some of its
more alarming excesses, excesses sometimes fuelled by parents' deluded
dreams of their children playing in the NHL (National Hockey League).
Karl Subban's (2017) book, *How We Did It: The Subban Plan for Success
in Hockey, School, and Life*, outlines how he and his wife produced three
NHL-drafted hockey players. When he and I met, I joked that while he
had written the How We Did It take on hockey, my book would be more
of a WHY Are We Doing This?

I surprised myself by being very taken in with Karl Subban's motivational talk at the Hockey Conference's closing event in June. My brother and his Olympian friends have long made a living from these kinds of speaking tours, and I tend to be skeptical. I see such talks as one of the few ways to turn sport success into post-sport income. However, Subban's emphasis on articulating dreams and finding a support crew and working hard to realize potential resonated with me. He was charming and funny, charismatic and inspiring, and though I continued to doubt that parents could be responsible for creating NHL players—or that the NHL should even be a goal in the first place—I did find myself liking Karl and wanting to read his book. I found myself putting my cynicism aside. I started to look forward to meeting him in Moose Jaw.

Home Ice, my nonfiction book, is critical of aspects of hockey culture. It suggests ways the sport needs to evolve. Through the personal narrative of a year in my life as a hockey mom, the book calls out coaches for hypermasculine and aggressive behaviours. It tells stories of implicit sexism in the change room, on the ice, and in the stands. It questions the lack of racial diversity. Mostly, *Home Ice* calls out pushy parents and emphasizes that parents do not create athletes. This lesson comes from John O'Sullivan's (2013) *Changing the Game*, which suggests the only thing a parent should ever say to an athlete after a practice or a competition is "I love to watch you play." This hands-off stance to raising athletes seems radically at odds with Karl Subban, who has written a book explaining how he created his three NHL athletes.

However, in Moose Jaw, Karl Subban and I became instant friends. Our joint Festival of Words session was full of laughs and shared insights. We both nodded vehemently through each other's talks. In the end, the how-we-did-it and why-are-we-doing-this books had far more overlap than I imagined. Mostly we both agreed that passion for a sport comes from the child. Parents can support children's enthusiasms and help children focus their energies and commit to a dream. But that essential love for a sport—or any activity—does not come top-down (parent to child); it comes from within. Karl and I also agree that the lessons of sport—discipline, work ethic, passion, goal setting—can be transferred to many areas of life, especially school and career. In that regard, sport has much to teach children, and therein lies the true value of hockey and any sport. Karl Subban also surprised me by saying that he pursued hockey for his kids not as a path to fame and fortune but as a way of spending time together. He and I agree: sports should be about family, fitness, and fun. In the end, Karl and I decided that our takes on hockey complement each other. Each book looks at hockey from a different end of the story. His retrospective account pulls the lessons from his hockey-parenting experience after its conclusion. My immersive account struggles to make sense of the hockey-parenting experience while I'm deep in the thick of it. I bought his book. He congratulated me on my forthcoming work. I declared that the two of us make a good team, and we promised to do future hockey-parent talks together.

After this successful meeting, I left with an optimistic bounce in my step. I felt buoyed by our shared attitude, our simple: "let's put our heads together and figure out what's good about hockey and how parents can help create positive experiences for their kids and for the whole family." Karl Subban did not dismiss me as just a girl, or my son as only an average, small-town Atom hockey player. He did not dismiss me— or my family or my project—in any way. This kindness and generosity came as a surprise because his acceptance of me sat at odds with my usual experience at the rink. The hockey arena, as I have experienced it, is still a man's world with little tolerance for a woman's presence, let alone a woman's voice. In *Home Ice*, I offer an exploration of this silencing of the female voice, and I, therefore, didn't expect the book to be received well by the particular men in my son's hockey world or by the wider hockey culture of which they are a part. My encounter with Karl Subban gave me (false?) hope that maybe all the hockey dads—even those of the most elite players—would be equally open to my perspective, equally willing to listen and engage.

Maybe I, as a mother committed to my son's sport of choice, would be allowed a voice in this important conversation about the state of youth hockey and what its future might look like. What I most wanted for *Home Ice* was for it to work as a bridge from the research being done in the academy to the parents sitting in the stands. An average hockey mom might pick up *Home Ice* on a stroll through Walmart and read it for the immersive, honest account of another woman's life—and along the way pick up quotations and ideas from the leading hockey studies scholarship, studies about the dangers of specializing too young, the benefits of playing multi-sports, the need for awareness about head injuries, and the best practices in sport parenting. I hoped the book—and the research woven throughout my personal story—would start conversations. Surely, we could at least talk about change. After my time at the Saskatchewan Festival of Words with Karl Subban, I believed such conversations could happen, smoothly and without conflict.

That hint of optimism flowered in the week before my book's release. Kevin Sylvester took an interest in *Home Ice* and had me on CBC Radio's *Sunday Edition* for a lengthy, in-depth conversation about some troubling aspects of youth hockey culture (such as exorbitant cost, early focus on high-level competition, inaccessibility, abusive coaches, forced specialization, a prevalence of athlete selection rather than athlete identification, head injuries, and strains on family life). The next day I received a surprising email. Jeff Turner, a member of the Ontario Hockey Federation's board of directors, wrote to say his wife had heard me on *Sunday Edition*, and he would like to meet me. He told me that declining enrolment in hockey has become a concerning problem. "I'd like to hear your ideas," he wrote. I had to laugh. I had long been attempting to be heard in my own home town—in particular, I had repeatedly suggested dividing the kids into two equal teams, instead of an A and B team, so we could have some home games rather than always travelling three hours each direction for a regular league game. After years of my hockey-mom ideas gaining no ground in my small home town, the possibility that someone in a prominent hockey role at a provincial level wanted to hear from me was delightful. I headed into the book's publication week feeling truly excited about the role I might have in these conversations.

My excitement and my optimism proved misplaced and naive. Almost as soon as the book hit the shelves, I faced the wrath of disapproving coaches. One of my son's former coaches (let's call him "The Coach") began posting aggressively on my Facebook page, challenging my version of events, calling my book fiction. He made ambiguously threatening comments about looking forward to my return to town, where I would have to answer to him personally. Most of The Coach's complaints were vague and emotional. I had put him in a bad light, he said, I didn't care about good people. To be honest, his anger surprised me. I have nothing against The Coach, and I could not think what in my book might have caused him such distress.

His one concrete complaint about *Home Ice* came in response to a particular scene. My son attended a hockey academy associated with an independent school. The program did not suit my boy. In a nutshell, my son finds transitions challenging, so leaving school in the middle of one class for hockey practice, and then returning from hockey in the middle of another class, caused him stress. The drills at the hockey practice did not come easily to him either, which added pressure to his already trying days. In *Home Ice*, I tell the story of me realizing: Why on earth is my grade four child stressed out?! That's wrong! This realization comes right alongside the story of my son leaving that particular hockey program. The scene shows an altercation with an unnamed coach and then shows my son losing his temper and skating his own head into the boards. I am the main target of the criticism in the scene. I regret that it took such a dramatic incident—my son attempting to break his own neck—for me to realize that the "more, more, more" approach to sport was not working for us.

But The Coach saw himself in the scene; he felt I portrayed him negatively. He insisted that the two things—the coach-player altercation and the self-harm incident—did not happen at the same practice. He kept repeating his version of the chronology as if it alone undermined everything about my book. Okay, so I remember the two incidents happening the same day; The Coach remembers the two incidents happening different days—really it doesn't matter. Not to me. I present the scene as a memory, and it is true to my memory. The altercation describes the kind of thing that happened at this hockey school and why my son found it stressful. My son skating into the boards marks the grand finale of his time in that hockey school, as well as the beginning of my changing attitude to pressure and sport. My point is simply that in sport more is not always better, and if my family is to stick to its "Have fun! Try hard!" philosophy of hockey, we must know to back away when we have run clear out of fun. As any reader will see, for my son, the fun had long gone out of these hockey academy sessions. I should have noticed before my own child, in deep frustration, ran the risk of seriously hurting himself.

Beyond the complaints about this specific scene, The Coach's comments tended to run toward the emotional. He reminded me of a drunk at closing time, chest puffed out and looking for a fight. "You don't know anything about this sport," he wrote. And: "Truthfully you have no idea what it's like to be a hockey parent today. But that's my opinion. I live in the world of hockey and u truly have no idea what's out there." And: "Why don't u ask someone who knows." And: "I'm not the only one in this community that have issues. I'd be prepared. It's not good." Over and over again, The Coach made his point loud and clear: you, dumb lady, shut up. *Or else. Be prepared. It's not good.*

I have been trained well by sport's patriarchal culture. When a man tells me I don't know anything—when a man tells me to shut up—I cower. Only much later would I think: my son has been in the sport for six years, I come from a family of elite athletes, I spent a year reading cutting-edge research for my book, so surely I must know something. I did not say any of that to The Coach. The moment The Coach told me to shut up, I did exactly what he wanted me to do. I shrank. I emailed Jeff Turner, from the Ontario Hockey Federation's board of directors, and told him he probably did not want to meet with me after all: "I think people who heard the interview on CBC might be coming to the book expecting an objective journalistic account of hockey. *Home Ice* is not that. It's a very personal memoir—the kind of story women readers like." There was no real reason for me to think my book would only appeal to female readers. Instead, this was me demoting myself and belittling my own efforts. I am familiar with masculine intimidation tactics, but I am not immune to them. As soon as a male coach yelled at me (even virtually), I relegated myself to the "just a girl" role. I silenced myself. I obediently stepped out of the big boys' conversation.

An early scene in *Home Ice* highlights this kind of sexism in the hockey locker room. In Atom (ages 9–10), coaches discourage parents, especially mothers, from coming into the change rooms. However, kids mostly cannot tie their own skates yet. I tend to scurry into the locker room apologetically, tie the skates, and scurry back out. One coach especially hates mothers in the change room. He has a way of waving his head from me to the exit. It is a gesture that says "GIT!" Well conditioned by this kind of patriarchal muscle move, I always do as he says and I GIT. Post-publication, I recognized The Coach's "you don't know anything about this sport," his "shut up," as just another manifestation of "GIT!" With the publication of *Home Ice*, I wanted to talk about ways hockey could evolve to be more enjoyable for children, healthier for families, and accessible to all. I thought, in my role as a concerned hockey mother, I could have a voice. How did my home-town hockey culture receive me into this conversation? With an unambiguous GIT!

The Coach's social media attacks cropped up a few weeks later, this time on Twitter. I had been on CTV's *The Social*, talking about *Home Ice*. In response to an innocuous CTV tweet with a link to my eleven-minute segment, The Coach responded:

@TheSocialCTV The fact that you promote a book like Angie Abdou's "Home Ice" shows the type of program you have. Maybe before you praise such garbage you should see the affect [*sic*] its [*sic*] had on the people in her community. I guess if it's written it must be valid and true.

Normally, I would ignore this type of tweet. I have learned that engaging with outrage on social media never leads anywhere worthwhile. But The Coach's post came through as I stood, tired and hungry, in a hallway at the Banff Mineral Springs Hospital, waiting for my husband to be rolled out of emergency surgery. I expected to have gotten the okay to take him home hours ago, and I had put off eating dinner or finding a place for us to stay. It was very late, and I hadn't received a clear update on his status. I was stressed and perhaps more than a little "hangry." After two months of taking the high road in response to personal attacks on me and my work—two months of staying largely silent—I lashed out. My husband has made me well aware that, when angry, I have the annoying habit of correcting people's grammar. "It never looks good on you, Ang." It's true. He's right. I know that. Yet I responded,

Hi [name deleted]. It's "effect." Affect is a verb. The book is creative nonfiction, a memoir. I don't see how it can have a negative effect on a community. I suspect you over-estimate the power of me expressing my opinion. I'll take that as a compliment, I guess.

As you can imagine, the exchange didn't go well from there, but I did resist the urge to continue correcting his grammar. Here, for your viewing pleasure, I include the entirety of our "conversation," not the kind of conversation I had naively hoped my book would encourage:

HIM: Thanks for the clarification. My mistake. Your arrogance is truly unbelievable. You're the farthest thing from a hockey mom yet you have all the answers. You attack good people and blow it off like it doesn't matter. Keep riding this high while it lasts. It won't last long.

ME: You might need to read the book to have an opinion. I don't claim to have the answers. I don't attack anyone. The goal of the book is to start a nice civil conversation (you're clearly uninterested in civility). Contrary to your opinion, I'm allowed a voice in that conversation.

HIM: I have read it. I love fiction. And yes, you have every right. I also have a right to express my opinion.

ME: I'm scared to ask what, in your opinion, makes me not a hockey mom. Is Ollie not a hockey player? Or am I not his mom? Remind me again, which one of us has astounding arrogance. If you're trying to disprove my points about hockey and sexism, you're not doing the best job.

HIM: There are amazing hockey mom's [sic] out there. I meet new ones every weekend. There are also amazing women involved in the sport that I have the utmost respect for. You however don't help the sport at all or give anyone a greater understanding of the benefits of playing the game.

ME: [Name deleted], I get the sense you haven't read the book. Reviewers call it a love letter to sport. I've had productive meetings with Ontario Hockey Federation ppl, 1 of whom said he wished every hockey family could read it. Taking it too personally may have interfered with your impression.

HIM: Enjoy it while it lasts.

ME: You're very combative. I'm not at war with you. I find your aggression and insults confusing. Marty says hi. Docs just wheeled him out from surgery. Thanks for the chat. It's helped me pass the time at the hospital.

HIM: He's a very patient man. Hope he's well.

I love the way the parting tweet about my husband's patience gets in a dig at my competence as a wife to complement the earlier assessment of my competence as a (hockey) mother. According to The Coach, I fail at all my womanly roles, it seems. As far as The Coach's insistence that I am riding a high that will soon come to an end (another of his vague threats), I am not sure he understands my job. I write a book and then I work for a season to promote that book—to launch it into the world— and then I go back to my desk, where I brainstorm an idea for a new book and begin writing again. Fall 2018 had not been a "high" that I had been "riding." Fall 2018 had been a whole lot of exhausting promotional work. Yes, it would soon come to an end, and I would breathe a sigh of relief and go back to the part of the writing life I more fully enjoy—the research, the thinking, the writing. The Coach might make the same complaint of me: that I do not understand his job. Perhaps we could bridge this gap with some face-to-face time, but when I, in response to his first Facebook posts, invited him to sit down to talk over coffee, he declined with a terse no thanks.

The Coach's tweets, as a response to a mother's book about her own life as a hockey mom, offer up much material for analysis. The part that gets me the most, though? The "you're the farthest thing from a hockey mom." The farthest thing from a hockey mom *in his estimation*. The Coach positions himself as the one with power to define "hockey mom." Being the mother of a hockey player does not, apparently, qualify me. Based on the objections he voiced to me, I have to assume a "hockey mom" is one who falls in line, does not question the hockey establishment, does not share her own story unless it coincides verbatim with The Coach's story, and does not represent anyone involved in hockey culture in a way that might be construed as "a bad light."

Good to know. Of course, that criteria would make the task of writing a memoir impossible. I think of memoir as the anti-Hallmark genre. As a memoirist, my job is not to encourage sentimental notions about hockey or to reinforce deeply ingrained stereotypes. My job is not to make everyone involved feel good. *My job* as a memoirist is to question, to explore, to challenge. A hockey-parent memoir is not advertising copy for Hockey Canada or for the Fernie Minor Hockey Association or for Fernie's Hockey Academy. A hockey-parent memoir is not a Tim Hortons commercial. Rather, a hockey-parent memoir creates the space to rethink the role of youth hockey in Canada.

I see now my early mistake in putting myself on the same page as Karl Subban and his *How We Did It* book. First, as a father, Karl Subban's voice has a place. Second, *How We Did It* does not challenge the hockey status quo or call into question the NHL dream and the strain it puts on hockey families (and family pocketbooks). Karl and I both have "a take" on youth sports, but I alone "take on" hockey culture. In response to my question about why The Coach felt so attacked by *Home Ice*, and why the two of us could not have a civil conversation, one friend said, "It's his livelihood. Your book challenges his livelihood. You can't expect him to respond rationally. He will react with pure emotion."

Therein lies the problem: youth sport has become big business. In 2017, drawing on data from WinterGreen Research, *Time Magazine* reported that youth sport had become a fifteen-billion-dollar industry (Gregory, 2017). In my altercation with The Coach, he chided me for my book's references to Ken Campbell's (2014) *Selling the Dream: How Parents and Their Kids Are Paying the Price for Our National Obsession.* Campbell and his co-writer Jim Parcels examine hockey as a business and build an argument about the harm to families and to the game. The Coach told me: nobody in hockey respects Campbell. I wonder if he meant: nobody earning a living off hockey respects Campbell. To change, or even to have a conversation about change, the advocates for a new and improved hockey will have to somehow circumvent those who benefit from hockey as business, those who stand to gain financially from hockey staying its current course. Unfortunately, for the most part, those who have power to effect change are also those standing in its way.

But I want to end on a positive note. Remember Jeff Turner from the Ontario Hockey Federation's board of directors? Remember my email trying to back out of our meetings on the grounds that I am just a girl and therefore disqualified from a voice in the conversation? He did not let me back out. He responded to my email:

My motivation for wanting to talk to you, which I am sure will be reinforced upon reading the book, comes from your CBC interview. You said something to the effect of: let's put some ideas on the table and let's discuss them. Some of what you suggested I totally agree with and some I don't. But whether I agree with your ideas or not, is irrelevant. It is ideas we need. Nobody has a monopoly on good ideas. My job is to assemble ideas. Some will be good and some bad. Nobody is smart enough to only have good ideas. I want them from all sources, not just old white guys who think they know everything. You are particularly intriguing because unlike most people whose ideas are anecdotally and not empirically driven, yours have some research to back them up. In addition, as a hockey parent, you are as qualified as anyone else to offer an opinion. So no, I won't change my mind about meeting.

Jeff and I met at a Starbucks on the corner of John and Queen in Toronto and sat at a table outdoors, braving the fall chill. He had read *Home Ice* by then and we talked for ninety minutes.

He listened to me, and I listened to him. The weeks leading up to our meeting had taught me not to take such respect for granted, and I did not. Jeff explained that he had been tasked with accumulating knowledge about declining enrolments in hockey. We know participation in hockey in Canada goes down at age thirteen, but does it really decrease any more than other sports? Do we know why teenagers leave the game? Can we do anything to retain them? Those initial questions have morphed into a study being conducted through Wilfrid Laurier University that will provide hard data to determine whether hockey does have a problem and, if so, what can be done to fix it. On a more personal level, Jeff is gathering information from people with two simple questions: What do you think is wrong with hockey? and What would you do to fix it? His main job? Listening. I found his openness so very refreshing.

Jeff and I did not agree about everything, but we talked. He changed my mind on some things and made me reconsider others. He told me change is hard, maybe particularly so in Canadian hockey. Parents who hope their child might be the next "Great One" do not want Hockey Canada's experiments to get in the way of that potential. However, Jeff also told me that in times of crisis it is always easier to make change, and Canadian hockey is in crisis. He took notes when I spoke and asked questions about the ideas in which he saw potential. I also asked him what he would do to change hockey. He said, "You mean if I was Czar? If I was Czar, I would..." He lit up with enthusiasm as he shared his strategies for keeping more kids in hockey longer and decreasing some of the costs and allowing kids to play a wide variety of sports rather than specializing too young.

I decided to hold onto Jeff's enthusiasm as I headed into phase two of touring *Home Ice*, and as I engaged in the conversations this book had started for me. I would also hold fast to the hint of optimism that re-emerged during that ninety-minute meeting. At the end of January 2019, I participated in a Sport for Life conference in Gatineau, Quebec. Richard Monette (managing director and editor-in-chief of Active for

Life) and Carolyn Trono (director of long-term athlete development at Sport for Life) invited me to join their panel on the benefits of multi-sport. As the author of *Home Ice*, I would speak from the grassroots parents' perspective. I felt like I'd found my people. Rooms full of sport administrators, coaches, and parents agreed that:

1. kids shouldn't specialize in sport too young;
2. kids don't need to be going to expensive hockey camps in the summer but would instead benefit from playing a variety of sports; and
3. parents have lost the sense of fun and play that should be the focus of youth sport.

Richard Monette reminded me that we, the parents who understand the importance of balance in sport and the importance of fun, are the quiet majority, but too often we let the vocal minority take charge of how sports are run in our communities. That needs to change.

Monette said another thing that struck me. He said that parents often act on a small sound bite rather than taking time to understand a full concept. For example, in *Outliers* (2008), Malcolm Gladwell argues we need ten thousand hours of practice to be good at something. Gladwell is, in fact, referencing a 1993 article by Ericsson, Krampe, and Tesch-Römer, a study that focused on chess and music, not sport. Nonetheless, parents fixate on that ten-thousand-hour rule and enroll their six-year-olds in year-round hockey. Nobody ever argued that success depends on reaching those ten thousand hours before we hit puberty. Even if we were to agree that the ten-thousand-hour model (based on chess and music) also applies to sports—which experts do not—there would be no reason to think that all ten thousand hours must be in the same sport. Rather than researching deeper to find the value of multi-sport or the dangers of too many hours of the same activity at too young an age, parents act on that one phrase: ten thousand hours. An easy (but misguided) sound bite.

Monette made me realize that I had reduced Karl Subban's book to a sound bite. Because Subban called his book *How We Did It*, I assumed his goal was to tell parents how to turn their children into NHL stars (or that his publisher's goal was to sell books on the premise that parents actually could take steps to guarantee that their kids have successful careers in hockey). I focused on a single story, the one I hear readers repeat most often, about Karl putting kindergartener P.K. Subban to bed in his snowsuit and waking him up for late-night shinny. Both these ideas of the book, my interpretation of the title and my focus on the six-year-old boy practising hockey at midnight, reinforce dangerous misconceptions in sport. They suggest parents can create athletes and that the earlier a child specializes the better. However, a careful, thorough reading of Subban's *How We Did It* shows his message to be quite different. He took P.K. to the outdoor rink late at night only because P.K. loved it, because they were having fun together. Karl Subban used sport to infuse his kids' childhood with joy, to build their confidence, and to steer them away from trouble. He built a backyard rink and set up stickhandling drills in the basement, not so his kids would become rich and famous but because that's how they spent time together, that's how they enjoyed each other's company. Even now, when Karl talks about taking his granddaughter skating every day, I hear his voice fill with love. I would argue that, for him, sport is about love. In that, our hockey books are in absolute agreement.

In April 2019, Karl Subban and I went on tour together. I knew that he—as the hockey dad of famous NHL players—would legitimize these events. He would be the one who drew a crowd, but he and I would both have a voice. Together we talked about how healthy attitudes toward children's hockey can improve family life. We asked people to reconsider their more destructive attitudes toward youth sport.

I am encouraged by the way men at the elite level of the sport—men like Jeff Turner and Karl Subban—enthusiastically make space for me as a woman speaking from the most grassroots level. They give me hope for the future. We can have conversations about the future of hockey. We can imagine change. We can think about the health of the sport— and the role it plays in healthy family life. We can talk about how hockey can be better for our kids. Parents—all parents—can have a voice in this conversation. In order for the change to be meaningful, we must.

References

Abdou, A. (2018). *Home ice: Reflections of a reluctant hockey mom.* Toronto: ECW Press.

Campbell, K., & Parcels, J. (2014). *Selling the dream: How parents and their kids are paying the price for our national obsession.* Toronto: Penguin.

Ericsson, K.A., Krampe, R.T., & Tesch-Römer, C. (1993). The role of deliberate practice in the acquisition of expert performance. *Psychological Review, 100*(3), 363–406. https://doi.org/10.1037/0033-295X.100.3.363

Gladwell, M. (2008). *Outliers: The story of success.* New York: Little, Brown and Company.

Gregory, S. (2017, September 4). How kids' sports became a $15 billion industry. *Time Magazine,190*(9).http://time.com/magazine/us/4913681/september-4th-2017-vol-190-no-9-u-s/

O'Sullivan, J. (2013). *Changing the game: The parent's guide to raising happy, high-performing athletes and giving sports back to our kids.* New York: Morgan James.

Subban, K., & Colby, S. (2017). *How we did it: The Subban plan for success in hockey, school, and life.* Toronto: Random House.

3

"I want justice and more"

Loreto, Carcillo, and Dominant Narratives of Hockey Culture on Twitter

CATHERINE HOUSTON, KYLE RICH, TAVIS SMITH & ANN PEGORARO

HOCKEY CONTINUES TO OCCUPY a significant place in the production of a "national identity" in Canada. The production and dissemination (through various media) of the sport and the spectacle surrounding it have been important aspects of Canadian identity for decades (Gruneau & Whitson, 1993; Whitson & Gruneau, 2006). For Robidoux (2002), national identity construction is an ongoing process in Canada, where "what it means to be Canadian is often scrutinized, lamented, and at times even celebrated...Yet through all of this, there has been one expression of nationalism that has remained constant since confederation, that being the game of ice hockey" (p. 209). Hockey is an important part of the construction of social and community identity, in both local (e.g., rural) communities (Rich, 2021; Rich, Bean, & Apramian, 2014) and across the country as a whole (Robidoux, 2002, 2012). Beyond the familiar connections made within communities, even people who do not know, or have not known, each other can connect and create an imagined collective identity (Anderson, 1991) through important cultural activities like ice hockey (Robidoux, 2002). However, the construction of these identities through sport media, and particularly through highly mediatized events (e.g., those involving tragedy), can be contentious and offer only a narrow representation of local and national identities (Kennedy, Silva, Coelho, & Cipolli III, 2019).

Alongside the traditional television and journalistic coverage of hockey (and sport in general) in Canada, social media platforms (e.g., Facebook, Instagram, Snapchat, and Twitter) have become significant sources of sport coverage. Social media has altered the way that sport events are consumed and the ways that conversations about sports occur (Pegoraro, 2014). Audiences turn to social media in real-time for commentary, news, and to see others' reactions. Also, it has altered the ways that communities (online and otherwise) negotiate and construct their identities and carry on conversations to produce or challenge various discourses.

In light of this book's focus on the neutral zone trap, the purpose of this chapter is to consider the trajectory of two instances where individuals called out and challenged the normative, mythologized, romantic narratives of hockey in Canada. Social media in general, and Twitter in particular, provides the forum for questioning the shape of conversations in, and about, hockey. The chapter will draw on two case studies that have received prominent media attention: first the Humboldt Broncos hockey team tragedy, and, second, bullying and hazing activities in junior hockey. We deploy a contextualized discourse analysis to consider two pivotal and contentious moments as reactions to these two cases unfolded on Twitter.

First, we discuss the case of Nora Loreto, who during the response to the Humboldt tragedy and amid the $15 million GoFundMe campaign—the largest crowdsourced fundraiser in Canadian history—commented on the maleness, youthfulness, and whiteness of the victims. Second, we look to the case of Canadian former National Hockey League (NHL) player Dan Carcillo. During the fallout of revelations of hazing and assault of football players at St. Michael's College

School (a prestigious all-boys private school in Toronto, Ontario), Carcillo commented in a Twitter thread that he "moved away from home, family & friends, to play hockey in the @OHLHockey for the @StingHockey [and] endured daily bullying/abuse at the hands of veteran players" (Hayes & Gibson, 2018). He went on to detail some aspects of the abuse in the original Twitter thread and other disclosures through Twitter and various media outlets.

This chapter considers the discourse that shaped the narratives that unfolded in the wake of these two Twitter threads. The type, timing, and content of responses to both of these threads shed light on the fallout of challenges to the dominant narratives in and of junior hockey in Canada. Further, the responses provide some telling insights into how, and which, "agents of change" are privileged and policed in digital spaces.

Deploying Discourse Analysis

Critical discourse analysis is a way of examining text that allows us to explore how meaning is constructed, specifically when language is used to explain, describe, and depict. It looks to "systematically explore often opaque relationships of causality and determination between (a) discursive practices, events and texts, and (b) wider social and cultural structures, relations and processes" (Fairclough, 1995, p. 132). By deploying critical discourse analysis in this context, we are particularly interested and aware of how practices, events, and texts are shaped ideologically, by relations of power (Fairclough, 1995). Through these two cases studies, we will begin to understand the contextual significance of the formation of these two different conversations around hockey culture, nationalism, and the Twittersphere, as well as how social media and technology do not merely report or comment upon the world, but how they effectively shape the meanings and perspectives we come to know. In this chapter, we use critical discourse analysis to interrogate this meaning-making, by examining both what issues are discussed, how perspectives are taken up (i.e., liked, challenged, supported, or rejected), as well as what social norms or practices enable these conversations to take place (Fairclough, 2001). Importantly, our analysis takes place through the reading of texts collected through Twitter. Twitter presents a platform whereby the structure and form of the interactions are easily quantified, mapped, and examined; additionally, the use of Twitter allows for the integration of text, images, video, and other forms of commentary.

The scope of the conversation, which took place on Twitter between Nora Loreto and Twitter users, included an original thread consisting of four tweets by Loreto and a total of approximately five thousand replies. In total, seventeen exchanges were analyzed between Loreto and Twitter users. Additionally, the scope of the conversation between Daniel Carcillo and Twitter users included an original thread consisting of fifteen tweets by Carcillo, with a total of 341 replies. In addressing the online interactions between Carcillo and Twitter users, eighteen conversations and exchanges were analyzed.

Individual tweets and exchanges within reply threads on Twitter allowed for a nuanced visualization of both case studies and the conversations that unfolded within them. For this chapter, tweets were gathered through software called Treeverse. Treeverse, an add-on to Google Chrome, allows for the collection and examination of escalating Twitter conversations. They are imagined as a tree, with each node representing individual tweets in reply to either an original tweet or to subsequent replies, and lines between tweets indicating the temporal arrangements of replies. This picturing of the conversations allows for information such as the timing of responses, the engagement with each specific tweet, and the responses between Twitter users to be seen. For example, one tweet with fifty unique replies would be visualized as a flat/horizontal structure, whereas a series of back-and-forth interactions would present as a very long vertical structure. By using Twitter and Treeverse, we were able to appreciate and further understand unique and complex communications, as this medium represents distinctive communication and contact opportunities (Earl & Kimport, 2011); however, new forms of communication and media do not come without challenges and intricacies. One such challenge, which we explore below, is maintaining a complex balance between freedom of expression and the defense of human dignity, as these systems open space for discourses that can be harmful, threatening, and aggressive. While social media allows users a congenial platform to freely express their thoughts, opinions, and responses, it can also serve to create spaces of antagonism and violence, where perpetrators are able to hide behind the anonymity of screen names and avatars.

Through critical discourse analysis, we examine the way people accepted, challenged, respected, and resisted Nora Loreto's critique of the response to the Humboldt tragedy, and Dan Carcillo's critique of hazing culture within junior hockey. Through this analysis, we were able to locate responses and criticisms to conversations that disrupted hockey's romanticized place in the formation and ongoing nature of Canada's national (sporting) identity. In particular, we were concerned with the ways in which Twitter users confronted Loreto and Carcillo's responses to these significant events within the hockey community and their association with an imagined national identity, understood through the idea of the wider "hockey family." In politicizing the public engagement with these two moments on and through Twitter, the implications of time, sport, authority, and nationalism are explored to understand and acknowledge the way that power operates in and through discourse in digital spaces. The concept of power is relevant throughout this analysis for two major reasons: first, locating the power that shapes the discourse gives important insight into the way that community identity is negotiated—in other words, who gets to decide the terms of the conversation; and, second, understanding the way that power functions in these Twitter exchanges shows the processes by which challenges to dominant norms are taken up or rejected by the broader public.

The Social Context: Sports and the Digital World

Contemporary cultural consumption and community interactions have been fundamentally changed by the evolution of technology and social media (Pegoraro, 2014). How people construct national identities, engage in societal exchanges, and create individual connections has been altered through our communal use of social media and mobile communication. The creation of online platforms and digital spaces of engagement has transformed the way society engages and participates in social issues, as the case studies in this chapter demonstrate.

Within the network of activities and practices that include hockey, "Hockey Twitter," and broader online processes of national identity construction, the social implications of digital communications are important. In the social construction of contemporary issues, debates and conversations, social media, and online platforms play a significant role in the framing and production of these issues (e.g., Kennedy et al., 2019). The existence of these online social spaces has actively affected how issues are being produced and engaged in, creating a network of social advocacy, potential aggression, and interactions that would not have typically taken place outside of these digital spaces.

Beyond the unique nature of instantaneous consumption of news and conversations through social media, the implications of events or reactions "going viral" are important to consider. *Virality* is a social information flow process where many people simultaneously share a message over a short period within their social networks. The message spreads beyond their own social networks often to distant networks, resulting in a sharp acceleration in the number of individuals exposed to the message (Nahon & Helmsley, 2013). As noted by Allsop, Bassett, and Hoskins (2007), virality happens in the context of a specific situation and occasion, indicating that virality is topically and temporally bound. Therefore, "a viral information event creates a temporally bound, self-organized, interest network in which membership is based on an interest in the information content or in belonging to the interest network of others" (Nahon & Helmsley, 2013, p. 79). With this in view, when Loreto tweeted in response to the overwhelming support for the crowdsourced funding campaign, her commentary was also caught up in the virality of the campaign to support the Humboldt Broncos. In order to conduct a discourse analysis, it is necessary to consider the implications of both Loreto's and Carcillo's tweets "going viral" as part of broader online engagement with the events and issues in general.

Finally, the network of practices operating in this discourse analysis calls us to consider the implication of insular online communities. The nature of social media allows people to curate their exposure to various online sources in a way that diverges from a traditional media model. In other words, most things that we see online are things that we are likely to agree with unless we are actively seeking out opposing opinions. This is an important consideration when analyzing the construction and maintenance of community identities, and the challenges to dominant narratives (Gruzd & Roy, 2014). By virtue of these challenges "going viral," they are introduced to audiences that are not necessarily inclined to agree, thereby challenging an even more rigid concept of community and identity than an objective observer might consider.

Nora Loreto and the Humboldt Broncos

On April 6, 2018, a bus carrying the Humboldt Broncos Junior Hockey Team and its staff collided with an oncoming semi-trailer on a highway in rural Saskatchewan after the truck did not yield at an intersection. Sixteen people were killed and another thirteen were injured, all associated with the team. The media coverage of the tragedy was almost omnipresent. From jerseys, shout-outs, and moments of silence in professional sports leagues like the National Basketball Association and Major League Baseball, to green-and-yellow sprinkled donuts at Tim Hortons coffee shops, and a solidarity movement of "putting your sticks out for the boys," exemplifying the real (i.e., monetary) and symbolic support for those involved in the accident was immense.

Among the social media buzz, Quebec-based writer and activist Nora Loreto commented—in a short series of four tweets—that the maleness, the youthfulness, and the whiteness of the victims were, of course, playing a significant role in this uptake (Loreto, 2018a). She went on to clarify, "I don't want less for the families and survivors of this tragedy. I want justice and more for so many other grieving parents and communities" (Loreto, 2018b). Public response to these tweets was swift and included thousands of replies, death threats, an attempted boycott of her work, and multiple editorials. While the majority of responses were perfunctory, trolling, or intended to incite emotional reactions, conservative political groups were more strategic in decontextualizing these statements and accusing Loreto of weaponizing identity politics. Yet others, such as Murphy-Perron (2018), wrote pieces eloquently acknowledging that other tragedies (e.g., the Quebec City mosque shooting in 2017, the Lac-Mégantic disaster in 2013, or the Southern Ontario crash involving migrant workers in 2012) did not receive the same widespread attention or a generous emptying of pocketbooks.

As the responses poured in, many of which were direct attacks or dismissals, Loreto removed herself from the conversation. Indeed, her only further comment was, "If you are responding to this thread to make this into a horse race, which it most certainly isn't, go away" (Loreto, 2018c). As our interest here is in examining discourses within these exchanges, both the structure and content of this thread are worth noting to understand how discourses were constructed and enacted in the digital space of the Twittersphere.

When looking at the Treeverse produced by the thread, an extremely flat structure is noticeable. This structure indicates that the majority of responses were direct responses to Loreto and did not seek to engage in any sort of dialogue or nuanced conversation about the issues involved. Although Loreto removed herself from the conversation, even responses that appeared to support her critique were shut down with superficial comments and attacks, preventing any sort of further engagement and discussion. In one of the few exchanges that took place, user Mike responded, "oh fuck off," to which Haze responded, "well said Mike, well said," and Donna: "thank you, Mike...my words exactly." When user Diana challenged Mike with " Why did u write that can't u just ignore her if u don't like it...?," user Tex chimed in with " You can fuck off too, Diana." The brevity and dismissal in these responses do not allow for any sort of meaningful engagement with the issues at play. This may be reflective of the polarization of political opinions and the way that critiques or diverse perspectives are taken up in the "echo chambers" that emerge within pockets of Twitter users with homogenous views (Gruzd & Roy, 2014). Further, in later tweets, Loreto shared several disturbing responses, attacks, and direct messages she received from Twitter users, for example, one response where a user referred to her as a "pseudo intellect postmodern dyke."

In the responses and the few discussions that did take place, several discourses emerged that constructed and policed what was acceptable within the discussions about hockey, tragedy, family, and sometimes even Canadian nationalism. For example, the idea of time was often implicated in these responses, suggesting that, immediately following such a tragedy, critical readings of events in public platforms are inappropriate. This is ironic, given that these platforms enable the widespread, often real-time sharing of information about these events in the first place. As such, social media users appear to desire to only consume news of tragedy and satisfy their desire to do good online through what can be called virtual activism (i.e., by liking, sharing, posting a solidarity photo of a hockey stick, or perhaps donating), without engaging meaningfully with issues involved (Vlavo, 2012). Ironically, users do not seem interested in having these activities scrutinized.

There was also a strong sense of communal identity and family associated with Canadian hockey, which emerged within the responses. While Loreto's critique was explicitly about those who were not implicated in such a community, readers actively responded with a defensive response about the integrity of this hockey community and provided compelling individual stories to demonstrate the inclusiveness of the hockey community—which ostensibly directs attention away from Loreto's point. For example, user Cole explained, "As a mom of a hockey-playing Aboriginal son. . .My son played until he was almost 18 years old, the hockey community is like a family regardless of race or religion. We grieve for our family." This user's story shifts the focus away from the manner in which the public was responding to the event and focuses on a very individual story of acceptance within a specific hockey context. Indeed, responses tended to promote these types of individual feel-good stories and attacked or dismissed those that took up the conversation about broader social processes.

Finally, through these discussions, it became apparent that the politicizing of the tragedy and the public response was unacceptable to the Twitter public. At the same time, the politicizing of sport, nationalism, and an imagined community was used to justify the public response to the tragedy and dismiss Loreto's critique. Although the public narrative is typically one of sport as apolitical, in this instance, we saw the opposite. Many tweeters explicitly recognized hockey as a site of nationalism and social support, in some ways reiterating Loreto's initial point that those outside of these circles would likely not receive the same response.

Cumulatively, the Twitter response to Loreto's critique demonstrates the way that constructions of sporting nationalisms are complex and invoke many elements, including time, place, family, and community. Despite the public's willingness to swiftly consume and respond to news of the tragedy, a swiftly delivered critique of this process did not appear to be readily acceptable. Thus, we might infer that increases in the speed and rate of information sharing also involve a policing of what perspectives are shared and enabled within digital spaces (Nahon & Helmsley, 2013). This case study demonstrates that the effects of these responses extend far beyond the digital realm, evidenced by the GoFundMe campaign and the systemic attack on Loreto and her work. Here, Loreto was attacked for politicizing a tragedy and reflecting on macro-social processes surrounding it. Hockey appeared to be a construct around which many people rallied and defensively lashed out. The severity of this response suggests that perhaps the relationship between hockey and the imagined Canadian identity is changing.

Dan Carcillo, the Sarnia Sting, and Hazing in the OHL

On November 24, 2018, in the wake of news coverage involving hazing incidents and allegations of abuse at St. Michael's College School, Dan Carcillo published a fifteen-tweet thread that outlined, in some detail, the hazing and abusive treatment he experienced during his rookie season in the Ontario Hockey League (OHL) (Hayes & Gibson, 2018). Carcillo played four seasons in the OHL and was drafted seventy-third overall in the 2003 NHL Entry Draft. His career in the NHL remains infamous, with Carcillo leading the NHL in penalty minutes during the 2007–2008 regular season. However, following his retirement from professional hockey in 2015, Carcillo became an outspoken proponent for mental health issues and post-concussion syndrome among hockey players. Following the death of a teammate, Carcillo founded Chapter 5, a not-for-profit organization focused on aiding athletes in their transition out of sport and into life after the game (Chapter 5 Foundation, 2019). Carcillo maintained a significant presence on social media, utilizing Twitter to confront injustices and challenge the perceptions of hockey culture he feels are perpetuating mental health issues and dangerous behaviours.

Carcillo's Twitter thread is an account of the experiences he endured during the 2002–2003 hockey season with the Sarnia Sting of the OHL. Across fifteen tweets, he recounts moving away from home, living with a billet family, going to a new school, and coping with the physical and mental rigours of elite sport. This is a familiar narrative within junior hockey, and one that has been increasingly normalized and glamourized over the last few decades. However, Carcillo diverts from the traditionally celebrated storyline of success and achievement that accompanies the journey to the NHL (MacDonald, 2014). In his third tweet he starts to uncover several darker aspects of his experience within hockey; he comments that having your "teammates beat you on a daily basis with the sawed off paddle of a goaltender's hockey stick, takes both a physical & mental toll on a teenager" (Carcillo, 2018a). Carcillo goes on to recount a particularly disturbing scene, where he remembers being "stuffed inside the bus washroom with 6–7 other rookies, while veterans hurl[ed] their spit from chewing tobacco through a vent in the door at you" (Carcillo, 2018b). This description of the "hot box treatment" showcases the horrific incidents of abuse and bullying that are often disguised as hazing within youth sport.

Following his descriptions of abuse and torment, Carcillo goes on to discuss how the power dynamics of the team, coaching staff, and management personnel left him feeling as though he did not know who to trust. Beyond his concerns about speaking out, Carcillo describes the stigma and reality of the toxic masculinity perpetuated within hockey culture, leaving him with the very real fear of jeopardizing his chances to go on to a professional career. He thus decided that rather than making complaints to the team or organization, he would write a letter to the OHL commissioner. Carcillo then concluded his Twitter thread, speaking to his hazing experience within the OHL, by stating, "Everything happens for a reason! Don't discredit times of suffering, Through pain, both emotional & physical, I have discovered who I am, If u r experiencing bullying/abuse of any kind & u don't know what to do, confide in someone you trust for advice #MentalHealth" (Carcillo, 2018c).

Carcillo's Twitter thread began with a hashtag, #BullyingAwarenessWeek, ostensibly in response to the ongoing news coverage of high school sports hazing incidents that were breaking across Canadian news cycles (Porter, 2018; The Canadian Press, 2018). Within this context, we consider the influences that shaped the responses to this original thread.

Carcillo's disclosure, on Twitter, once again reflects the importance and influence of social media, and Twitter in particular. In the broader aftermath of Carcillo's tweets, traditional media outlets like CBC, *The Hockey News*, and Rogers Sportsnet picked up the story and contributed to the discourse as it unfolded. Importantly, public engagement with Carcillo through Twitter also played a prominent role.

The initial responses to Carcillo's tweets, and his challenge to the dominant narratives surrounding junior hockey in Canada, were telling in a number of ways. The visual representations of the threads produced by Treeverse show a clear difference between Carcillo's conversation with his audience and Loreto's conversation with hers. Visually, and in real-time, the conversation between Carcillo and his Twitter followers is significantly more vertical than Loreto's. Carcillo contributes to this shape by repeatedly engaging with the responses to his original tweets and the overall Twitter thread; additionally, separate conversations flow from his tweets, creating further discourse and engagement among a variety of Twitter users. The majority of responses to Carcillo's tweets and the content of the conversations between Carcillo and Twitter users are notably cordial. At times, though, responses appear argumentative or concerned with pushing back on Carcillo's narrative, and competing discourses do emerge in response to Carcillo's tweets. First, users confront Carcillo's record as a player and enforcer during his time in the NHL, in particular appealing to hockey's "code." For example, when another former NHL player tweeted, "Make sure if you speak about hazing you have a squeaky clean track record with your teammates" (O'Neil, 2018). Second, and more prominent, is the congratulatory and respectful tone of Twitter users as their responses are laced with admiration and deference for Carcillo's inclination to challenge the "culture of silence" within hockey. These two competing discourses raise questions about the functioning and politics of the hockey family, and the imagined community that sport creates, upholds, and reproduces.

Reflections on Loreto, Carcillo, and the Social Order

While both of the cases reviewed in this chapter provide examples of individuals redirecting conversations about sport toward more critical perspectives, much can be said about a juxtaposition of these two stories and how they were taken up in the Twittersphere. In conclusion, we reflect on these two stories and pick up on a few of the threads that we have already introduced regarding sport, nationalism, and critiques in digital spaces. Within this reflection, we consider social positions within and outside of imagined sport and national communities, and reflect on ideas of insider-outsider status, paying attention to issues related to gender within sport. Additionally, we leverage ideas related to time and structure, considering how digital spaces have come to influence conversations, perpetuate discussion, and spark social movements and campaigns.

In defining what it means to be a member of a family, community, or any unit of identity, it necessarily involves defining what it means to not be a member (Spracklen, 2013). In the cases reviewed above, it is relevant to consider the apparent insider-outsider tensions and how the social, political, and professional positions of the individuals involved influenced the way their perspectives were taken up and responded to. As evidenced by the two critiques provided, the "hockey family" as an imagined community can be leveraged in different ways. One's status within the family directly affects how their opinions, decisions, and critiques are received by the public, which can be exacerbated online due to the nature of social media. If an individual is considered part of the family, as we see with Dan Carcillo, that person has the authority and legitimacy that allows them to confront it and lead difficult, perhaps uncomfortable, conversations about it. Conversely, if one is not a member of the community, which was the case with Nora Loreto, such a person is presumed to have no understanding of the inner workings of the family. This typically results in backlash and reminders of the position of the "outsider" and someone who is in no place to criticize the wider community. The respect and admiration Carcillo received, compared to the threats, counterattacks, and abuse Loreto endured, showcase the reality of insider-outsider status, and how one's intimate involvement within a perceived cultural "family" allows for their critique of the same family.

Within these two case studies, insider-outsider status is particularly prominent and likely further amplified by gender. It is well established that gender legitimizes "insider" status within sports, especially masculine sporting spaces such as the world of ice hockey. Women's marginalization from sporting circles, and their lack of legitimation and authority within sporting culture as experts, journalists, and athletes are relevant to this conversation (Cooky, 2018). As a woman, Loreto received significant gender-based criticism, with Twitter users choosing to respond with sexualized, graphic attacks. In contrast to this response, Carcillo's bravery and truthfulness around incidents of hazing and abuse are celebrated, with many Twitter users thanking him for his willingness to speak out, breaking a significant stigma around men confronting issues of toxic masculinity, mental health, and violence in hockey. The positions of Carcillo and Loreto are very different. Carcillo's status within the hockey family, his experiences within the sport at the highest professional level, and his so-called wisdom as an ex-NHL player left his insider status within the space as unquestionable. Yet Loreto was attacked based on her status as a woman who existed outside of the imagined hockey community.

The way that time was employed as a mechanism for policing the perspectives that were given attention within the respective broader conversations was also interesting. Time and timing come into play as prominent elements of the response to both of these Twitter episodes. As discussed, Loreto's comments were roundly criticized for coming "too soon"; part of the discourse that she had violated a social norm by commenting how and when she did. In contrast, the response to Carcillo's tweets included a discursive element that suggested this challenge to the normative sporting culture (especially hazing) was long overdue. Importantly, we recognize that Carcillo's comments came just days after the news of sexual assaults (represented as hazing rituals) of high school athletes in Ontario became mainstream news. It is notable, then, that where Loreto's comments were deemed "too soon," Carcillo's were not. This speaks again to the location of power within the formation of discourses in response to devastating events.

The structure of the Treeverse visualizations of these two case studies is instructive in several ways. First, as noted above, the "shape" of the conversation (i.e., vertical vs. horizontal) provides some insight into the dynamics of the discourses at play and the location of power in their construction. Where the engagement with Loreto's tweet is obviously flat/horizontal, it is indicative of an overwhelmingly uniform discourse, formed in opposition. Single-tweet responses that range from dismissal to overt threats characterize the general trend. Where the engagement with Carcillo's tweets is more layered/vertical in shape, it is indicative of at least an appetite or willingness to exchange or share perspectives. Many of these perspectives are supportive, speaking to Carcillo's social and cultural capital and therefore his credibility as a member of the hockey culture and with the identity that most prominently characterizes it. Carcillo does, of course, contribute to this shape by remaining engaged in this conversation.

Taken together, these two cases and their comparison provide a few insights into the role of Twitter in the construction and maintenance of imagined community identities in sport in general, and of hockey in Canada in particular. First, social media has become an important part of the way we associate with and consume hockey; in addition, hockey and social media are connected in the ways that people challenge, negotiate, scrutinize, and celebrate national identity (Norman, 2012; Szto, 2016). Second, challenges or critical commentary (through social media) concerning that national identity, and the hockey community that contributes to it, are important and informative spaces to consider the politics and power that maintain that identity. Third, critical analysis of both Nora Loreto and Dan Carcillo's comments shows that the discourses that develop in response to those challenges depend in large part on the insider or outsider status of those who voice the challenges. It provides some insight into what happens when someone challenges the perceptions that characterize hockey in Canada. Insiders have more power to determine the content, and timing, of acceptable challenges to dominant narratives; perceived outsiders do not. Finally, we note that both the Humboldt Broncos accident and various incidents of assault and hazing, including Dan Carcillo's experiences, were and continue to be devastating. Neither Loreto's nor Carcillo's comments sought to diminish these tragedies or others that occur across Canada. This chapter demonstrates how the responses to their tweets may be shaping the conversation about hockey and social issues, and may provide insights into the discourses framing the maintenance of community, national identity, and the culture of hockey in Canada. Undoubtedly, this conversation will continue to develop as changing ideas of sport and its role in Canada and Canadian identity continue to evolve.

References

Allsop, D.T., Bassett, B.R., & Hoskins, J.A. (2007, December). Word-of-mouth research: Principles and applications. *Journal of Advertising Research, 47*(4), 398–411.

Anderson, B. (1991). *Imagined communities: Reflections on the origin and spread of nationalism.* London, UK: Verso.

Carcillo, D. [@CarBombBoom13]. (2018a, November 24). 3/ teammates beat you on a daily basis with the sawed off paddle of a goaltender's hockey stick, takes both a physical & mental toll on a teenager I remember being so confused at the beginning of the yr I remember thinking to myself, "If this is part of the process, just shut [Tweet]. https://twitter.com/carbombboom13/status/1066383598499086342

Carcillo, D. [@CarBombBoom13]. (2018b, November 24). 6/ when you are sitting in a bus seat If you are stuffed inside the bus washroom with 6–7 other rookies, while

veterans hurl their spit from chewing tobacco through a vent in the door at you,
45 mins can feel like an eternity. 2 of us had had enough... [Tweet]. https://
twitter.com/carbombboom13/status/1066383598499086342

Carcillo, D. [@CarBombBoom13]. (2018c, November 24). 15/ Everything happens
for a reason! Don't discredit times of suffering Through pain, both emotional
& physical, I have discovered who I am If u r experiencing bullying/abuse
of any kind & u don't know what to do, confide in someone you trust for
advice #MentalHealth [Tweet]. https://twitter.com/CarBombBoom13/
status/1066383627817312261

Chapter 5 Foundation. (2019, January 28). Who we are [Mission statement]. http://
www.chapter5foundation.com/about-us/

Cooky, C. (2018). Sociology of gender and sport. In B.J. Risman, C.M. Froyum, & W.J.
Scarborough (Eds.), *Handbook of the sociology of gender* (pp. 459–469). Basel,
Switzerland: Springer.

Earl, J., & Kimport, K. (Eds.). (2011). *Digitally enabled social change: Activism in the
internet age*. Cambridge, MA: MIT Press.

Fairclough, N. (1995). *Critical discourse analysis: The critical study of language*.
London, UK: Longman Group.

Fairclough, N. (2001). *Language and power*. London, UK: Pearson Education.

Gruneau, R., & Whitson, D. (1993). *Hockey Night in Canada: Sport, identities, and
cultural politics* (2nd ed.). Toronto: Garamond Press.

Gruzd, A., & Roy, J. (2014). Investigating political polarization on Twitter: A
Canadian perspective. *Policy and Internet, 6*(1), 28–45.

Hayes, M., & Gibson, V. (2018). Toronto police charge six St. Michael's students with
sexual assault. *The Globe and Mail*. https://www.theglobeandmail.com/canada/
toronto/article-toronto-police-arrest-charge-six-st-michaels-students-
for-video-of/

Kennedy, L., Silva, D., Coelho, M., & Cipolli III, W. (2019). "We are all Broncos":
Hockey, tragedy, and the formation of Canadian identity. *Sociology of Sport
Journal, 36*(3), 189–202.

Loreto, N. [@NoLore]. (2018a, April 8). I'm trying to not get cynical about what is a
totally devastating tragedy but the maleness, the youthfulness and the whiteness
of the victims are, of course, playing a significant role [Tweet]. https://twitter.
com/nolore/status/983159952264003584

Loreto, N. [@NoLore]. (2018b, April 8). I don't want less for the families and
survivors of this tragedy. I want justice and more for so many other

grieving parents and communities [Tweet]. https://twitter.com/nolore/ status/983159952264003584

Loreto, N. [@NoLore]. (2018c, April 8). (If you're responding to this thread to make this into a horse race, which it most certainly isn't, go away) [Tweet]. https:// twitter.com/nolore/status/983159952264003584

MacDonald, C.A. (2014). Masculinity and sport revisited: A review of literature on hegemonic masculinity and men's ice hockey in Canada. *Canadian Graduate Journal of Sociology and Criminology, 3*(1), 95–112.

Murphy-Perron, M. (2018). We mourned Humboldt differently than other tragedies. Let's talk about that. *Huffpost*. https://www.huffingtonpost.ca/ mathieu-murphyperron/humbolt-crash-nora-loreto_a_23412639/

Nahon, K., & Helmsley, J. (2013). *Going viral*. Cambridge, UK: Polity Press.

Norman, M. (2012). Saturday night's alright for tweeting: Cultural citizenship, collective discussion, and the new media consumption/production of Hockey Day in Canada. *Sociology of Sport Journal, 29*(3), 306–324.

O'Neil, J. [@odognine2]. (2018, November 27). Make sure if you speak about hazing you have a squeaky clean track record with your teammates [Tweet]. https:// twitter.com/odognine2/status/1067553640850890754?lang=en

Pegoraro, A. (2014). Twitter as disruptive innovation in sport communication. *Communication and Sport, 2*(2), 132–137.

Porter, C. (2018). St. Michael's, a Toronto all-boys school, is rocked by accusations of sexual assaults. *The New York Times*. https://www.nytimes.com/2018/11/23/ world/canada/toronto-st-michaels-college-school-hazing-sexual-assault.html

Rich, K.A. (2021). Rural sport spectacles: Ice hockey, mythologies, and meaning-making in rural Canada. *Leisure Sciences*. http://doi.org/10.1080/01490400.2 020.1870591

Rich, K.A., Bean, C., & Apramian, Z. (2014). Boozing, brawling, and community building: Sport-facilitated community development in a rural Ontario community. *Leisure/Loisir, 38*(1), 73–91.

Robidoux, M.A. (2002). Imagining a Canadian identity through sport: A historical interpretation of lacrosse and hockey. *Journal of American Folklore, 115*(456), 209–225.

Robidoux, M.A. (2012). *Stickhandling through the margins*. Toronto: University of Toronto Press.

Spracklen, K. (2013). Leisure and community. In K. Spracklen (Ed.), *Sport, leisure & society* (pp. 102–114). London, UK: Palgrave Macmillan.

Szto, C. (2016). #LOL at multiculturalism: Reactions to Hockey Night in Canada Punjabi from the Twitterverse. *Sociology of Sport Journal, 33*(3), 208–218.

The Canadian Press. (2018). Timeline of events on assault allegations at St. Michael's College School. *Global News.* https://globalnews.ca/news/4681026/ timeline-st-michaels-college-assaults/

Vlavo, F. (2012). "Click here to protest": Electronic civil disobedience and the imaginaire of virtual activism. In H. Breslow & A. Mousoutzanis (Eds.), *Cybercultures: Mediations of community, culture, politics* (pp. 125–148). New York: Rodopi.

Whitson, D., & Gruneau, R. (Eds.). (2006). *Artificial ice: Hockey, culture and commerce.* Peterborough, ON: Broadview Press.

4

Hockey Talks

Mental Health Faces off against the "Green Lantern" Mentality

BRETT PARDY

THE #HOCKEYTALKS INITIATIVE was launched in February 2013 as a collaboration between the National Hockey League (NHL) players and the seven Canadian NHL teams to emphasize "mental health and wellness awareness and education" (Epstein, 2013, para. 1). The work began as player-led activism with the Vancouver Canucks a year earlier, in the 2011–2012 season, after former player Rick Rypien died by suicide. Rypien's close friend and teammate Kevin Bieksa became an advocate for mental health, stating:

> Mental health is obviously an issue that is near and dear to my heart. I think people usually go to their friends first and their friends are usually that channel for the people suffering to vent to and they have to handle that responsibility the right way. Most times they don't want to break their friend's trust but it's so important to let the proper people know about what's going on. Everybody needs to help out. (as quoted in Epstein, 2013, para. 3)

The initiative sees each Canadian N H L team set up an information page on its website, dedicate one home game to "bringing awareness" to ending the stigma, and players wear apparel and #HockeyTalks helmet decals for the month.

The purpose of this chapter is twofold. First, it explores how the Hockey Talks initiative is promoted, how N H L players engage in it, and why the initiative has remained static since its 2013 inception. Second, it offers an analysis of what I term the "Green Lantern theory of hockey" and how this stalls the N H L's progress on addressing player's well-being. The superhero Green Lantern has a magic ring that can create anything they can imagine, if only they use enough willpower. Political scientist Brendan Nyhan (2009) introduced "the Green Lantern theory of the [American] presidency," which critiques media narratives that the president either succeeds or fails to implement policy by how much they want to dedicate themselves to it. Nyhan critiques the media for failing to address the checks and balances of government and offering a simple, compelling, but false picture of how politics works. The Green Lantern concept is also the ethos of the N H L, where coaches, media, fans, and other players praise players' use of their "willpower" to create goals, block shots, and hit opponents. Anything that suggests a lapse in this willpower is suspect (Wyshynski, 2018). The continual celebration of Green Lantern hockey carries with it an undercurrent that is the very thing that makes talking about mental health and illness difficult for N H L players. The N H L is committed to talking about mental health, but in a vacuum away from factors that make people hide mental health in the first place.

As an outsider to the N H L, I will rely upon published interviews and autobiographical articles to understand the N H L's internal culture concerning treatment of mental health and illness. While active N H L players mainly talk around mental health and illness, inspired by Hockey Talks and Bell Let's Talk Day, several former players have written narratives sharing their mental illness experiences: Clint

Malarchuk, who played in the NHL between 1981 and 1992 (Malarchuk & Robson, 2014); Stéphane Richer, who was active in the league from 1984 to 2002 (Cowan, 2015); and Corey Hirsch (2017), who played between 1992 and 2003. More recently, Nick Boynton (2018) and Dan Carcillo (Chiarito, 2018), who played from 1999 to 2011 and 2006 to 2014, respectively, have also publicly expressed a history of mental health issues.

Some of the narratives are decades old and presumably there has been some improvement in the NHL's approach to mental illness in that time. Former Canuck and then-team president Trevor Linden alluded to this progress in a video that the Vancouver Canucks (2017) produced that featured Corey Hirsch. Linden said he understood Hirsch's silence because an NHL locker room "was an unforgiving place in those days," with the connotation that things have changed. Presumably, because of Hockey Talks, things have changed and players are more likely to address their mental health and would listen to a teammate's discussion of mental health/illness, but we also have little public evidence of this. I will focus not on the internal workings of the teams as much as how media and fans create discursive environments around the NHL that both reflect and influence how coaches and players think and speak. The media and fan discourse are a feedback loop to hockey culture (Adams, 2006; Stead, 2010).

The former players' mental illness discussions, emerging one or two per year, may be the slow trickle that begins a breakthrough. The pieces suggest there is an appetite for players' experiences to be heard. Most importantly, they show that mental illness is not a barrier to success. While Hockey Talks aims to normalize mental illness, it inadvertently makes mental illness seem more limiting than it is, because only one of seven hundred-plus active NHL players discusses their own mental illness. In September 2018, New York Islanders goaltender Robin Lehner (2018) became the first active player to publicly discuss mental illness by writing about his bipolar diagnosis and how his manic highs and depressive lows affected his life and play. His performance during 2018–2019 was his career best and members of the Professional Hockey Writers' Association voted Lehner as the recipient of the Bill Masterton Memorial Trophy, awarded for perseverance and dedication to hockey. Given that this award has often gone to players returning from a serious physical injury, his candidacy was a positive sign of treating mental illness like physical injury, as the Hockey Talks campaigns stress. Perhaps, by the time you read this, there will have been more brave players.

Hockey Talks...about Talking?

On their Hockey Talks webpages, the Canadian NHL teams each present a short summary emphasizing four key points: 1) one in five Canadians experiences a mental health or addiction problem; 2) 70 per cent of mental health problems have their onset during childhood or adolescence; 3) mental health is the leading cause of disability in Canada; and 4) identifying signs and getting help early are important for effective treatment (Winnipeg Jets, 2020). Each team provides web links to local and provincial sources of mental health information. Teams also may post videos or testimonial stories from players about how it is important to listen and be supportive of other people's experiences. The teams collectively put out a public service announcement video featuring players saying, "If you are worried about yourself or someone else, you should reach out...You are not a burden, this is not a weakness, and there are ways to get help" (Vancouver Canucks, 2019, 0:14–0:23).

Notably, the NHL teams go with the terminology "mental health," using it nearly interchangeably with mental illness. I will instead be following the definitions of the Canadian Mental Health Association. *Mental health* refers to emotional well-being and is affected by circumstances such as stress, personal relationships, and work (Canadian Mental Health Association, 2018a). *Mental illness* is caused by "a complex interplay of genetic, biological, personality and environmental factors" (Canadian Mental Health Association 2018b, para. 3). It is a category that includes anxiety disorders, bipolar disorders, schizophrenia, major depression, and personality disorders, which often require medical treatment.

Terminology issues aside, such a program was an exciting development for the NHL, as the league usually lags behind social progress (Jhaveri, 2017; Shoalts, 2017), but here positioned itself as a leader in creating empathy and understanding around mental health and illness. The intensely masculine culture of the NHL actually made it a perfect fit to be a leader in discussing mental health/illness, as a masculine belief in not showing "weakness" often leads men to not seek outside help in addressing their mental health (Rogers & Pilgrim, 2014). The Canadian Mental Health Association (2018c) reports that 75 per cent of suicides in Canada are men. I am not suggesting that women and nonbinary fans are not encouraged by the NHL's initiatives. Rather, it is that the NHL's assumed fan has been, as Andrew Ference, the NHL's first director of social impact, growth, and fan development, puts it, "middle-aged white dudes" (Wyshynski, 2018, para. 4).

While I am wary of the emphasis on hockey players as role models, sports fandom is a form of communication, with audiences sending and receiving a variety of messages on topics such nationalism (Gruneau & Whitson, 1993), masculinity (Allain, 2008), race (Szto, 2011), and sexuality (MacDonald, 2018). This is why I was so excited about Hockey Talks, as it has great potential to snap the silence over mental health often being conflated with toughness; however, the tensions between the more conservative elements of hockey and the emotional honesty necessary to grapple with mental health/illness have not been resolved.

The result of these unresolved tensions is that, after more than six years of events, players continue to discuss only the importance of treating mental illness like physical injury and stressing the need to listen rather than judge. Discussing the importance of talking (as opposed to showing how to talk) is an acceptable start, but only a start, rather than a satisfying outcome for the program. Talking about talking rather than showing how to actually talk ultimately makes this "safe" in ways that do not challenge the institutions and structure of the league as a business or culture, as is typical of the NHL's charity efforts (Szto, 2011). The significant problem of talking about talking is it always assumes that NHL players are role models for being allies, but never role models for dealing with mental illness. That there is silence about being the role model for handling mental illness sends a disturbing message that, despite the call to talk, the response is a promise to be an ally who listens, but never someone who had success by being listened to. Such silence can be read the wrong way: as if there are no NHL players with mental illness, as if mental illness is a barrier that prevents success. Rather than instilling strength in someone who is struggling, this silence may instead further worry them.

The biggest example of how NHL players contribute to "talking" is through Bell Canada's Let's Talk Day in late January. Let's Talk Day began in 2010 as an effort to encourage public discussion around mental health. Bell pledges to donate five cents for each tweet and retweet on Twitter that includes the hashtag #BellLetsTalk. In 2018, the hashtag received over 138 million interactions and raised nearly $7 million (Forani, 2018), which was donated to hospitals, community groups, and mental health foundations. Bell was a league sponsor at the initiative's beginning, is now a current sponsor of several Canadian teams, and the rise of Hockey Talks is surely linked to Bell's efforts to "talk." It has become an annual tradition for NHL teams to tweet the hashtag, as well as retweet current players and draft picks that used the hashtag. In 2018, the thirty-one NHL teams retweeted 186 players, but only one— Toronto Maple Leafs minor league player Rich Clune, said anything about personal experiences. Clune (2018) tweeted, "Don't be afraid to ask for help. Hang in there another day, hour, or minute if that's all you can get. I know how hard it is." Clune (2015) had previously written for The Players' Tribune about how his depression led him to alcohol and drug addiction. Beyond Clune, the tweet content is, at best, platitudes like "reach out," but 139 of the 186 player tweets retweeted by NHL official team accounts were just the hashtag. The NHL has come a long way in recognizing that mental health advocacy is something that players should be at least seen to be doing; however, they are more comfortable when money stands in for empathy and honesty.

While fundraising is noble, mental illness advocacy is a rare instance where "slacktivism" and "raising awareness" have positive effects. *Slacktivism*, which is largely known as online support and offline inaction, is often criticized for creating strong opinions but lacking commitment to politically engage with the subject (Morozov, 2012). Instead, slacktivist campaigns, after acknowledging the issue, turn either to collecting names for petitions or raising money, both greatly aided by internet technologies (Morozov, 2012). While raising awareness alone about the atrocities of a Ugandan terrorist creates little change, raising awareness about mental health/illness has positive effects. Money alone will not create change in how society thinks about mental health because the problem does not solely lie in underfunding.

Speaking for my own Canadian context, society does need healthier and more honest discussions about mental health because much of the current system is a stopgap (Canadian Mental Health Association, 2018d). We need solutions that also address the sense of fear and shame that goes along with mental health. While this is not the place, nor am I the person, to outline a new system, my goal for this chapter is to outline how media and fans, the aspects of professional hockey I participate in, can change how we talk about certain aspects of hockey—predominantly toughness—in ways that would facilitate an honest discussion around mental health. I follow Kalman-Lamb's (2018) suggestion that "perhaps in the cultivation of empathy, compassion and community between athletes and spectators we can begin to imagine a new form of social relations" (p. 174). Hockey Talks's stagnation is inevitable unless we see wider changes in NHL culture (as well as the hockey culture that feeds into it), where players, executives, media, and fans all challenge the norms of masculine individuality and toughness to truly destigmatize mental illness. As I will outline, the concept of honest, open discussion of mental health remains too incongruous with central tenets of NHL hockey culture to occur. Instead, talking about talking has been the solution to this impasse, an acknowledgement that some form of change should happen, but a reticence to commit to any specific change.

One of the scariest parts of talking about mental illness is the potential for judgment, that people will not believe you or treat you differently in perpetuity after your revelation. That it is so rare for a player to discuss can send the wrong message. As each team's website emphasizes one in five people will deal with mental illness, but only one NHL player apparently does, it could be interpreted that mental illness is indeed a barrier to success. However, analysis of how NHL culture's glorification of rugged individual masculinity and achievement of everything through dedication and "hard work" makes it easy to understand why most active NHL players would not want to make such illness public. This culture is what Hockey Talks should also work to change.

Green Lantern Hockey and Physical Injury

Former Toronto Maple Leafs head coach and mental health advocate Mike Babcock reflected,

> When you think of someone like [long distance speed skater] Clara Hughes, as mentally tough of an athlete as she is and was, she had mental illness. Mental toughness and mental illness have nothing to do with one another. (Proteau, 2017, para. 16)

Uncoupling the link between hockey's vaunted "mental toughness" and mental illness is essential but easier said than done. Disturbingly, after the Maple Leafs fired Babcock in November 2019, former player Johan Franzen described Babcock as a bully who made him terrified of being at the rink (St. James, 2019). The context provided by Franzen makes Babcock's above quote read in a different light, as if mental illness is a completely separate issue from what professional hockey players are expected to endure as part of the culture. Such an approach is why the NHL does not make substantial progress addressing mental illness.

Part of mental toughness is not being a "distraction," or, as Andrew Ference recalls, "If you're getting involved in other things outside of the game itself, you open yourself up to criticism, even if it had nothing to do with the game that you play" (Wyshynski, 2018, para. 2). If players cannot be people, but just single-minded hockey players, then it is difficult to address their personal needs. Ference emphasizes that the fans play as much a role in such surveillance and criticism as the coach and general manager, which supports the necessity of shifting how we as fans talk about the game. If we are going to treat mental illness like a physical injury or illness, as Corey Hirsch (Sabatino, 2019) and Clint Malarchuk (Brophy, 2014) have suggested, then we must first change the way we see even physical injury.

The Toronto Maple Leafs' website feature on Bell Let's Talk Day included the statement, "professional hockey players are renowned for their ability to shake off injuries and vulnerability to push forward competitively, but, thanks in part to the annual social media awareness initiative, those same athletes are far more willing to come to terms with injuries to, and diseases of, the mind" (Proteau, 2019, para. 5). The problem is "the ability to shake off injuries and vulnerability to push forward competitively" (Proteau, 2019, para. 5) is the most insidious way the Green Lantern mentality shows itself in hockey. The pain of physical injury is something that can be played through with sufficient willpower. By contrast, a failure to play through this injury is a lack of mental toughness. While Babcock states mental illness and mental toughness have nothing to do with each other, it is easy to imagine that a player not playing through mental illness would be criticized for a lack of mental toughness. Kalman-Lamb (2018) argues that professional sport requires the alienation of the athlete to produce "social reproductive labour...

[which] generates the meaning fans crave and around which they can form community" (p. 17). The athlete as a human is outside this community and fans generally ease their conscience of this by thinking about the salaries (elite, male) athletes make. NHL fans particularly pride their sport for "their" athlete's toughness and ability to play through pain to win. The popular "hockey vs. basketball" meme often compares basketball players' injuries, like leg cramps, against hockey players covered in blood after being hit with a puck, finishing a penalty-killing shift while on a broken leg, or the most egregious—in the words of the meme a hockey player "dies on bench, is revived, and asks to be put back in the game" (Petchesky, 2014). Given the masochistic celebration of an NHL player's ability to play through injury, the suggestion that hockey should treat mental illness like physical injury does not seem like a solution. Until hockey fans take the physical suffering of the athletes as a source of concern rather than pride, it is difficult to imagine making a similar jump to mental illness.

Playing through injury is often done not purely for the love of the game but because it is entrenched in what hockey players "do." In Kalman-Lamb's (2018) interviews with ex-players, he finds "the athlete must be willing to treat his physical body as an object he is willing to destroy in order to fulfil his duty to his team" (p. 25). If the player is unable to play, he is unable to fulfill this duty and no longer has value. Players' own awareness of their value creates significant anxiety. Goaltender Ben Meisner (2018), who played pro hockey in the East Coast Hockey League and in Germany's Deutsche Eishockey Liga, calls attention to the precarity involved in much of professional hockey. While the sport's household names make millions over careers that can last nearly two decades, every off-season hundreds of players scramble to find a job in the professional men's hockey landscape in North America, Europe, and Asia. While NHL contracts are guaranteed, contracts in many leagues are not, and being cut, which could occur at any time, may mean the end of a career. Meisner (2018) writes,

For a lot of guys down in the minors, deciding whether to reach out for help becomes a lose-lose proposition. If you speak up and tell someone that you need to miss time for an injury that's not necessarily visible—no broken ankle or sprained wrist—not only do you lose your spot on the roster while you're out, it could mean that you lose your job as a professional hockey player altogether. (para. 3)

He notes that although players' unions have ensured players cannot be cut because of injury, the same protection does not apply to something like less predictable "recovery" timelines associated with conditions such as depression or anxiety. Meisner adds that even if a team was willing to do that, anxiety and depression can lead to assuming a worst-case scenario of losing your position with the team.

Physical injury, particularly concussions and/or dependency on pain-killers, also plays a significant role in mental health/illness and any effort to seriously talk about mental illness should emphasize prevention as much as treatment. One of the effects of chronic traumatic encephalopathy (CTE), a degenerative brain condition in people who have sustained multiple concussions, is increased risk of depression, anxiety, and personality changes (Hart Jr. et al., 2013). NHL Commissioner Gary Bettman continues to deny the linkage between concussion and CTE and blames the media instead for creating a panic (Belson, 2018). Former NHL player Dan Carcillo, now an advocate for taking concussions more seriously in hockey, asserts that by having such an approach, "the NHL is killing human beings because they are by not properly diagnosing and treating these concussions" (Chiarito, 2018). Nonetheless, as Silverwood (2015) notes, "Society seems to have an obsession with finding a medical cause for increased suicide ideation in current or retired players" (para. 4). The linkage to concussions specifically and the analogy to physical health in general focuses on mental illness as a form of injury, which allows the NHL to ignore the social factors of mental health. Hockey Talks never interrogates the myriad ways NHL culture's obsession with stoic, rugged, individualist masculinity could lead to poor mental health.

What Could Success with Hockey Talks Look Like?

A good example of how to move Hockey Talks forward can be found in the professional women's hockey leagues—the Canadian Women's Hockey League and the National Women's Hockey League (NWHL). Players from both leagues are also active members in Bell Let's Talk Day on social media, but some players do more than just fundraise. In 2018, Connecticut Whale player Anya Battaglino (2018) tweeted, "I would be lying to tell you that I don't still struggle with mental health." Madison Packer (2018) of the Metropolitan Riveters tweeted a picture of her semicolon tattoo, a popular anti-suicide symbol that indicates choosing not to end a sentence but to keep going. Her teammate with the Riveters, Tatiana Rafter (2018) posted on Instagram, "Bell Lets Talk has inspired me to share my ongoing battle with depression. I've tried to post about my personal struggle the past few years but wasn't quite ready and would hit delete." Rafter discussed how opening up after years of trying to hide it has made her feel stronger. She continued to share how she manages her depression on social media. These examples from the NWHL follow the gendered pattern in broader society of willingness to discuss mental health (Rogers & Pilgrim, 2014), and are also likely possible due to not being the large business that men's hockey is. Still, this is exactly the type of content NHL players should be comfortable sharing during #HockeyTalks, and until it occurs, it is hard to see the initiative as accomplishing its goals.

Toward Possible Solutions

Hockey Talks is an idea that has already created progress just by asking people to think and talk about mental health/illness, *yet the way* it talks about mental health/illness reveals how far the NHL has left to go—players are comfortable being allies, but evidently less so when it comes to being the public's role model for living with mental illness. The NHL players' foray into player-led activism has partially revealed the cultural barriers to actually addressing change.

To avoid continued stagnation, conditions need to be created where an NHL player could say, "I deal with a mental health issue," rather than "I would listen to a friend who has one." This burden is on hockey executives, media, and fans. Kalman-Lamb (2018) argues that professional sport requires the viewing of athletes as products that will supply fans with dreams of sharing collective victory with their imagined community. As this relationship remains profitable, there is little hope for a top-down solution from the NHL to address mental health and illness. Instead, it is up to fans to work to create a climate where honest conversation about mental health can occur. This is unfortunate in the sense that the NHL will not be the leader in creating empathy for mental health/illness that they positioned themselves to be when the initiative began. The NHL's call to action on mental health/illness may be going nowhere, but fans can take the invitation to talk back to the NHL.

Engaged fans would do well to learn to talk about hockey in ways that do not dehumanize players. Indeed, behind every player, every injury, every trade, and every "bad" contract is a person. The glass that separates spectator from athlete should not be thick enough to block one's sense of empathy. Athletes should not have to feel the persistent questionings that may accompany discussion of their mental health. They should be celebrated for healing properly, not for playing through injuries. Such change will not be immediate but, in the feedback loop of hockey culture, it will eventually alter how athletes are valued. When players are seen as people first, they will then be capable of being role models for talking about mental health and will thus expand the benefits of talking further. Until then, it is just talking about talking.

References

Adams, M.L. (2006). The game of whose lives? Gender, race, and entitlement in Canada's "national" game. In D. Whitson & R. Gruneau (Eds.), *Artificial ice: Hockey, culture and commerce* (pp. 71–84). Toronto: University of Toronto Press.

Allain, K.A. (2008). "Real fast and tough": The construction of Canadian hockey masculinity. *Sociology of Sport Journal,* 25(4), 462–481.

Battaglino, A. [@battaglinoa]. (2018, January 31). I would be lying to tell you that I don't still struggle with mental health. Except now I don't call it struggling I call it battling, and I have a support system that loves me and understands me. Be that support system, start the conversation, save a life #BellLetsTalk [Tweet]. https://twitter.com/battaglinoa/status/958738810732347392

Belson, K. (2018, July 24). In N.H.L concussion lawsuit, Gary Bettman opts to fight. *The New York Times.* https://www.nytimes.com/2018/07/24/sports/nhl-concussion-lawsuit-gary-bettman.html

Boynton, N. (2018, June 13). Everything's not ok. *The Players' Tribune.* https://www.theplayerstribune.com/en-us/articles/nick-boynton-everythings-not-ok

Brophy, A. (2014, November 13). Ex NHL goalie Clint Malarchuk: Mental illness is tough opponent. *Samaritan Mag.* https://www.samaritanmag.com/features/ex-nhl-goalie-clint-malarchuk-mental-illness-tough-opponent

Canadian Mental Health Association. (2018a). Your mental health. https://cmha.ca/resources

Canadian Mental Health Association. (2018b). Fast facts about mental illness. https://cmha.ca/about-cmha/fast-facts-about-mental-illness

Canadian Mental Health Association. (2018c). Men and mental illness. https://cmha.ca/documents/men-and-mental-illness

Canadian Mental Health Association. (2018d). *Mental health in the balance: Ending the health care disparity in Canada.* https://alberta.cmha.ca/wp-content/uploads/2018/09/CMHA-Parity-Paper-Full-EN.pdf

Chiarito, R. (2018, June 28). Q&A: Daniel Carcillo on hockey and his crusade against traumatic brain injuries. *Chicago Magazine.* https://www.chicagomag.com/city-life/June-2018/Q-A-Daniel-Carcillo-on-Hockey-and-Traumatic-Brain-Injuries/

Clune, R. (2015, July 1). The battle. *The Players' Tribune.* https://www.theplayerstribune.com/en-us/articles/rich-clune-hockey-nhl

Clune, R. [@richclune]. (2018, January 31). Don't be afraid to ask for help. Hang in there another day, hour, or minute if that's all you can get. I know how hard it is

#BellLetsTalk [Tweet]. https://twitter.com/richclune/status/
958861085741785090

Cowan, S. (2015, January 29). Former Hab Stéphane Richer among those who have
battled depression. *Montreal Gazette.* https://montrealgazette.com/sports/
hockey/nhl/montreal-canadiens/former-hab-stephane-richer-among-those-who-
have-battled-depression

Epstein, E. (2013, February 1). #HockeyTalks launches to raise awareness for mental
health. NHLPA. https://www.nhlpa.com/news/1-12980/hockeytalks-launches-to-
raise-awareness-for-mental-health

Forani, J. (2018, January 31). Bell Let's Talk hits 138 million interactions as celebrities
join in. CTV News. https://www.ctvnews.ca/health/bell-let-s-talk-hits-138-million-
interactions-as-celebrities-join-in-1.3783948

Gruneau, R., & Whitson, D. (1993). *Hockey Night in Canada: Sport, identities, and
cultural politics.* Toronto: Garamond Press.

Hart Jr., J., Kraut, M.A., Womack, K.B., Strain, J., Didehbani, N., Bartz, E., Conover, H.,
Mansinghani, S., Lu, H., & Cullum, M. (2013). Neuroimaging of cognitive
dysfunction and depression in aging retired National Football League players: A
cross-sectional study. *JAMA Neurology, 70*(3), 326–335. http://doi.org/
10.1001/2013.jamaneurol.340

Hirsch, C. (2017, February 15). Dark, dark, dark, dark, dark, dark, dark, dark. *The
Players' Tribune.* https://www.theplayerstribune.com/en-us/articles/
corey-hirsch-dark-dark-dark

Jhaveri, H. (2017, September 25). Why hockey fans shouldn't look to NHL players to
be allies. *USA Today.* https://ftw.usatoday.com/2017/09/why-hockey-fans-shouldnt-
look-to-nhl-players-to-be-allies

Kalman-Lamb, N. (2018). *Game misconduct: Injury, fandom, and the business of sport.*
Halifax, NS: Fernwood.

Lehner, R. (2018, September 13). "I could not stand being alone in my brain": Islanders
goalie Robin Lehner opens up about his addiction and bipolar diagnosis. *The
Athletic.* https://theathletic.com/522117/2018/09/13/islanders-goalie-robin-lehner-
opens-up-about-his-addiction-and-bipolar-diagnosis-i-could-not-stand-being-
alone-in-my-brain/

MacDonald, C.A. (2018). Insert name of openly gay hockey player here: Attitudes
towards homosexuality among Canadian male major midget AAA ice hockey
players. *Sociology of Sport Journal, 35*(4), 347–357. http://doi.org/10.1123/
ssj.2017-0133

Malarchuk, C., & Robson, D. (2014). *The crazy game: How I survived in the crease and beyond.* New York: HarperCollins.

Meisner, B. (2018, August 14). I'm not Connor McDavid. *The Players' Tribune.* https://www.theplayerstribune.com/en-us/articles/hockey-ben-meisner-im-not-connor-mcdavid

Morozov, E. (2012). *The net delusion: The dark side of internet freedom.* New York: Public Affairs.

Nyhan, B. (2009, December 14). The Green Lantern theory of the presidency [Blog post]. https://www.brendan-nyhan.com/blog/2009/12/the-green-lantern-theory-of-the-presidency.html

Packer, M. [@madison_packer]. (2018, January 31). The struggles mental health presents have impacted my life and the lives of the people I love most. I will donate 10 cents for every like & 25 cents for every RT to @CGHelps. It's okay to ask for help, and it's okay to struggle. Start the conversation. Save a life #BellsLetsTalk [Tweet]. https://twitter.com/madison_packer_/status/958840776494075910

Petchesky, B. (2014, March 12). Hockey fans using Rich Peverley to shit on LeBron James are the worst. *Deadspin.* https://deadspin.com/hockey-fans-using-rich-peverley-to-shit-on-lebron-james-1542223654

Proteau, A. (2017, January 24). Babcock, Leafs, focus on mental health awareness. *MapleLeafs.com.* https://www.nhl.com/mapleleafs/news/babcock-leafs-focus-on-mental-health-awareness/c-286067874

Proteau, A. (2019, January 30). On Bell Let's Talk Day, Leafs are proud of evolution on mental health. *MapleLeafs.com.* https://www.nhl.com/mapleleafs/news/leafs-discuss-importance-of-mental-health-initiatives/c-304333250

Rafter, T. [@tatianarafter]. (2018, January 31). #BellLetsTalk has inspired me to share my ongoing battle with depression. . .[Instagram post]. https://www.instagram.com/p/BeomeYBhER-/

Rogers, A., & Pilgrim, D. (2014). *A sociology of mental health and illness* (5th ed.). London, UK: Open University Press.

Sabatino, G. (2019, February 21). Former NHL goaltender shares mental health struggles with Lake City students. *The Williams Lake Tribune.* https://www.wltribune.com/sports/former-nhl-goaltender-shares-mental-health-struggles-with-lakecity-students/

Shoalts, D. (2017, September 29). NHL can no longer keep its head in the sand. *The Globe and Mail.* https://www.theglobeandmail.com/sports/hockey/nhl-can-no-longer-keep-its-head-in-the-sand/article36447339/

Silverwood, V. (2015, September 25). The concussion scapegoat. *Hockey in Society*. https://hockeyinsociety.com/2015/09/25/the-concussion-scapegoat/

St. James, H. (2019, December 2). Ex-Red Wing Johan Franzen calls Mike Babcock "the worst (person) I have ever met." *Detroit Free Press*. https://www.freep.com/story/sports/nhl/red-wings/2019/12/02/detroit-red-wings-johan-franzen-mike-babcock-worst-person/2590915001/

Stead, D. (2010). Sport and the media. In B. Houlihan (Ed.), *Sport and society: A student introduction* (pp. 32–347). London, UK: Sage.

Szto, C. (2011, December 10). "Hockey is for everyone": A pretty good lie. *Hockey in Society*. https://hockeyinsociety.com/2011/12/10/hockey-is-for-everyone-a-pretty-good-lie/

Vancouver Canucks. (2017, February 15). Hirsch story: Struggle & recovery. https://www.nhl.com/canucks/video/hirsch-story-struggle--recovery/t-277437438/c-49452303

Vancouver Canucks. (2019, January 15). Hockey Talks: Together we can. https://www.nhl.com/canucks/community/hockey-talks

Winnipeg Jets. (2020, January 5). Hockey talks. https://www.nhl.com/jets/community/hockey-talks

Wyshysnki, G. (2018, March 26). Andrew Ference says NHL must reach beyond "middle-aged white dudes." *ESPN*. http://www.espn.com/nhl/story/_/id/22908289/nhl-andrew-ference-says-nhl-reach-middle-aged-white-dudes

Access and Support

5

"We have to work for it. For everything. Absolutely everything."

An Examination of the Gendered Structure of Ice Hockey in U SPORTS

CHELSEY LEAHY

SINCE THEIR INTRODUCTION TO SPORTS, girls and women have had to overcome the neutral zone trap by challenging the ideological belief of sport as a male domain (Bandy, 2016; DiCarlo, 2016). However, sport remains mainly sex-segregated and viewed as a masculine space, making it hard for some girls and women to gain the same respect and privilege as their male counterparts (Messner, 2002). The traditional emphasis on sport as a male domain has permitted the masculine institutional arrangement of sport to appear natural and unchallengeable (Messner, 2002). Giddens (1984), however, argues that individuals have the agency to create change, despite the naturalized elements of a system. The gender imbalance in sport has permitted boys and men to establish their own cultural practices, which individuals have come to understand and value as the most legitimate practices (Hall, 2002). In turn, girls and women have had to fight to gain and keep control over their own experiences, while trying to have their practices and activities viewed as legitimate by the privileged group and others (Hall, 2002).

The following chapter reports on a case study that was conducted to examine how the gendered structure of U SPORTS ice hockey impacts the experience of female players in this league. It is the result of a broader project in which the author examined the overall experiences of female varsity ice hockey players in U SPORTS from their introduction into the sport until the 2015–2016 season.

Methods

This case study used Messner's (2002) tri-level conceptual approach to studying gender in sport, which suggests looking at gender in sport from three levels: 1) social interactions; 2) structural context; and 3) cultural symbols. This chapter specifically focuses on how players' social interactions and the structural context of ice hockey in U SPORTS have shaped their experiences. The author took a qualitative multi-methods approach for this study to create a complete picture (Kirby, Greaves, & Reid, 2006). Kirby and colleagues (2006) argue that in social sciences there is debate "about who can be a 'knower' and what counts as legitimate knowledge" (pp. 63–64). For this reason, the author conducted two sets of semi-structured interviews and a document analysis.

The primary dataset was built of five semi-structured interviews with women ice hockey players who played at Rankin University (a pseudonym has been applied) during the 2015–2016 season. Participants for this dataset were deliberately selected using convenience sampling (Markula & Silk, 2011) and their status as female ice hockey players in U SPORTS playing for the same institution. Of these participants, Avery and Caroline (pseudonyms have been applied to all participants) were both in their first of five years of eligibility, while Brooke was in her second year. Dayle and Elizabeth were in their fourth years of eligibility with the intention of it being their final season, as they were expecting to graduate in the spring of 2016. Secondary datasets were used to enhance and create a more complete picture using supplementary semi-structured interviews and through information gathered from

"We have to work for it. For everything. Absolutely everything."

secondary sources. These secondary datasets gave the author a better understanding of the structural context of the program and U SPORTS ice hockey. The supplementary interviews were conducted with the head coach (coach) of the team and the athletic director (AD), whereas the information gathered from secondary sources was gathered from Donnelly, Norman, and Kidd's (2013) *Gender Equity in Canadian Interuniversity Sport: A Biennial Report (No. 2)*, as well as the "Equity Policy 80.80" of the U SPORTS *Policy and Procedures, 80—Administration Manual*. Additionally, secondary information was collected from Rankin University's athletic department's annual budget between 2011 and 2015 (received through a request for information), the regional conference's Game Coverage and Medical Requirements document from the 2015–2016 season, and "U SPORTS Playing Regulations" for both women's and men's ice hockey, respectively.

The transcripts of the player interviews were coded first using open coding, which permitted the author to code using broad themes (van den Hoonaard, 2012); thirteen themes emerged at this stage. Following open coding, focused coding was used, allowing the broad themes to be placed into overarching themes within the data (van den Hoonaard, 2012). Through the focused coding, two main themes emerged: 1) common conceptions of female ice hockey players; and 2) comparison to men's ice hockey. The latter is the focus of this chapter. Although the common conceptions of female ice hockey players are important to discuss, the players demonstrated more concern surrounding the comparison to men. For this reason, the author believes it is important to highlight the area that appeared to be shaping the majority of the experiences of these players.

Further, although the player interviews provided details about how they perceived the differences in the programs, the players spoke in broad terms about regulations and financial matters, making it unclear where exactly the differences were present, if at all. It was at this stage that the author made the decision to use a multi-methods approach to gain greater insight on the ice hockey programs at Rankin University and the structural differences between women's and men's ice hockey at the U SPORTS level. These secondary datasets were coded using the two themes that emerged during the player interviews.

Ice Hockey as a Gendered Space

Female ice hockey players often have stories about moments they have faced different treatment than male players. These include historically having to hide one's female identity, such as Abby Hoffman did in 1955 when there were no girls' teams in Toronto to play on and girls were not yet welcome to play on boys' teams (Kidd, 2013), and Hayley Wickenheiser (2013) growing up hearing taunts from players and parents about girls not belonging in the game. Women's ice hockey has made great strides in its ability to access the sport (Adams & Leavitt, 2018; Weaving & Roberts, 2012). However, the fight for the same, or even similar, treatment is still happening today. Take, for example, the Chatham-Kent, Ontario, female ice hockey players who were kicked out of their locker room in late 2017, when the municipality had leased the room to an all-boys AAA team, the Chatham-Kent Cyclones (Terfloth, 2017), communicating to the young girls that they were less of a priority. In turn, this shaped their experiences as female ice hockey players.

People at the centre of the gender regime of sport tend to be the ADs, players, and coaches of male high-status sports (Messner, 2011), as was the case with the AAA team in Ontario. In each of the interviews, the players focused primarily on perceived gender differences between female and male ice hockey players. Three of the five participants started by playing ice hockey on boys' teams (or sex-integrated teams) before transferring to girls' ice hockey around the age that body checking is introduced. Body checking was permitted at the under-thirteen age level until 2013 when Hockey Canada banned it for this age group (SportMedBC, 2017). The participants' experiences playing youth ice hockey, in addition to how the players perceived support and resource allocation at the university level, helped to shape their experiences as ice hockey players.

Moreover, the structural difference between male and female ice hockey often influenced the players' experiences of the game. This chapter argues that women's university ice hockey in Canada is a gendered space (DiCarlo, 2016) based on the lack of body checking shaping women's ice hockey, the difference in funding at the university level, and players' (in)ability to follow their dreams in comparison to their male counterparts. In this chapter, when discussing ice hockey as a gendered space, the author is referring to how the experiences of female players are shaped based on their gender, with ice hockey being a male-dominated sport. The structural differences of the game based on gender shape the players' understanding of their experience as female ice hockey players.

Body Checking Shaping Ice Hockey

Individuals navigate the world (and sport) within socially constructed boundaries (rules)—both formal and informal—that have been predetermined through conventional values that impact how people behave (Paraschak, 2000; Suzuki, 2017). These parameters tell players (and others) what is appropriate play and what is not. The rules of women's and men's ice hockey, at most levels, differ and help to shape common beliefs surrounding ice hockey (Adams & Leavitt, 2018). These beliefs shape how individuals understand the game, and which game is seen as the most legitimate (Theberge, 1998).

Although there is little difference in the playing rules, there is one major rule that can change how people understand ice hockey: body checking. *Body checking* refers to contact by a player on an opposing team player that has as an objective to separate the opponent from the puck (International Ice Hockey Federation [IIHF], 2018). This part of the game, which many find entertaining in men's hockey, is prohibited in the women's game (Adams & Leavitt, 2018). This small difference in the rules of play may be a reason behind the further regulation differences between U SPORTS men's and women's ice hockey. For instance, in the 2015–2016 season, U SPORTS required men's ice hockey to have four officials on the ice. Further, the regional conference in which the institution plays requires security and an ambulance on site at every men's game due to the perceived high risk of the sport. In contrast, the women's game only required three officials during the 2015–2016 season, with no security or ambulance required on site. This could possibly be due to the more aggressive perception of men's ice hockey, leading to the assumption that it is more legitimate, in comparison to women's ice hockey (Adams & Leavitt, 2018).

Further, body checking is part of the style of play that is most often viewed as the legitimate style of play (Adams & Leavitt, 2018; Theberge, 1998, 2003). This style of play is "epitomized by the aggressive physicality of play in the [National Hockey League (NHL)], the version that really 'counts' in the subculture of Canadian Hockey" (Theberge, 1998, p. 186). Dayle, a fourth-year player at Rankin University, confirms this when discussing women's hockey being perceived as inferior to the men's game:

> [In] women's hockey there is no open ice hitting. There is bumping and stuff along the boards, but you can't go out and make those big checks. You can't go out hunting. You're not going out to fight, where [in] guys' hockey that is part of the game, [it's] part of the excitement. That's what the fans like…that excitement part of the game where it's the big hits and fights. Women's hockey it's about puck control. It's about running the systems. You can't take yourself out of the play to do certain things because then they're gone on a rush or you're in the [penalty] box. The biggest assumption is that women's hockey isn't as good as men's hockey.

Although body contact through pushing and leaning into other players, known as competitive contact, is permitted while in immediate proximity of the puck with a sole purpose of gaining procession of the puck (IIHF, 2018), the lack of body checking in women's ice hockey is justified mostly by the naturalized size difference between women and men (Theberge, 1998; Weaving & Roberts, 2012). The naturalized difference between women and men in regard to strength and size, also known as the *muscle gap* (Theberge, 1998), is an ideological construct used to justify the difference in athletic performance and ability between women and men. This ideology creates a belief that women should not be playing by the same rules as men, viewing women as inferior players who are marked by a broader cultural struggle concerning gender, sport, and physicality (Adams & Leavitt, 2018). The rules of the game, regardless of the actual physicality of a game, reinforce a belief that women are weaker, and therefore should not be permitted to body check. Adams and Leavitt (2018) and Weaving and Roberts (2012) argue that this difference in rules is in place to protect female players from injury and is patriarchal in nature.

Despite women's ice hockey having a rule against intentional body checking, which creates a game that is perceived as less physical (Weaving & Roberts, 2012), the coach of Rankin University did not believe this simple difference to be symbolic of the ability of the women to be physical, noting the fact that the men's team had been less competitive that season:

> There is nothing different between the men's and women's game.
> For a sport that has "no contact" there definitely is a lot of contact.
> People need to come watch it before they say, "oh it's women's
> hockey, it's boring." They go to the men's games and get upset,
> that they are always losing. Why wouldn't they rather come watch
> a game, where it is actually close, so you can get into it, and they
> pull out the win for you...And the game gets really physical and
> exciting because it's so close and either team could win in a matter
> of one slip-up.

This small difference in the rules changes how fans perceive the game (Adams & Leavitt, 2018) and potentially how organizers decide what is necessary or unnecessary at arenas on game day. For instance, the requirement governing the number of mandatory officials on the ice at the time of this study was not the same, although it has since changed. The level of certification is not the same for officials refereeing the women's games versus the men's, which may further shape how spectators perceive the sport based on gender categories. Furthermore, the difference in the level and the number of officials required adds to the cost of running a men's game over a women's, and may alter how female players view financial support they receive from their institution.

Disparity in the Budget

In Canada, university student bodies consist of a majority of female students (Fletcher & Bratt, 2015). Despite this, men's sports teams receive disproportionately more funding than women's teams. U SPORTS has not posted the amount of Athletic Financial Awards (AFAs) awarded since 2015, for which the 2013–2014 academic years' distributions were shared (Norman, Donnelly, & Kidd, 2019). In 2013–2014, male athletes were awarded 14 per cent more AFAs than their female counterparts. In U SPORTS during the 2013–2014 academic year, male athletes were awarded $9,124,047 (57 per cent), with female athletes receiving a total of $6,820,642 (43 per cent) (Norman et al., 2019). In 2012–2013, men's ice hockey AFAs in U SPORTS were valued at a total of $1,752,211, whereas women's ice hockey received AFAs valued at $945,789 (Donnelly et al., 2013). U SPORTS restricts AFAs to the amount of tuition and compulsory fees at the university where the AFAs are being awarded (Fletcher & Bratt, 2015). As reported by Cardwell (2013), four hundred female hockey players during a given season were reported leaving Canada for university to play in the National Collegiate Athletic Association (NCAA). In 2014, U SPORTS introduced a pilot project that would allow institutions to provide women's ice hockey players with more than the compulsory fees, providing them with residence fees and book expenses (Cardwell, 2013). The pilot project was put into place to try to keep the Canadian women's hockey pool in Canada for university (Cardwell, 2013). Although this pilot project was in place during the time of this study, through the interviews with the players, it was unclear if anyone was receiving AFAs based on this new pilot project, as none of the players discussed receiving more than tuition costs.

Despite not being able to obtain the amount of AFAs awarded at Rankin University for this period, the author was able to obtain the number of students based on gender for the academic year of 2014–2015 (Norman et al., 2019) and the budget for the athletic teams between 2011 and 2015. During the 2014–2015 academic year, the student body consisted of 70 per cent female students (Norman et al., 2019). Nonetheless, during the same academic year, the men's ice hockey team had a budget of $160,000, in comparison to the women's team's $90,000. Participants were aware that the men's team received more financial support and explained it based on the athletic department and community undervaluing the team. After speaking to the coach and AD, it was made clear that it is not as simple as looking at the numbers or favouring one team over the other.

At Rankin University, the AD makes the athletic team budgets out of two components: 1) operational budget; and 2) miscellaneous budget. The operational budget is a net amount that the AD can calculate based on what it costs for each game. This budget comprises the cost of travel (hotels, bus, food, etc.), referees, and other mandatory game-day operational expenses. For instance, men's ice hockey requires two referees and two linesmen that need higher qualification than the women's one referee and two linesmen. Higher qualification requires higher pay (see Table 5.1). The cost of referees and linesmen alone differs by $310 per game for a men's game over a women's game. In addition, as stated earlier, the regional conference of U SPORTS requires men's ice hockey teams to have security and an ambulance on site at each game, which is an additional cost that women's programs do not incur.

Table 5.1: U SPORTS Ice Hockey Officials Requirement and Pay (2015–2016 Season)

	Women's Ice Hockey	Men's Ice Hockey
Referee(s)	1 × $80	2 × $155
Linesmen	2 × $40	2 × $80
Total per game	$160	$470

On the one hand, we can partially explain the disparity in the budget by the difference in the cost of running a men's program versus the cost of running a women's program, based on the differences in U SPORTS and regional conference regulations. On the other hand, we can also understand these differences based on a more profound common perception of female athletes. For instance, the lack of body checking could cause individuals to view the women's game as less aggressive (Adams & Leavitt, 2018) and thus needing less attention to player conduct on the ice. This difference only takes into account the disparity in the operational budget. Regardless of the additional cost that the men's ice hockey team requires due to regulation differences, the coach believes the women's team has everything it needs. Players, however, believe that the men's ice hockey team receives disproportionately higher financial support than the women's team. For example, Dayle states,

> I think the biggest challenge is we don't get a lot of funding or support from the University as [the] men do, which is unfortunate because we have a better record than they do. I understand it's a different calibre of hockey, but we are still good hockey players. It is still good hockey...Sorry I'm really bad at trying to explain this. It's just we love it [hockey] more, because it's not given to us

on a silver platter. We aren't spoon fed everything from the time we are young, we have to work for it. For everything. Absolutely everything.

The AD notes that, in addition to the operational budget, "on the men's side, we have to try and compete with the budgets of other universities in the conference...[one of these teams] gets treated like professional players." Further, he adds that to be competitive in the conference, the men's team requires more money than is invested in the women's program for things like equipment. The AD believes that, due to the fact that most male players come from the Canadian Hockey League (CHL), they are accustomed to a higher standard and expect more as a result. The other participants also expressed similar inequalities, such as quality of sticks and mismatched gear. Dayle agrees when she states the following:

The men, they get new gear every year. They all match, all their gear matches, us none of our gear matches. We get [the men's] old practice jerseys. We get their old practice socks. They [athletic department] tell us we get all the same things, but we don't. They all have custom towels. We have these old ratty things that have bleach stains on them...it's really disheartening.

Avery furthers Dayle's statement when discussing the quality of their sticks. She states, "If the boys break all their sticks, they get a brand-new stick that [is] better than ours. We get the cheap version of the stick and they would get the better version...which is kind of shitty...but what can you do? It's just what you get."

The coach and AD justify the men requiring new equipment at a higher rate due to the size and weight difference between men and women. The coach notes, "Girls are less heavy than men and are less hard on their equipment." Although the coach believes that his players are smaller and less heavy in comparison to male players, he describes how he approaches the women's need for more funding. He states,

I show [the athletic department] by getting the girls to perform. You can't ask for more when you don't give more and you don't show that you need it…every year we get a little more, but right now we have everything we need.

To ask for more, the coach believes the team needs to be performing. The annual budgets obtained through the request for information show that the men's ice hockey budget only increased between 2012 and the 2013–2014 season, whereas the women's budget had increased twice between 2011 and 2015 (see Table 5.2). The table shows the planned budgets that were allocated by the athletic department for the men's and women's teams between 2011 and 2015, alongside actual expenses, donations and sponsorships, and net expenses.

As the budget demonstrates, the men's ice hockey team at Rankin University receives more money than the women's team; however, as the AD and coach justify, the men's team requires equipment at a higher rate because they tend to wear out their equipment faster. The coach adds that, although it may appear that the women's team only gets one set of equipment when they join the team, he provides the equipment on a case-by-case need. For example, the coach explains that most players' parents buy them new skates before they come to university, and for this reason the players only get one pair of skates paid for by the team. He adds that if a player arrives with old skates that are already starting to wear out, that player may get more than one new pair.

The coach explains that not every player wears out their equipment at the same pace and assumes that most players would prefer not to break in new equipment every year. The coach notes, "If [the athletes] just asked why the men get more, they would understand how the budgets are made."

Table 5.2: Annual Ice Hockey Budgets, Rankin University, 2011–2015

	Budget	Actual Expenses	Donations and Sponsorships	Net Expenses
2011–2012				
Women	$78,000.00	$91,519.08	$3,400.00	$88,119.08
Men	$150,000.00	$225,947.52	$2,000.00	$223,947.52
2012–2013				
Women	$81,000.00	$94,906.22	$5,150.00	$89,756.22
Men	$160,000.00	$166,264.03	$7,175.00	$159,089.03
2013–2014				
Women	$81,000.00	$122,381.81	$26,673.00	$95,708.81
Men	$160,000.00	$207,348.55	$14,610.00	$192,738.55
2014–2015				
Women	$90,000.00	$95,032.16	$12,530.60	$82,501.56
Men	$160,000.00	$146,223.64	$21,434.45	$124,789.19

As previously mentioned, the coach believes the women's team has everything it needs, and does not believe there is a lack of support from the athletic department. Despite the coach's belief, the players interviewed believe the men's team receives more, including higher quality equipment. Four of the participants discuss the men's unlimited supply of sticks, which Caroline suggests when she states, "I've actually been taking my sticks from the guys' team because I've broken so many."

In addition to the participants discussing their perception of disproportionate support, they also discuss the CHL financial packages male players may receive. The CHL's three regional leagues provide their former athletes with scholarships that cover post-secondary education costs for the number of years played in the CHL (Colpitts, 2018). These scholarships cover a minimum of tuition, books, and compulsory fees toward post-secondary education (Colpitts, 2018). This is a financial package that many U SPORTS male athletes receive—546 U SPORTS players in 2017–2018 to be exact (CHL, 2018)—that women do not by virtue of not having an equivalent league. This leads women to typically travel a different pathway to university hockey entirely.

Ability to Follow Her Dream

As mentioned above, many university male hockey players in Canada have spent their junior hockey careers in one of the three regional leagues of the CHL. Many understand the CHL as a feeder system to the NHL (Allain, 2008; Edwards & Washington, 2015; MacDonald & Lafrance, 2018). Additionally, it supplies more players to U SPORTS than any other league (CHL, 2019a). In the 2016–2017 season, 80 per cent of players in the U SPORTS men's ice hockey championship tournament were graduates of the CHL (CHL, 2019b).

We are aware of where the majority of U SPORTS male ice hockey players have played prior to their university careers, however the path of female U SPORTS hockey players prior to university does not always look the same from player to player. In the following subsections, the author discusses the differences in the paths of female study participants from their introduction to the sport until the 2015–2016 season, in comparison to their male counterparts. Snyder (2002) argues that an individual's past influences how they are able to imagine reaching current goals or imagine future goals. For this reason, the author argues that the past experience of the players is important to understand how they experience U SPORTS ice hockey.

Introduction to the Game

Since the 1980s, the participation of female players in Canada has been increasing at a rapid speed; despite this, they still face barriers in the sport (Stevens & Adams, 2013). The governance of hockey in Canada varies. For instance, in the province of Ontario, girls and women can play within either a semi-integrated model that sees girls and boys playing on the same team or within a segregated model with the Ontario Women's Hockey Association (OWHA) (Stevens & Adams, 2013). Ontario is the only Canadian province with separate governing bodies for male and female ice hockey at the provincial level (Stevens & Adams, 2013). Municipal-level hockey in the rest of the country tends to operate from an integrated model where girls and boys play together or a semi-integrated model where they do not necessarily play together but are governed by the same organization or governing body (Adams & Leavitt, 2018; Stevens & Adams, 2013). Four of the players in this study started their careers in integrated programs. Elizabeth, however, grew up in Ontario and played in organizations governed by the OWHA prior to leaving the province to attend a private high school.

Around the age of eight, players are introduced to the divisional ladder of competitive ice hockey—a ranking of tiers based on ability—where they begin to learn what it takes to "make it" (Gruneau & Whitson, 1993). Players at the highest level for their age group play A or AB, those in the middle group play B, and the lower but still competitive players play in the C division (Gruneau & Whitson, 1993). Divisions in some regions are called AAA, AA, and A, with AAA being the highest level of competitive hockey. For girls who start playing hockey together with boys, it is at this time that they become aware of the common understanding surrounding athletic ability and the normalized differences between boys and girls (Gruneau & Whitson, 1993). For instance, Brooke recounts her story growing up playing boys' ice hockey:

> I played with the guys, a year or two. Later I was still playing with them and tried out for the [competitive] team. I didn't make it, because I was a girl…it's like the usual there, I come from a small town, so there was like two girls that tried out and we both got cut because we were girls. We had to play on the B team, and we were like "no, I don't think so we are better than these guys," so we played ringette.

For Brooke, coming from a small town meant there were no girls' hockey teams available; therefore, she stopped playing hockey for two years during that time. She discusses, briefly, that she never thought she would return to hockey. She was being taught at this young age that only boys are able to play competitive hockey. Although Brooke left hockey for two years due to a lack of girls' teams in her region, she returned to the sport upon her parents finding a girls' team. Playing on this team did not come without barriers for Brooke and her family. For her to be able to play, she had to compete in the age group above where she was supposed to play, as well as travel over an hour for practices and games.

Alternatively, Caroline was always welcomed on boys' competitive teams. She also had the opportunity to play for the boys' competitive team while playing on her girls' high school team, however it was made clear from the start that "if two games conflicted you had to go to the boys [game]." Put differently, boys' hockey had to be prioritized. For Caroline, being good enough to prove herself on a boys' elite-level team was already a win in her books; however, she is aware that the boys' team had to be the one that came first, and that her experience playing girls' hockey around her male teammates was not considered an advantage to her training. Adams (2006) argues that experiences such as Caroline's demonstrate women's and girls' hockey are not valued to the same extent as men's and boys' hockey. This teaches female players from their introduction to the game all the way through to university that the hockey that matters is male ice hockey (Adams, 2006).

All the female players who played boys' hockey had a story about playing or not playing because of not making the team. For Dayle, this was a story of getting punished (or losing ice time) for making a simple mistake her male teammates made and being pushed away from her team by the coach. In her words, "I came off the ice, and my coach asked me if I was still going to play guys hockey next year, then told me to take a seat and didn't put me back on." Dayle believes her coach viewed her mistake as an opportunity to bench her; she notes, "If one of the boys had made the same mistake they wouldn't have been benched."

Regardless of talent or ability, Avery, Brooke, Caroline, and Dayle were being taught by their experiences that female ice hockey players are considered inferior and, in Caroline's case, that female-only teams are viewed as being detrimental to development, despite giving players more ice time. Prior to university, the participants have experienced barriers and challenges that have taught them that society undervalues women's ice hockey in comparison to men's, in turn possibly shaping how they perceive their support at the university level. For instance, when asked what it means to be a hockey player, Avery states, "I don't know. I don't know if it means anything," adding that for males "their goal from when they first stepped on the ice until whenever is to go to the NHL, but to be a female [player] it's different."

As mentioned earlier, Elizabeth started playing hockey in an organization governed by the OWHA. The OWHA provides opportunities for girls and women to develop in a female-centred space, where girls in the province of Ontario have more opportunity for elite-level coaching and competition while playing only with girls (Stevens & Adams, 2013). Unlike the other participants, Elizabeth always played on sex-segregated teams and compared her experience to that of her brothers, stating,

It's substantially different. . .When you think about [men's] careers versus our career it's completely different. [Men in U SPORTS] are all coming from the [Ontario Hockey League] or one of those [CHL] leagues, where all our girls are pretty much coming from midget. [The men] are exposed to more of a competitive nature, where some of our girls are coming from teams in a small town that may have only had three lines, everyone got to play. In the leagues the guys are coming from they are getting sat all the time, it's like a business.

Path to University

Gruneau and Whitson (1993) discuss how, from a young age, many boys dream of playing at the highest level of professional hockey, the NHL. The female players interviewed discuss the path of male players in comparison to their own. They discussed, in particular, how they believe that their male counterparts' dream of playing professional hockey appears to be attainable, having played semi-professional prior to university.

Comparatively, the dream for girls growing up would have been to compete on a national team in hopes of going to the Olympics (Stevens, 2006). Brooke highlights that once players do not make it to NCAA Division I hockey, the dream of playing at the Olympics dies. Further, Elizabeth notes, "[I] didn't see a future in hockey," with other participants making similar mentions of their (in)ability to play NCAA Division I, possibly alluding to NCAA Division I having been a goal at some point in their careers.

At the time of this study, players from university or college had a small chance of being picked up by either a Canadian Women's Hockey League (CWHL) team, which has since folded following the 2018–2019 season, or a National Women's Hockey League (NWHL) team. During the 2018–2019 season, the two leagues housed a combined total of eleven teams (CWHL, 2019; NWHL, 2019). The small number of teams leaves much less room for female players to realize their dreams in comparison to the roster space among the NHL's thirty-one teams (NHL, 2018). A new opportunity to play professionally may alter the dreams of some young girls; however, currently, there is still no equivalent to the CHL.

Furthermore, Stevens (2006) notes that it is often girls from middle-class families who can work their way up the ladder to professional women's hockey because they tend to have more access to additional coaching, equipment, skating camps, and private hockey schools. These extras are said to make the difference between a good player and an excellent player (Stevens, 2006). Elizabeth credits her privileged upbringing for her success in hockey:

> I luckily made this one team in grade eleven, when I went to a boarding school. I was the fifth player on the fourth line. I was brutal. We won nationals though and it motivated me to want to do more with hockey than just play for the fun. That following summer I spent training for hockey, doing power skating and things like that. I was fortunate that my parents could afford to send me to boarding school and for the training I did in the summers to get ready for my next season.

Despite her privilege, Elizabeth discusses how, for most U SPORTS female ice hockey players, the dream of going professional seems impossible. She highlights that, for a select few, going to Europe to play may be their only opportunity to play professionally. In her fourth season with the team, Elizabeth mentions the possibility of going to play professionally in Europe for a team that contacted her. This permits her to envision the possibility of continuing her hockey career, although she did not see Canada being an option to continue playing. As for those who played in the CWHL, it is important to note the marginal amount of money players receive. Until the 2017–2018 season, the CWHL did not pay its players and, once it did, players' salaries ranged from $2,000 to $10,000 a year (Sportsnet, 2017).

It was clear, however, that the other participants had given up on the dream of playing professional hockey because they believed the chances were low for players in their regional league of U SPORTS to make it to the CWHL or the NWHL after university. For instance, Brooke states,

> I was naive; I didn't want to give up the dream…the dream of playing professional has died. Second year has taken it out of me. The guys, they can still go to the NHL and make millions of dollars.

For us, there is no league that even comes close to comparing to the NHL, or even any league in Russia or like the [Kontinental Hockey League]. We can't compare in any way, once we are done university hockey we are done...It's only really Division I [NCAA] that would ever get these chances [of playing CWHL or NWHL].

While Brooke has correctly pointed out that the men are able to go on to the NHL following their U SPORTS careers, the odds of this occurring is a rarity (U SPORTS, n.d.). Nonetheless, the participants' point is that men are still able to maintain their dream, while women are less likely to do so.

Brooke and the other participants note that it is much more likely for players to get drafted to the CWHL or NWHL when playing NCAA Division I in the United States. The interviewees add that the same NCAA athletes are more likely to obtain a spot on the Canadian National Team roster as well. Indeed, according to the 2018 PyeongChang Olympic roster available on Hockey Canada's website, only two athletes had played their university careers in Canada (Hockey Canada, 2018). Shannon Szabados played for the MacEwan Griffins, which play in the Canadian Collegiate Athletic Association on its men's ice hockey team (Szabo, 2009). Mélodie Daoust, however, played in U SPORTS for McGill University (Daoust, 2019).

Conclusion

Women and girls' participation in ice hockey has grown tremendously over the last three decades (Stevens & Adams, 2013). Despite this, their experiences have not been the same as their male counterparts. This chapter argues that the experiences of female players are being shaped by the broad sport system, where ice hockey can be understood as a gendered space (DiCarlo, 2016). When considering the lived experiences of female players in this case study, it was important to look at both their personal experiences and the broader system in which they operate. The broader system, that of ice hockey, creates the boundaries in which individuals operate and limits what they are able to imagine as possible (Paraschak, 2000; Suzuki, 2017). For instance, imagining a future playing professional hockey was not part of the players' upbringing, as the CWHL and NWHL did not exist prior to 2007 and 2015, respectively (CWHL, 2019; NWHL, 2019).

The structural differences in the rules and regulations, in addition to the lived experiences of the players, gives a more in-depth understanding of how ice hockey in Canada and at the university level is a gendered space. The male players at Rankin University receive more funding on the basis of having played in the CHL, the perceived size difference, as well as the operational cost differences.

Further, the interviewed players' early hockey experiences shaped their understanding of their place within the game (Snyder, 2002). Three of the four players who started by playing on integrated or semi-integrated teams were made to feel like they did not belong within certain teams. Whereas Elizabeth, who played sex-segregated hockey her entire life, was aware that her experience of where hockey could lead her was not the same as that of her brothers (or other males). These differences are constructed through the gendering of the sport and extend to how the players' past experiences have potentially shaped their current university experience.

References

Adams, C., & Leavitt, S. (2018). "It's just girls' hockey": Troubling progress narratives in girls' and women's sport. *International Review for the Sociology of Sport, 53*(2), 152–172.

Adams, M.L. (2006). The game of whose lives? Gender, race, and entitlement in Canada's "national" game. In D. Whitson & R. Gruneau (Eds.), *Artificial ice: Hockey, culture, and commerce* (pp. 71–84). Toronto: Broadview Press.

Allain, K.A. (2008). "Real fast and tough": The construction of Canadian hockey masculinity. *Sociology of Sport Journal, 25*(4), 462–481.

Bandy, S.J. (2016). Gender and the "cultural turn" in the study of sport and physical culture. *Sport in Society, 19*(5), 726–735. https://doi.org/10.1080/17430437.20 15.1073950

CHL. (2018). CHL scholarship program investment tops $9.6 million in 2017–18. http://chl.ca/article/chl-scholarship-program-investment-tops-9-6-million-in-2017-18

CHL. (2019a). About the CHL. http://chl.ca/aboutthechl

CHL. (2019b). CHL grads well represented at 2016–17 U SPORTS awards and University Cup. http://chl.ca/article/chl-grads-well-represented-at-2016-17-u-sports-awards-and-university-cup

Cardwell, M. (2013). CIS hopes to score big with women's hockey pilot project. https://www.universityaffairs.ca/news/news-article/cis-hopes-to-score-big-with-womens-hockey-pilot-project/

Colpitts, I. (2018). CHL scholarship program setting players up for life after hockey. http://hockey-now.live.publishwithagility.com/college/chl-scholarship-program-setting-players-up-for-life-after-hockey

CWHL. (2019). The Canadian Women's Hockey League.

Daoust, M. (2019). About me. http://melodiedaoust.com/about-me

DiCarlo, D. (2016). Playing like a girl? The negotiation of gender and sexual identity among female ice hockey athletes on male teams. *Sport in Society, 19*(8–9), 1363–1373.

Donnelly, P., Norman, M., & Kidd, B. (2013). *Gender equity in Canadian interuniversity sport: A biennial report (No. 2)*. Toronto: Centre for Sport Policy Studies (Faculty of Kinesiology and Physical Education).

Edwards, J.R., & Washington, M. (2015). Establishing a "safety net": Exploring the emergence and maintenance of College Hockey Inc. and NCAA Division I Hockey. *Journal of Sport Management, 29*(3), 291–304.

Fletcher, T., & Bratt, D. (2015). Sport and physical activity in Canadian educational systems. In J. Crossman & J. Scherer (Eds.), *Social dimensions of Canadian sport and physical activity* (pp. 205–229). Toronto: Pearson.

Giddens, A. (1984). *The constitution of society: Outline of the theory of structuration*. Los Angeles: University of California Press.

Gruneau, R.S., & Whitson, D. (1993). *Hockey Night in Canada: Sport, identities, and cultural politics*. Toronto: Garamond Press.

Hall, A. (2002). *The girl and the game: A history of women's sport in Canada*. Peterborough, ON: Broadview Press.

Hockey Canada. (2018). National women's team. https://www.hockeycanada.ca/
en-ca/Team-Canada/Women/National.aspx

IIHF. (2018). *IIHF official rule book 2018–2022*. https://www.iihf.com/IIHFMvc/
media/Downloads/Rule%20Book/IIHF_Official_Rule_Book_2018_Web_v2.pdf

Kidd, B. (2013). Homage to the sisterhood. In G. Demers, L. Greaves, S. Kirby, & M. Lay
(Eds.), *Playing it forward: 50 years of women and sport in Canada/Pour celles qui
suivront: 50 ans d'histoire de femmes en sport au Canada* (pp. 15–26). Ottawa:
Feminist History Society/Société d'histoire féministe.

Kirby, S., Greaves, L., & Reid, C. (2006). *Experience research social change: Methods
beyond the mainstream* (2nd ed.). Peterborough, ON: Broadview Press.

MacDonald, C., & Lafrance, M.E. (2018). "Girls love me, guys wanna be me":
Representations of men, masculinity, and junior ice hockey in *Gongshow*
magazine. *The International Journal of Sport and Society, 10*(1), 1–19.

Markula, P., & Silk, M. (2011). *Qualitative research for physical culture*. London, UK:
Palgrave Macmillan.

Messner, M. (2002). *Taking the field: Women, men and sport*. Minneapolis: University
of Minnesota Press.

Messner, M. (2011). Gender ideologies, youth sports, and the production of soft
essentialism. *Sociology of Sport Journal, 28*(2), 151–170.

NHL. (2018). Teams. https://www.nhl.com/info/teams

Norman, M., Donnelly, P., & Kidd, B. (2019). *Gender equity in Canadian
interuniversity sport: A biennial report (No. 3 & 4) 2014–15, 2016–17*. Toronto:
Centre for Sport Policy Studies (Faculty of Kinesiology and Physical Education,
University of Toronto).

NWHL. (2019). Official site of the National Women's Hockey League. https://www.
nwhl.zone/

Paraschak, V. (2000). Knowing ourselves through the "other": Indigenous people in
sport in Canada. In R. Jones & K. Armour (Eds.), *Sociology of sport: Theory and
practice* (pp. 153–166). Essex, ON: Longman.

Snyder, C.R. (2002). Hope theory: Rainbows in the mind. *Psychological Inquiry,
13*(4), 249–275.

SportMedBC. (2017). Hockey Canada announces ban on body checking in peewee
hockey. https://sportmedbc.com/news/hockey-canada-announces-ban-body-
checking-peewee-hockey

Sportsnet. (2017). CWHL announces it will pay players in 2017–18. https://www.
sportsnet.ca/hockey/nhl/cwhl-announces-will-pay-players-2017-18/

Stevens, J. (2006). Women's hockey in Canada: After the "gold rush." In D. Whitson & R.S. Gruneau (Eds.), *Artificial ice: Hockey, culture, and commerce* (pp. 85–100). Toronto: Broadview Press.

Stevens, J., & Adams, C. (2013). "Together we can make it better": Collective action and governance in a girls' ice hockey association. *International Review for the Sociology of Sport, 48*(6), 658–672.

Suzuki, N. (2017). A capability approach to understanding sport for social inclusion: Agency, structure and organisations. *Social Inclusion, 5*(2), 150–158. https://doi.org/10.17645/si.v5i2.905

Szabo. P. (2009). Interview with Shannon Szabados: One-on-one with Team Canada's youngest star goalie. *In Goal Magazine.* https://ingoalmag.com/interviews/interview-with-shannon-szabados-one-on-one-with-team-canadas-youngest-star-goalie/

Terfloth, T. (2017). Forcing girls out of hockey locker-room sparks outrage. *The Windsor Star.* https://windsorstar.com/news/local-news/dressing-room-decision-in-ridgetown-slammed

Theberge, N. (1998). "Same sport, different gender": A consideration of binary gender logic and the sport continuum in the case of ice hockey. *Journal of Sport & Social Issues, 22*(2), 183–198.

Theberge, N. (2003). "No fear comes": Adolescent girls, ice hockey and the embodiment of gender. *Youth & Society, 34*(4), 497–516.

U SPORTS. (n.d.). Alberta's Ryan latest CIS grad to reach NHL. https://presto-en.usports.ca/sports/mice/2015-16/releases/20160303-2

van den Hoonaard, D.K. (2012). *Qualitative research in action: A Canadian primer.* Don Mills, ON: Oxford University Press.

Weaving, C., & Roberts, S. (2012). Checking in: Analysis of the (lack of) body checking in women's ice hockey. *Research Quarterly for Exercise and Sport, 83*(3), 470–478.

Wickenheiser, H. (2013). Skating in the drainage ditches. In G. Demers, L. Greaves, S. Kirby, & M. Lay (Eds.), *Playing it forward/Pour celles qui suivront* (pp. 75–76). Ottawa: Feminist History Society/Société d'histoire féministe.

6

#BeBoldForChange

*The 2017 US Women's National Hockey Team Player Boycott, Twitter,
and (Neo)Liberal Feminism*

NOAH UNDERWOOD & JUDY DAVIDSON

HOCKEY, as one of the quintessential sporting exemplars of white,
hegemonic masculinity,[1] has historically been hostile to participation
by girls and women, who have participated in large enough numbers
to develop an elite game in only the last quarter century. For decades,
women's hockey (along with most elite female sports) in the United
States has been underfunded by the national governing body, and under
covered by mainstream media, perpetuating its minority gender status
in the sport (Berkman, 2017a; Messner, Duncan, & Cooky, 2003); however,
in March 2017, members of the US women's national hockey team
(USWNT from hereon in) sought to change both of these minority
conditions, using the threat of a player boycott of the International Ice
Hockey Federation (IIHF) Women's World Ice Hockey Championship
in an attempt to get USA Hockey to pay serious attention to reducing
the structural inequalities that have existed in women's and girls'
hockey. Their job action campaign was not only publicized on Twitter
(and subsequently picked up and covered by the mainstream media),

but some of their boycott demands were met before the tournament commenced, including promises for increased funding for the women's game.

In this chapter, we do several things to build our analysis. The first section traces the story of the players' job action as it unfolded on Twitter, and how those tweets (and their content) was subsequently amplified by mainstream sports media. To make our analysis, we use tweets by members of the USWNT, responses from USA Hockey, and other media representations. We suggest that the player boycott was successful due to player solidarity and fan support, and an imminent international hockey tournament on home ice. In the next section, we analyze four key themes that emerge from our tweet analysis, and which we argue contributed to the success of the boycott by building a neoliberal feminist brand. Those themes are deploying the promise of a bright future for women's hockey, negotiating fairly in good faith, celebrating female athleticism, and, finally, subtly promoting American patriotism. We end the chapter by arguing that the USWNT was somewhat successful in advancing the cause of gender equity in women's elite sport, but this was only made possible due to a concomitant reiteration of dominant, privileged discourses of race, class, and nationalism.

To conduct an analysis of the Twitter representational tactics used in these labour negotiations, we focus on the team's digital media presence and the themes mobilized during its boycott. The team's use of social media, specifically Twitter, was its primary medium for public relations and information sharing. Messages were carefully coordinated and timed by almost all members of the team, and message content was clear, poignant, and seemingly feminist. Close reading techniques and thematic coding were used to examine nine coordinated tweets from the USWNT, complemented with select statements from USA Hockey and mainstream media coverage of the boycott. From those themes, we argue that the team's solidarity and careful social media strategy were large reasons why it received assurances from USA Hockey for a deal to which it could agree. We conclude the chapter by suggesting the team was able to resist the typically "heterosexy"[2] representations of female athletes that digital media often demands (Bruce & Hardin, 2014; Lavoi & Calhoun, 2014) by mobilizing now common-sense discourses of liberal athletic feminism through middle-class aspirational slogans and white patriotic American nationalism.

The Unfolding of a Successful Player Boycott

Prior to the start of the 2017 World Championship, the team and its governing body had been in labour negotiations for almost twelve months with no movement, let alone resolution, toward meeting key demands for equitable treatment for the women's squad, including financial compensation and program development. The two sides had arrived at an impasse, and on March 15, 2017, the athletes of the USWNT took a stand to, as they strategically tagged it on social media, "#BeBoldForChange." The team threatened to stage a labour boycott of the tournament, which was scheduled to begin March 31 on home ice in Plymouth, Michigan. Through this action, and with unequivocal and unusual player solidarity, the team successfully pressured USA Hockey to meet some of its demands after many months of stalled negotiations.

Exactly sixteen days before the start of the Women's World Championship, twenty of the twenty-three players on the USWNT roster announced, on Twitter, in a coordinated set of individual tweets, that they would not represent their country in the tournament under the existing agreement with USA Hockey. The first set of tweets, posted on March 15, 2017, stated the following:

> The members of the U.S. Women's National Hockey Team announce that we will not be playing in the 2017 IIHF Women's World Championship in Plymouth, Michigan unless significant progress has been made on the year-long negotiations with USA Hockey over fair wages and equitable support.

We have asked USA Hockey for equitable support as required by the Ted Stevens Amateur Sports Act.[3] Specifically, we have asked for equitable support in the areas of financial compensation, youth team development, equipment, travel expenses, hotel accommodations, meals, staffing, transportation, marketing, and publicity.

The goals of our requests are to achieve fair treatment from USA Hockey, to initiate the appropriate steps to correct the outlined issues, and to move forward with a shared goal of promoting and growing girls and women in our sport while representing the United States in future competitions, including the Women's World Championship.

Putting on the USA jersey represents the culmination of many years of hard work and sacrifice that reflect our love of both hockey and country. In making these requests, we are simply asking USA Hockey to comply with the law. (Duggan, 2017a)

This message laid out the opening position of the USWNT and centred its two main issues with USA Hockey—fair wages and equitable support. The team was demanding basic remuneration for individual player salaries, and reasonable funding for gear, travel costs, and other forms of team needs, all of which it was not receiving. "Equitable support" referred to youth team development, marketing, and publicity that would bring the women's program budget to be commensurate with levels of funding and support that the US men's national team received.

For its part, USA Hockey responded to the team's boycott threat through Twitter the same day (March 15) with a statement of its own. In it, USA Hockey explicitly attempted to counter the team's claim that it was not treating the women fairly, invoking its own version of equitable treatment. It pointed to support for the 2018 PyeongChang Winter Olympic Games, including three main points:

1. "a 6-month training camp, additional support stipends, and incentives for medals that could result in each player receiving nearly $85,000 in cash over the Olympic training and performance period";
2. "USA Hockey is invested in the growth and development of girls and women at every level of play"; and
3. "USA Hockey's international programs have enjoyed amazing success in women's hockey." (USA Hockey, 2017a)

It concluded its position by outlining the triumphs of the team over the previous two decades. The organization's statement suggested that USA Hockey's financial support for the women's team was more than adequate, represented the individualized earnings as clearly generous, and suggested it was demonstrably running a very successful program, domestically and internationally.

The rebuttal on Twitter from the national team was swift and concise, contextualizing and justifying the team's resolve to sit out the international tournament. The team's tweets consistently countered USA Hockey's statements, not allowing what it claimed was misleading information to linger in the digital public space on its own. The resulting responses on Twitter denied that an offer of $85,000 per player was ever proposed by USA Hockey, noting that $60,000 per player comes from the United States Olympic Committee for gold medal winners. The short time frame of a six-month pre-Olympic training period was highlighted, and that for three and a half out of four years the players are unpaid, including during international tournament cycles. It ended its counter-response with "Lastly, it does nothing to address the marketing and training support that is not on par with what it provides to the men's and boys' teams" (Duggan, 2017b). This squarely positioned a gender equity argument at the centre of this dispute. Twenty of twenty-one players tweeted the opening tweet, while ten tweeted the rebuttal responses.

The next day (March 16, 2017), twenty-four hours after the boycott was announced, it was revealed that USA Hockey officially asked each of the players on the USWNT senior team to declare their individual intentions as to whether or not they would be participating in the World Championship under the current agreement (Perez & Allen, 2017). Consistent with their initial boycott statement, each player indicated they would not play. The women reiterated their stance: "We are aware of USA Hockey's deadline and we have allowed it to pass. We are focused on the issue of equitable support and stand by our position. We continue to be grateful for the encouragement and loyalty of our fans" (USWNT as quoted in Perez & Allen, 2017).

The USWNT anticipated that USA Hockey would attempt to create a "strike breaker" replacement lineup. In a statement sent to *USA Today*, the players addressed USA Hockey's attempts to field a replacement team: "We have heard that USA Hockey is attempting to field an alternative team to play in the World Championship games. We regret that they have not instead chosen to reconsider their treatment of the current World Championship-winning team" (USWNT as quoted in Perez & Allen, 2017). Key members of the senior team had been strategically proactive, contacting all of the reserve players, around ninety people in total, securing their commitment to the boycott. As defense star Monique Lamoureux-Morando reported,

We've discussed this with every single player in the player pool from the past year, and they are all on board with us. And we had an entire conference call with the U18 team last night and it included a lot of their parents and they are all on board with us as well. (DiCaro, 2017)

The team had effectively rallied the players in the US women's elite hockey system, eventually receiving commitments from almost all of them, including the National Collegiate Athletic Association (NCAA)

college and university hockey level, professionals, and former reserve members.

USA Hockey issued a press release, to which it tweeted out the link, two days after its initial statement in response to the boycott threat. On March 17, in what was to be its final public communication about the dispute, USA Hockey's then Executive Director Dave Ogrean issued an extensive statement published on USA Hockey's website. In it, he essentially conceded defeat in the attempt to create a scab replacement team. "We remain committed to having the players that were selected to represent the US in the upcoming women's world championship to be the players that are on the ice when the tournament begins" (USA Hockey, 2017b). In this, USA Hockey realized that its attempts to recruit any elite women's players had been futile, and it pivoted to reiterating its earlier claims. It highlighted its financial contributions again, and suggested it was not USA Hockey's job to pay female players a living wage.

As with the previous USA Hockey communications, the USWNT's representatives quickly released a counter-statement (retweeted by fifteen of the twenty-one players on Twitter), claiming "USA Hockey issued a press release with patently false information about the status of the negotiations" (Duggan, 2017c). This expedient response to USA Hockey again shows the preparedness and organization of the team and its legal advisors, and this, along with almost total player solidarity to not join a replacement team, was one of the keys for the USWNT to gain the changes it pursued in the negotiations.

It becomes clear at this stage in the Twitter battle that the team started to mobilize two distinct categories of goals to build off each other. The social media campaign started with a focus on the team-based goals in order to get USA Hockey's attention, and accordingly, to get the public's attention. The team then gradually expanded its reach to use the systemic-based goals as the messaging catalyst. This second, scaffolded strategy was ambitious and inspirational in its content because it addressed issues of inclusion and entrenched sexism. The progressive and consistent messaging laid the groundwork for the team's negotiating strategy and public relations battle with USA Hockey.

After March 17, and USA Hockey's final statement, the women's team's Twitter content changed focus. It no longer had to foreground and actively rebut USA Hockey's claims, or keep demonstrating that its treatment by USA Hockey was unjust; however, during this period, the majority of the team's tweets on social media (three out of five final tweets, which were tweeted out fifty-four times between the players' personal accounts) still included a reference to the team's ongoing negotiations with USA Hockey. As an example, "The discussions were productive and will continue this week, with the goal of reaching an agreement that would allow the players to get to camp in time to train for and compete in the World Championships" (Duggan, 2017d). This messaging strategy clearly reiterated the team's commitment to continue to actively negotiate in good faith. It also had the effect of carefully counteracting any sense that it was attempting to hold the governing body hostage with its demands. There was another change in strategy, however—one that targeted a different sort of image building. The team's messages became more often aspirational, grander in scope, and aimed at a broader public. The tweets now seemed to be targeted at people sympathetic to a mild feminist message—the team's fan base, young female hockey players, their families, and allied parties beyond. A CBS Chicago headline, "U.S. Women's Hockey Team Is Fighting For Your Daughter," demonstrates the effectiveness of its strategy, distilling its message from Twitter to mainstream media coverage (DiCaro, 2017).

The USWNT was able to end its boycott successfully on March 28, 2017, almost two weeks after it had started, and three days before the official IIHF World Championship commenced. USA Hockey agreed to an unprecedented deal with the USWNT, which included a four-year term, additional resources for the team, and a new advisory group to run the promotional aspect and growth of girls' and women's hockey (USA

Hockey, 2017c). A looming tournament on national home ice, and the team's unwavering solidarity and support for the boycott[4] forced USA Hockey to hasten the negotiations and broker a deal. On the one hand, for its part, the USWNT was able to shift a power dynamic with USA Hockey (by stopping the governing body's stonewalling), and gain public exposure through a Twitter social media campaign. That Twitter campaign was immediately picked up by the mainstream media and was an important element in striking the new deal. On the other hand, USA Hockey did not completely "lose" the negotiations; it was able to field its best team for a world championship tournament, it avoided financial loss for not being able to have a team in the tournament, and it regained control of representing and marketing the team during the tournament. While the USWNT ended up winning the gold at the 2017 World Championship, and a subsequent gold medal at the 2018 PyeongChang Winter Olympics, the more important victory may be that it reshaped the athletic labour landscape on liberal feminist pay equity terms for American women's hockey. This player dispute put gender equity successfully in the spotlight, with articles in the *New York Times* (Berkman, 2017b), ESPNW (Foudy, 2017; Granato, 2017), and *USA Today* (Jhaveri, 2017) among others, highlighting this issue after the team went public with its initial boycott threat.

How to Build a Liberal White Feminist Athletic Brand on Twitter

For this part of our analysis, we focus on a set of messages collectively sent out by members of the USWNT on Twitter during the two-week period of the boycott. Because Twitter is a microblogging website where users can discuss "what's happening in the world and what people are talking about right now" (Twitter, 2017) in messages then limited to 140 characters or less, it lends itself to be useful to promote social action, and therefore analyze that social action (Schmittel & Sanderson, 2015). We examined every identical tweet (matching text in all cases, and similar themed images) sent out by at least ten players on the team between the first announcement of the boycott on March 15, 2017, to its conclusion on March 28, 2017. This dataset included nine tweets in total, sent out a total of 152 times across twenty-one different players' Twitter accounts. All of these tweets were sent as part of the second messaging strategy we highlighted earlier, where the team focused on larger issues beyond just the labour negotiation details, and after USA Hockey ceased responding on Twitter. Using close reading techniques, we have thematically coded this dataset (Schmittel & Sanderson, 2015). The USWNT utilized a variety of different themes in its tweets to garner public support and improve its negotiating position. The main themes we focus on are futurity, negotiations, female athleticism on athleticism's terms, and American nationalism.

The most common theme (used in at least 50 per cent of the tweets) utilized by the team was to imagine what the prospects could be for the growth of girls' hockey, if they could be treated equitably. The team tactically put its demands for the future of the sport front and centre in its campaign. Examples of this theme can be seen in the tweets sent out on March 15. " The goals of our requests are to…move forward with a shared goal of promoting and growing girls and women in our sport" (Duggan, 2017a), and March 23, with "A forward looking agreement will benefit the next generation of players even more than the current players" (Duggan, 2017e). This lens was used as a frame five times out of the nine coordinated tweets, and was the most common theme the players tweeted. One of the most shared sets of tweets read, "She said she wanted to be just like me. I told her, 'Be better.' Taking a stand today for their tomorrow" #BeBoldForChange" (Duggan, 2017h). Every player who posted this text added pictures of themselves with the real girls who would benefit—keen, eager, bright-eyed, primarily white girls were imagined as future national team hockey players.

These tweets embody what Lee Edelman (2004) has called *reproductive futurism*—the idea that our participation in political struggle is motivated by a belief in, and a desire for, creating better futures for our innocent children—in this case, young girls in hockey. Edelman suggests this strategy is one that keeps a middle-class, white, heteronormative ideal intact, one where we fight for our children against various queer threats. This theme points to who the USWNT thought its target supportive audience might be, one we suggest makes up most girls' hockey families—middle-class, white, and likely liberal—a group that is typically more willing to accept messages of individualized feminist inclusion through increased support for the sport from USA Hockey (Donnelly & Harvey, 2007). The USWNT tweets invoked a rhetoric not designed to radically change USA Hockey's operational structure, but one that was trying to open the possibilities for girls and women who were already included in USA Hockey's framework.

The team's negotiations with USA Hockey constitute the second most common theme consistently utilized by the USWNT, appearing in four of the nine analyzed coordinated tweets. The team made it clear that it was willing to take concessions on its position in order to avoid missing any games in the 2017 Women's World Hockey Championship. Tweets like "We ask that [USA Hockey's board of directors] approve the original agreement that, the players believed, was acceptable to both parties after Monday's meeting" (Duggan, 2017e), and "Those terms reflected 15 months of negotiations and significant compromise by parties on both sides" (Duggan, 2017i) show that the team was not attempting to fulfill a ransom list of demands through a complete boycott of the World Championship, but rather wished to negotiate in good faith with USA Hockey. The USWNT retained the national legal firm Ballard Spahr, known for representing elite professional and amateur athletes, with prior successes for gender.equity wins with women's soccer (Ballard Spahr, 2017). Its lawyers effectively advised the team to walk the balance between being both flexible and conciliatory, while not wavering on its strong negotiating position (Ballard Spahr, 2017). While avoiding bargaining in public, the team members' tweets kept the public of the digital realm (and those following the mainstream media's reiteration of the social media content) apprised that conversations at the bargaining table were ongoing, ensuring that USA Hockey's Twitter silence was not left to morph into a different story.

After those two main themes, there were several different subthemes employed more sporadically through the USWNT tweets. We draw together two of these themes now to suggest, through a cumulative and layered analysis, how this Twitter campaign about female athletes playing a highly masculinized game was able to support the team in successfully making feminist demands in this era of retrograde, unbridled sexism and misogyny on digital media platforms, especially in female sporting contexts (Bruce & Hardin, 2014; Lavoi & Calhoun, 2014). The two subthemes we explore are female athleticism on athleticism's terms and American nationalism.

As sport feminists (Cooky, 2018; McClearen, 2018, among others) have recently argued, despite the promise of digital social media to democratize the internet and potentially create more space for progressive, feminist representations of female athletes and media coverage of women's sport, things in the digital world for female athletes do not look very good. One of the strongest themes that comes through in this scholarship is that a particular version of neoliberal/third-wave/post-feminist "agency"[5] is noted in female athletes' self-representational strategies on social media. Thorpe, Toffoletti, and Bruce (2017) use the example of surfer Alana Blanchard to demonstrate how very skilled, athletic, and strong women must sell themselves as sex objects primarily for heterosexual male consumption. This twenty-first century iteration of the female apologetic[6] operates under the guise of empowerment through exercising the freedom to sell their bodies and brands to the highest patriarchal bidder. For the most part, sexual objectification and trivialization of female athletes continues unabated in the sports media digital realm. We argue that this is one place where the USWNT does successfully resist the standard social media expectations and trends in its player boycott.

At no time in their Twitter campaign were the USWNT players airbrushed, pushed up, scantily clad, or hypersexualized. In fact, they were quite the opposite. On March 24, the team released a series of photos on Twitter. Each of the players on the senior team sent out a tweet with the text " The players of the USWNT are..." accompanied by an informal headshot photo of each player, holding up unique, handwritten signs denoting what the team's social media hashtag #BeBoldForChange meant to them (Duggan 2017f, 2017g).

In some cases, players chose language typically reserved for male athletes (bold, strong, limitless), while others used more typically feminine words (family, together, devoted). The players were in a variety of casual clothes like hoodies, sweaters, and T-shirts. They wore glasses, they had on toques and ball caps, and there was no apparent makeup. There were still classic touches to ensure they appeared appropriately heterosexually feminine. If there was a hat on, a ponytail was visible over one shoulder (Musto & McGann, 2016). Subtle, understated jewellery was worn, most often a light chain necklace. Many of the photos were taken in the domestic, private sphere such as living rooms, and were not framed in public arena dressing rooms or on the ice. The classic female apologetic was upturned here. The players' self-presentation was not afraid of gender or sexual ambiguity, it was not designed for the desirous male gaze, nor did it defensively ward off the threat of the lesbian bogeyman (Griffin, 1998). The overall effect spoke to the team's entire point—they were athletes, just like their male counterparts, and they expected to receive equitable compensation. The players did not apologize for playing an aggressive, physical game, and they did not try to recuperate or justify their athleticism by overcompensating with over-the-top expressions of conventional femininity.

The second subtheme we draw on is that of American nationalism, which can be seen in several of the tweets through usage of the American flag and patriotic messaging. In its first coordinated message, the USWNT explicitly foregrounded devotion to nation: "Putting on the USA jersey represents the culmination of many years of hard work and sacrifice that reflect our love of both hockey and country" (Duggan, 2017a). The team continued to foreground patriotic nationalism by including the stars and stripes of the American flag as a backdrop in its second coordinated tweet on March 16, 2017. The text read, in part, " We are thankful for the outpouring of support from across the country" and "we are extremely hopeful that we will...defend our title as world champions" (Duggan, 2017b). These American booster strategies anticipated and neutralized any criticism that its labour boycott was "un-American," a hot topic button in the Kaepernick-inspired, "take a knee" National Football League context of 2017. By "claiming" the flag and pledging its national allegiance, the women's team outmanoeuvred USA Hockey, mobilizing and maintaining fan support for the team and its cause (Cavalier & Newhall, 2018; Scherer & Koch, 2010).

We have chosen to highlight these two subthemes in conjunction with our two main themes to forge an analysis about why the USWNT was successful in its player boycott action. Several sport feminists have suggested that in this "postfeminist" moment, we need to consider how feminist demands are making a comeback and/or how neoliberal governance is mobilizing feminist ideals for corporate gain (Cooky, 2018; Toffoletti, Francombe-Webb, & Thorpe, 2018). As McClearen (2018) asks, " What happens when sports media popularizes rhetorics of feminism?" (p. 942). We think this is an excellent question to answer in the context of the USWNT's boycott and the Twitter campaign that popularized its struggle. We suggest that, logistically, the team had several key components in place—enduring and unequivocal solidarity among almost one hundred elite female hockey players throughout the United States, a looming international hockey tournament being hosted by USA Hockey, and the economic and cultural capital within the team to be able to hire a large, skilled, powerful law firm. The clearly feminist and collectivist demand for pay equity, and the group cohesion to not fold in the face of USA Hockey's control are particular feminist victories; however, we argue those victories come at a representational cost.

Remarkably, intense backlash to the USWNT Twitter campaign was almost negligible. Morris, MacDonald, and Pegoraro (2017), in an analysis of the comments section on the USA Hockey Facebook page, found that support for the players' cause was high, and conversation centred on what ought to constitute equal pay. Given the vitriolic and violently misogynistic responses to feminist causes online, this response is quite muted.[7] One way to understand this understated response is to consider how the USWNT Twitter campaign used class and race privilege to leverage its white feminist cause.

Other than the player boycott for gender equity, everything else about the team's Twitter campaign appealed to the dominant interests of the hegemonic white middle class in America. The team invoked a picture of the sport to come, where particular young girls were hailed to join a worthy legacy of players. This imagined future was carefully curated on Twitter—young white girls in hockey arenas with successful mothers and fathers supporting them. Their heroes were young women who were independent, brave, and determined. They were the confident, white female subjects who stood their ground and held up aspirational signs. These kinds of women go on to take up positions within the dominant and elite business and professional classes. This is a nonthreatening future for those already ensconced within it.

While the players' depiction of their feminine subjectivities pushed a small envelope by not hypersexualizing themselves, and, concomitantly, by not deferring to USA Hockey, they clearly positioned themselves as docile American patriots. Every player's photo looked a lot like the "girl next door" in a well-off suburb in white middle America. These were good female subjects of the American empire, in clear alignment with the ideals of US nationalism. The players mobilized in such a way so as to continue to reap the benefits and privileges that came with aligning themselves with the ideologies of the ruling class. This boycott was in many subtle ways safe, and therefore winnable. It appeared not to be explicitly about race, it was not explicitly about class, but discourses of whiteness, American nationalism, and middle-class respectability were all deftly deployed to assure fans and allies that this was a worthy cause, not a radical intersectional feminist revolution.

The USWNT's willingness to be embedded in the privileges of a white neoliberal feminism was reiterated after its Olympic gold medal win in PyeongChang, Korea, in 2018. Following its Olympic performance, the team received an invitation to the celebration for the USA Winter Olympic Team, hosted by the Trump White House. After Donald Trump took office in 2017, numerous athletes and teams began declining invitations to the White House, including the entire National Basketball Association (NBA) championship-winning Golden State Warriors team, in protest of the forty-fifth president's racist, sexist, and homophobic actions and policies. Several Winter Olympians also chose not to attend this event, including the first openly gay male American figure skater, Adam Rippon, and decorated alpine skier Lindsey Vonn. Given the trend of athletes boycotting White House events under the Trump administration, and the very public feminist labour boycott undertaken by the USWNT the prior year, one may have expected the entire team to show solidarity with other athlete activists and not patronize this event. However, the majority of the USWNT team attended the White House event, with only two players not in attendance (Brennan, 2018).

This action demonstrates the ultimate neoliberal nature of the USWNT labour boycott in 2017, and perhaps points to why the team was successful in securing some of its demands. It did not ask for substantial enough change to shift the culture at USA Hockey to open women's and girls' hockey to more diversity or inclusion; rather, it was about ensuring that those who were already able to enter and succeed in the USA Hockey system were treated equally regardless of gender. As

Eileen Narcotta-Welp (2015) notes concerning the 1999 US Women's Soccer team, "the team was celebrated as an emblem of American womanhood that includes all women, [but] closer inspection reveals it actually worked to maintain the narrow ideals of nationalism, gender, and race" (p. 390). The USWNT can be understood in a similar light, as it represented its collective labour action as a celebration of a progressive, equality-based movement to mainstream publications. It demanded only resource equity with the primarily white men's hockey team, which did not disrupt the sport, its culture, or how USA Hockey had operated for the prior decade. Seeking recognition from the Trump White House both solidified the team's commitment to American patriotism and highlighted the limits of white liberal feminist activism to effect systemic change and reduce barriers for those who are not currently welcome in the American women's hockey community.

Conclusion

In this chapter, we have examined the USWNT's Twitter campaign in which it successfully mobilized public support for a labour boycott of an international women's hockey tournament to extract some gains for women's elite hockey from its governing body, USA Hockey. We argue that the boycott was successful because of an impending international tournament in Michigan, and almost complete player solidarity for the cause, where elite female hockey players across the United States refused to join a replacement team when approached by USA Hockey. The team's two-week-long Twitter campaign in late March 2017 was also picked up by various mainstream media sources and highlighted negotiation updates and the promise of a rosy future for women's hockey. Our analysis also revealed that by mobilizing other key themes such as celebrating female athleticism on athleticism's terms (rather than hypersexualizing it), and aligning the USWNT with American patriotism, the team was able to produce a neoliberal white feminist athletic brand that resonated with women's hockey fans and allies. Ultimately, the two sides reached a deal, but it still lacked substantive change. While the agreement covers a four-year period, pays the players of the USWNT a wage, and claims to provide equitable coverage to the women's and girls' teams, it does not change the systemic hierarchy within USA Hockey. There are still many more high-performance teams for boys' and men's hockey, with more events being played by those teams. However, the agreement was more than what the team had prior to the stonewalled negotiations and the labour action. The USWNT laid a foundation for singular gender equity in its boycott campaign. The challenge in front of women's hockey is to determine the next course of action to continue making the sport more equitable for all who might play.

Notes

1. *Hegemonic masculinity* refers to the current hierarchy of power, authority, and recognition among men, which rewards its practitioners with the patriarchal dividend. Men's sport practices, and select male athletes, are often held up as exemplars of hegemonic masculinity. In this historical moment, it is characterized by a capacity for violence, engaging in aggressive physicality and force, and adhering to entrenched heteronormative performatives (Scott, 2014).

2. Pat Griffin (1998) coined the term *heterosexy* to denote a default representational strategy that female athletes deploy, not in a manner to celebrate athleticism but to convey conventionally white feminine and heterosexualized performatives.

3. The Ted Stevens Olympic and Amateur Sports Act requires national sporting bodies to "provide equitable support and encouragement for participation by women where separate programs for male and female athletes are conducted on a national basis" (Warren, 2017).

4. USWNT alternate captain, Monique Lamoureux-Morando, outlined how the team had started forming a player coalition before it announced its boycott. It had secured player commitments from approximately ninety women from all NCAA teams and National Women's Hockey League players prior to its boycott. When USA Hockey started to reach out to Division III and high school players to field a replacement team, the USWNT was in contact with every one of the organizations and/or Division III coaches that were going to Nationals. "From what we know,

we have heard of possibly one to three players that have said 'yes'" (Lamoureux-Morando as quoted in DiCaro, 2017).

5. Baer (2016) addresses neoliberal/third-wave/postfeminist agency in this way. What "are the specific political investments of digital feminism, which has emerged in tandem with the global hegemony of neoliberalism...Will structural change result from the 'microrebellions' of digital feminism, which often appear to work in concert with neoliberal subjectivities and entrepreneurial forms of self-promotion, self-reliance, and self-governance?...By what means do we measure the efficacy of political action in an age when inequalities are tolerated, upward redistribution of wealth is the norm, and alternatives to capitalism are increasingly unimaginable?" (p. 18).

6. The *female apologetic* is defined by Hardy (2015) as any "behavior in sport...by female athletes that emphasizes a female athlete's femininity. This behaviour is in response to the masculine and/or lesbian stereotypes associated with female sport participation" (p. 155).

7. As Lavoi and Calhoun (2014) suggest, "Digital media provides a space for unmediated content and sexist, homophobic, and misogynistic backlash to flourish" (p. 327). Sanderson and Gramlich (2016) describe the social media misogynist backlash produced when the NBA San Antonio Spurs hired Becky Hammon in 2014, the first woman to ever assume a full-time, paid assistant coaching role in men's professional, mainstream North American sport.

References

Baer, H. (2016). Redoing feminism: Digital activism, body politics, and neoliberalism. *Feminist Media Studies, 16*(1), 17–34.

Ballard Spahr. (2017). Ballard Spahr, Faegre Baker faceoff over women's hockey. https://www.ballardspahr.com/eventsnews/mediacoverage/2017-03-16-ballard-spahr-faegre-baker-faceoff-over-womens-hockey.aspx

Berkman, S. (2017a, March 15). U.S. women's hockey team plans to boycott World Championships over pay dispute. *The New York Times.* https://www.nytimes.com/2017/03/15/sports/hockey/team-usa-women-boycott-world-championships.html

Berkman, S. (2017b, March 20). U.S women's hockey team sees "a lot of progress" toward a deal. *The New York Times.* https://www.nytimes.com/2017/03/20/sports/hockey/us-womens-hockey-team-sees-progress-toward-deal.html

Brennan, C. (2018, April 26). Many of Team USA's biggest names will bail on White House visit, meeting with Trump. *USA Today.* https://www.usatoday.com/

story/sports/christinebrennan/2018/04/26/us-olympic-team-big-names-skip-white-house-trump/550302002/

Bruce, T., & Hardin, M. (2014). Reclaiming our voices: Sportswomen and social media. In A.C. Billings & M. Hardin (Eds.), *Routledge handbook of sport and new media* (pp. 311–319). New York: Routledge.

Cavalier, E.S., & Newhall, K.E. (2018). "Stick to soccer": Fan reaction and inclusion rhetoric on social media. *Sport in Society, 21*(7), 1078–1095.

Cooky, C. (2018). What's new about sporting femininities? Female athletes and the sport-media industrial complex. In K. Toffoletti, J. Francombe-Webb, & H. Thorpe (Eds.), *New sporting femininities: Embodied politics in postfeminist times* (pp. 23–41). London, UK: Palgrave Macmillan.

DiCaro, J. (2017, March 27). U.S. women's hockey team is fighting for your daughter. CBS *Chicago.* http://chicago.cbslocal.com/2017/03/27/dicaro-u-s-womens-hockey-team-is-fighting-for-your-daughter/

Donnelly, P., & Harvey, J. (2007). Social class and gender: Intersections in sport and physical activity. In K. Young & P. White (Eds.), *Sport and gender in Canada* (2nd ed.). Don Mills, ON: Oxford University Press.

Duggan, M. [@mduggan10]. (2017a, March 15). US WNT will not play in the 2017 IIHF World Championships [Tweet]. https://twitter.com/mduggan10/status/842013144826429440

Duggan, M. [@mduggan10]. (2017b, March 15). US women's hockey response to statement by @usahockey [Tweet]. https://twitter.com/mduggan10a/status/842143397490106369

Duggan, M. [@mduggan10]. (2017c, March 17). Statement from USWNT. #BeBoldForChange [Tweet]. https://twitter.com/mduggan10/status/842903123194757120

Duggan, M. [@mduggan10]. (2017d, March 20). No text [Tweet]. https://twitter.com/mduggan10/status/843975863913857026

Duggan, M. [@mduggan10]. (2017e, March 23). #BeBoldForChange [Tweet]. https://twitter.com/mduggan10/status/845081637201367040

Duggan, M. [@mduggan10]. (2017f, March 24). The players of the USWNT are... #BeBoldForChange [Tweet]. https://twitter.com/mduggan10/status/845259230756159489

Duggan, M. [@mduggan10]. (2017g, March 24). Show us what #BeBoldForChange means to you [Tweet]. https://twitter.com/mduggan10/status/845335806285877253

Duggan, M. [@mduggan10]. (2017h, March 25). She said she wanted to be just like me [Tweet]. https://twitter.com/mduggan10/status/845738400783237127

Duggan, M. [@mduggan10]. (2017i, March 26). Hoping for a game changer [Tweet]. https://twitter.com/mduggan10/status/846147375102115840

Edelman, L. (2004). *No future: Queer theory and the death drive*. Durham, NC: Duke University Press.

Foudy, J. (2017, March 16). It's time for USA Hockey to wake up and support the women's team. ESPN. http://www.espn.com/espnw/voices/ article/18908360/time-usa-hockey-wake-support-women-team

Granato, C. (2017, March 28). What U.S. women's team accomplished is nothing short of heroic. ESPN. http://www.espn.com/espnw/voices/article/19027162/ us-women-hockey-team-why-cammi-granato-proud-women-landmark-deal

Griffin, P. (1998). *Strong women, deep closets: Lesbians and homophobia in sport*. Champaign, IL: Human Kinetics.

Hardy, E. (2015). The female "apologetic" behavior within Canadian women's rugby: Athlete perceptions and media influences. *Sport in Society, 18*(2), 155–167.

Jhaveri, H. (2017, March 15). The U.S. women's hockey team is boycotting over unfair wages. Here's why that's the right thing to do. *USA Today*. https://ftw.usatoday. com/2017/03/usa-womens-national-hockey-team-refuses-to-play-in-2017- world-championship

Lavoi, N.M., & Calhoun, A.S. (2014). Digital media and women's sport. In A.C. Billings & M. Hardin (Eds.), *Routledge handbook of sport and new media*. (pp. 320–330). New York: Routledge.

McClearen, J. (2018). Introduction—women in sports media: New scholarly engagements. *Feminist Media Studies, 18*(5), 942–945.

Messner, M.A., Duncan, M.C., & Cooky, C. (2003). Silence, sports bras, and wrestling porn: Women in televised sports news and highlights shows. *Journal of Sport & Social Issues, 27*(1), 38–51.

Morris, E., MacDonald, C.A., & Pegoraro, A. (2017, November). *#BeBoldForChange: A social media analysis of the US women's national hockey team's fight for pay equity*. Paper presented at the meeting of the North American Society for the Sociology of Sport, Windsor, ON.

Musto, M., & McGann, P.J. (2016). Strike a pose! The femininity effect in collegiate women's sport. *Sociology of Sport Journal, 33*(2), 101–112.

Narcotta-Welp, E. (2015). A black fly in white milk: The 1999 Women's World Cup, Briana Scurry, and the politics of inclusion. *Journal of Sport History, 42*(3), 382–393.

Perez, A.J., & Allen, K. (2017, March 16). USA Hockey issues deadline for women to declare World Championship intentions. *USA Today*. https://www.usatoday.com/story/sports/hockey/2017/03/16/usa-womens-national-team-boycott-world-championship-iihf-deadline/99247726/

Sanderson, J., & Gramlich, K. (2016). "You go girl!": Twitter and conversations about sport culture and gender. *Sociology of Sport Journal, 33*(2), 113–123.

Scherer, J., & Koch, J. (2010). Living with war: Sport, citizenship, and the cultural politics of post-9/11 Canadian identity. *Sociology of Sport Journal, 27*(1), 1–29.

Schmittel, A., & Sanderson, J. (2015). Talking about Trayvon in 140 characters: Exploring NFL players' tweets about the George Zimmerman verdict. *Journal of Sport & Social Issues, 39*(4), 332–345.

Scott, J. (2014). Hegemonic masculinity. In J. Scott (Ed.), *A dictionary of sociology* (4th ed.). Oxford University Press online.

Thorpe, H., Toffoletti, K., & Bruce, T. (2017). Sportswomen and social media: Bringing third-wave feminism, postfeminism, and neoliberal feminism into conversation. *Journal of Sport & Social Issues, 41*(5), 359–383.

Toffoletti, K., Francombe-Webb, J., & Thorpe, H. (2018). Femininities, sport and physical culture in postfeminist, neoliberal times. In K. Toffoletti, J. Francombe-Webb, & H. Thorpe (Eds.), *New sporting femininities: Embodied politics in postfeminist times* (pp. 1–19). London, UK: Palgrave Macmillan.

Twitter. (2017). About. https://about.twitter.com

USA Hockey [@usahockey]. (2017a, March 15). USA Hockey supports the equitable treatment of our female athletes [Tweet]. https://twitter.com/usahockey/status/842089809808130051

USA Hockey. (2017b, March 17). Update on women's national team issues. http://www.usahockey.com/news_article/show/771106?referrer_id=752796

USA Hockey. (2017c, March 28). USA Hockey & USWNT moving forward together. https://www.usahockey.com/news_article/show/773291

Warren, E., et al. (2017, March 27). Senators call on USA Hockey to treat women's national hockey team fairly [Letter]. https://www.warren.senate.gov/files/documents/2017_3_28_Women's_Hockey_Letter.pdf

7

Desirable Disability

My Journey from Upright Hockey to Sledge Hockey, and Back Again

KIERAN BLOCK with CHERYL A. MACDONALD

AS LONG AS I CAN REMEMBER, I wanted to play in the National
Hockey League (NHL). Hockey was my dream and my passion. As I grew
up, I quickly fell in love with the sport, partly thanks to my older
brother. He was four years my senior and seemingly always four steps
ahead of where I wanted to be in life. He played in Canada's Western
Hockey League (WHL)—a developmental league that feeds the NHL—
when he was sixteen years old. As such, I, too, wanted to play in the
WHL at sixteen years old, and I did. My path would diverge from my
brother's though. As it turned out, I could not follow in his next steps. In
fact, there came a time when I literally physically could not; I became
unable to walk, much less skate. Unplanned and permanent disabilities
have a particular way of quickly dismantling one's NHL dreams. Having
said that, my brother did not make it either, so I suppose we are even in
some ways. I had to "settle" for the title of world champion sledge
hockey (or para hockey) athlete instead. The story of how I got there is a
good one—I even co-authored a book about it (Belzil & Block, 2017)—
but my story has also left me contemplating the ways in which

disabilities are defined and the extent to which those definitions are inclusive of a population that is already marginalized in society. I came upon these questions because I am categorized as both too disabled and not disabled enough, depending on the sport and the decision makers within it. I felt for a long time like I was not welcome in sledge hockey or upright hockey. I felt, quite frankly, "paralyzed." Let us go back to 2007 where it all began.

Monday, August 6, 2007

Following my WHL career, my best option was to pursue a post-secondary education. I enrolled in an education degree at the University of Alberta in Edmonton and earned a spot on the nationally ranked Golden Bears varsity ice hockey team. I was in top shape and working hard in preparation for my second season, when some friends and I decided to get out of town for a few days before the school year and hockey season began to ramp up. We headed out to the mountains for some camping, campfires, cliff jumping, swimming, and relaxation in Alberta's Jasper National Park. This trip was destined to be one of those memorable ones with good friends as summer faded away. I was young, healthy, adventurous, and up for anything. Looking back, it was certainly memorable; more than I had expected, to be sure. It was a bright and sunny day at Horseshoe Lake and I was vibrating with anticipation. I can still recount every detail as if it happened this morning.

After a few successful cliff jumps into the lake, I took a leap of faith, both figuratively and literally; I ran and jumped in without looking. I thought I was in the same place from which I had jumped minutes before, but that would have made for a boring story, apparently. As soon as my foot touched the rock from which I was supposed to propel myself, everything felt different. I knew instantly I was somewhere else and, consequently, I did not know where I was going. In retrospect, my friend shouting at me to wait should have been an indication.

I remember realizing there was no water and yelling, "Oh F%#K!" as I descended ten metres to land on hard rock. I also recall having enough time to hold an internal conversation with myself as I fell, about the real possibility that I would die when I hit the ground. I thought I might be paralyzed or a quadriplegic if I was lucky. Luck was certainly on my side because I "only" shattered my right leg and broke my left foot and heel. The impact was so severe that I had a compound fracture; my bone was sticking out of my skin. I was bedridden for three months and did not take a step with my right foot for an additional month. I was in devitalizing pain until I finally had my ankle fused in 2013—it had taken six years to regulate it properly. I was miserable after my accident; I had no hockey and I was unwilling to accept that I had a disability.

Introduction to Sledge Hockey

My injury led me to become dear friends with Matt Cook, a fellow Edmontonian who, like me, had to find another option for hockey due to a disability. A cancer-related leg amputation took him away from junior hockey, so I was able to relate to him. A few years after my accident, he introduced me to a peculiar sport, at best, in which individuals played hockey from the seat of their pants—quite literally sitting down. This was sledge hockey, a sport with a Paralympic scope played by people with varying lower body impairments. It is an opportunity for people with physical limitations to compete at nearly all age levels, but the pinnacle is the World Championships. Matt played on the Canadian National Team and said, "You need to give it a shot." I met his suggestion with considerable resistance. I was an elite hockey player and there was no way I was playing a disabled sport. Or so I thought. Fast-forward a few years and I am now a multiple-medal-holding Paralympic athlete who learned to love sledge hockey. For me, the sport served as a way to stay in shape and still be able to maintain some sort of normalcy by competing in a sport with a similar set of rules and methods. I learned that the Paralympics are not a consolation prize for those who cannot make it to the Olympics; this is its own proper sporting event, and competing at the highest levels could prove to be a real and fun challenge for me.

Reflection
Connecting with Matt was really special. Matt was an amazing young man who taught me so much about myself and what it means to be "disabled." He truly let his light shine and, in doing so, showed me that I was able to do the same thing. Matt is my inspiration, my guide, and my saviour. Without his mentorship I might still be stuck trying to figure out what being disabled means to me.

What Matt did not tell me in the beginning was that it would technically be in my best interest to never truly heal physically if I wanted to qualify as disabled enough for the National Team. As it turned out, I had been recovering quite nicely from my injury before I entered the sport. I decided to start training to maximize my potential because I thought it would help me. I wanted to be the best in the world. I hired a trainer, Ethan—who knew and understood the sport—to get me to the next level. I worked out with him at Fitness Garage, a garage converted to a training facility on his parents' acreage. Training quickly became my priority as I headed into summer before my first tryout camp with the Canadian National Team. At the beginning of the summer, I was training six days a week, eating healthily, and living an active lifestyle in order to give myself the best opportunity to crack the roster of the top sixteen sledge hockey athletes in the country. I did not realize this would actually hold me back in the future.

Not Disabled Enough for a Disabled Sport

Many problems ensued with my eligibility for the National Team because my healing process led me into a grey area, where multiple doctors categorized me as too able-bodied for competitive sledge hockey but too disabled for competitive upright hockey. As a result, I missed many major sledge competitions due to my ineligibility and this ultimately affected my position within the national program. In 2011, my ankle had not yet been fused and walking always caused debilitating pain. When I was headed to tryouts that year, feeling healthy and strong for someone who was in pain and had limited mobility, I had not given any thought to the fact that I might not actually be classified as disabled. I had ten degrees of movement in my mangled ankle and apparently this does not constitute a disability. I even walked with a limp similar to Batman's arch nemesis the Penguin—only probably with far more pain. Pain is an interesting concept here because it is not typically considered a medical phenomenon (Dekkers, 2015). As such, it was not considered a determinant of my disability.

Reflection

I trained and worked so hard to get back to being healthy. I did everything in my power to get myself ready to play sledge hockey. But I became too healthy and too strong, despite having finally accepted that I felt disabled. How can this be a thing? It was so confusing and very frustrating. It was a bigger blow than breaking my legs. I felt helpless. My passion for the sport began to diminish after this experience.

Ironically, I required an ankle fusion in order to be considered disabled enough for sledge hockey, and my ankle had begun to fuse itself prior to surgery, but until my ankle was fully fused, I was not disabled enough to qualify for the team. You read that correctly: my pain and difficulty walking did not constitute a disability, while my fused ankle, which alleviated my pain and even assisted me enough to return to upright hockey, would allow me to classify as disabled and to qualify for the National Team. At least that is what I understood until I arrived in South Korea for the World Championships. I had recently seen the doctor and he informed me that I was growing new bone that would solidify my ankle's location, eliminate its mobility entirely, and confirm my place as a disabled person in sledge hockey. I eventually decided during my consultation with my surgeon that it was in my best interest to surgically fuse my ankle instead of waiting for it to do so itself. The date was set for June 12, 2013, two months after the World Championships. After failing countless tests to confirm that I was disabled during the previous two years, I thought there would be no question that I would make the team. I should also add that once an athlete has qualified as disabled at the national level, they are not required to undergo further testing no matter how much their body changes over time.

Able-Bodied in the Neutral Zone Trap

My first trip to South Korea was a memorable one. At the time, all eyes were on North Korean leader Kim Jong-un, who seemed to be gearing up for war against the world (United Nations Human Rights Council, 2013) and it was all over the news. I recall being told not to post too much on social media in order to avoid somehow being implicated in the political tension at the time. It was on this trip that doctors informed me, just before the tournament began, that I still had not qualified as disabled and the team staff thought it was best for me to head home to Canada so I would not be a distraction to the team. I was also asked not to do any media engagements on the subject (I did not listen). Nine days later, Team Canada was once again the world champion in sledge hockey. I woke up early the morning after the last game and quickly checked the outcome online. I had a storm of emotions rush over me—anger, excitement, frustration, hurt, joy, jealousy, pride—so many conflicting feelings at once. The team achieved its biggest goal and I felt left out. It was the first time I felt like I truly was no longer a member of the team. To add insult to injury, for three months that summer I (im)patiently waited and waited and waited for both the return of my hockey gear and my seasonal exit interview.

Reflection

On one hand, I became "permanently disabled" when I fused my ankle. On the other hand, I never felt so "able-bodied" in my life since I broke my legs. My pain was gone and my ankle became strong. I was able to do anything. To be honest, all I wanted to do was go back into stand-up hockey. I wanted to make a push to play professional hockey in Europe or somewhere. In retrospect, maybe I should have tried to play professionally. I spent my first game as a verified "disabled athlete" on the National Team in the stands because my coach designated me a healthy scratch after warm-ups. To make it worse, that was also the first time my brother ever came to watch me. I was so embarrassed.

Once I received the phone call for my exit interview, I was told how poorly my year had gone. I asked whether or not my gear would be returned to me so I could begin training for the next year. This was the summer before a Paralympic year so I had missed three months of training for it. The interviewer's response caught me off guard: "Oh, you don't have your gear?" It arrived a week later after having sat in a storage unit in the main office all that time. There was some good news, however; I could be brought to Russia for a test event the following month. I was very excited until I found out before even having left for the tournament that there was no one there to test me and I would continue to be ineligible. I had assumed this would mean I had to stay home again, but the team brought me anyway. I did not understand the disability classification system, or why I had been sent home from South Korea and then brought to Russia, despite knowing that I would not qualify. At this point I was confused and depressed and my attitude began to reflect that.

For better or worse, I decided to start using my voice to draw attention to my situation. In November of 2011, I had done an interview with CTV prior to going off to compete with the National Team. It was a positive story about finding myself. In the video, I proudly exclaimed, "Not for one second do I feel sorry for myself now. I love my life so much so that I look at other people and go 'you know, you can do what I can do'" (CTV, 2011). Fast-forward to almost two years later and the same footage was used to introduce me in a video titled, "Local Sledge Hockey Player's Disability Denied," in which I spoke on television about the grey area that I and other athletes occupied as not disabled enough to compete (CTV, 2013). I am sure that the National Team was not pleased that I had cast a somewhat negative light on the sport, but I felt the need to take the opportunity to make this issue of defining disabilities visible, because it is more common than many would guess.

I recall another athlete at tryouts one year who had a degenerative hip disorder with a 5.5-centimetre hip differential and an impaired arm—someone far less physically capable than I was—who also did not qualify as disabled enough. His hip differential was not big enough to qualify. What is worse, he was regularly taking medication to prevent muscle atrophy. Had he stopped taking this medication, his hip differential would not have improved and he would have continued to classify as disabled enough to compete. It may sound silly, but as athletes who lived for sledge hockey, it really begged the question as to whether or not it was worth it to try to improve our health and abilities if it meant no longer being able to play. He is an impressive sledge hockey athlete and he now has no one to play against because he is too skilled for regular sledge but is not allowed to compete at the national level.

Structural Barriers to Sledge Hockey

I recognize that it is imperative to apply parameters that ensure the inclusion of disabled athletes in the Paralympics so that able-bodied athletes do not take those opportunities. After all, able-bodied athletes have the Olympics. The issue lies in the ways in which disabilities are defined and measured, because every case is different, as is every degree of disability. No two impairments will ever be the same and no two bodies will ever be the same; they are as independent as the people who house them. Disability cannot be defined by an arbitrary set of black-and-white rules. The World Health Organization (WHO), a leader in international public health, defines disability as follows:

> The International Classification of Functioning, Disability and Health (ICF) defines disability as an umbrella term for impairments, activity limitations and participation restrictions. Disability is the interaction between individuals with a health condition (e.g., cerebral palsy, Down syndrome and depression) and personal and environmental factors (e.g., negative attitudes, inaccessible transportation and public buildings, and limited social supports). (WHO, 2018, para. 1)

Canada's *Federal Disability Reference Guide* references the WHO and takes the definition a step further, proposing two approaches to disability: biomedical and social. The guide states,

> According to the traditional, bio-medical approach, disability is viewed as a medical or health problem that prevents or reduces a person's ability to participate fully in society. In contrast, the social approach views disability as a natural part of society, where attitudes, stigma and prejudices present barriers to people with disabilities, and prevent or hinder their participation in mainstream society. (Human Resources and Skills Development Canada, 2013, p. 2)

According to these definitions and approaches, I am disabled. On August 6, 2007, I shattered my leg and along with it my identity. It permanently changed my life trajectory and the way people understand me and interact with me to this day. I could no longer do the things I was doing before my accident and, to some extent, still cannot. Having said that, both the definition and the ways in which it describes me become complicated when applied to the Paralympics.

The International Paralympic Committee (IPC) seeks to regulate the definition of a disability by creating levels of impairment. The goal of this classification system is to ensure that the less impaired bodies do not pose impossible challenges to those who are more severely disabled (IPC, n.d.a). In other words, grouping athletes according to their level of impairment (called classes) is supposed to create an even playing field, which is not entirely different from age, sex, or weight classifications in sport. In order to classify athletes, the IPC has sport-specific guidelines with "Minimum Disability Criteria" (IPC, 2013), and, unfortunately for me, sledge hockey only has one class. According to the World Para Hockey (WPH) website, to qualify for sledge hockey, impairment must prevent the athlete from being able to play stand-up hockey (WPH, n.d.), which is far more specific than the definitions laid out by the WHO and the federal reference guide. I am capable of playing stand-up hockey, but it certainly does not go over well with an ankle that has no mobility, so my goal to be in the NHL is a pipe dream. Simply getting my foot into a skate is challenging enough—a challenge that does not exist in sledge hockey because there are no skates.

The main reason that sledge hockey has no hierarchy of impairment classifications is that the flow of the game does not allow for it to adhere to the points system by which most disability sports operate. For example, in wheelchair basketball, players are assigned up to 4.5 points each based on their abilities and there can be no more than fourteen combined points among five team members at any given time (IPC, n.d.b). Coaches and officials have time to confirm the point calculations during wheelchair basketball because line changes happen during the stoppage of play. In hockey—in both its stand-up and sledge forms—athletes change on the fly. It may be feasible to change the style of play so as to allow the points system to function properly, but this would take away the sport's intended closeness to stand-up hockey.

The sister sport to Canada's official winter game, one of the most popular sports in the Paralympic Winter Games (*The Hockey News*, 2014), only has one class of impairments. While I see the reasoning behind it, this does contradict the inclusive spirit of the Paralympics and thus renders my playing field already unfair to an extent. The same could be said about the gentleman I mentioned earlier, who was more disabled than I was, who also did not make the cut. This situation creates the belief that, in order to compete at the very top level of sledge hockey, an athlete must be as disabled as possible so as not to jeopardize their opportunity to play as a result of being too able-bodied. For example, if someone got into a tragic accident and wanted to succeed in sledge hockey, their best course of action would be to get classified immediately so they are considered disabled enough, despite whether or not they heal later on, because the classification will not change. Even in 2008, had I classified, I would have been able to compete despite feeling better physically and no longer being in pain. Moreover, if someone is born with a disability that likely will not change over time, they have to hope that it is a grave enough condition that falls within the qualifying definitions of disability for sledge hockey. Otherwise, there is no place for them at top levels of the sport.

Another structural challenge that adds to barriers against participation in sledge hockey is the general difficulty of accessing reasonable opportunities to participate. I do not know if this is a cause or an effect, but sledge hockey—at least in Alberta—can have inconvenient ice times in faraway places and the participation fees can seem unreasonable at times. I recall some local practices being on Saturday nights and sometimes nearly thirty minutes away from Edmonton. For a sport that is still in its infancy, despite increased awareness about it, one would think that the goal would be to attract participants, not turn them off or away from the sport.

Reflection

I truly do not understand, in a disabled sport, why they would get so specific about what constitutes a disability. How can they set parameters around every disability? What I learned in sledge hockey is that, intentionally or not, they find ways to prevent people from playing. They seem to want to keep it small and insular. Every year the sledge hockey programs in Edmonton stay the same size or shrink. There were more members in the first organization I joined within my first year than any other year. I have met many disabled people, much more disabled than I am, that will never classify for the sport.

Including the Excluded

I was bitter for a long time about having been turned away from a sport that had essentially helped me find myself and love myself again; however, the more distance I get from sledge hockey, the more I appreciate the time I did have in it and the more I seek to shed light on the sport's issues to improve it for those coming up behind me. The definitions, rules, and classifications around disability in sledge hockey are arguably too specific in a world where disability seems impossible to define. I may not be disabled enough for the National Team, but I was welcome to be involved with Alberta Sledge Hockey as a coach. Many coaches are able-bodied transplants from stand-up hockey who understand the game but do not always understand disability. Moreover, many of the athletes will likely never have the opportunity to try out for the National Team, let alone qualify. With this in view, I wanted to use my experience with disability and with international competition to fill those gaps and improve the sport at lower levels. I know I am not the only athlete who has had to navigate what it means to be disabled, both personally and on paper, so the best I could do was help those who are still in the midst of it while continuing to share my story.

I hope that the IPC can develop more opportunities and classifications for individuals with all sorts of disabilities to participate in sledge hockey, since the sport is only becoming more popular. More recently, the sport has received increased attention due to the addition of Ryan Straschnitzki, a former member of the Saskatchewan Junior Hockey League's Humboldt Broncos. The team was involved in a bus crash in 2018 that killed sixteen people (Lough, 2018). Much like I was "lucky" to only have shattered my leg and broken my ankle, Straschnitzki was also "lucky" to have only fractured part of his spine, paralyzing his lower body. Months later, the National Team had him out on the ice teaching him to play sledge hockey, and he was quoted by Global News as having said, "I still wanted to be part of the game and I told my parents that I'm going to win a gold medal for Canada someday" (Lough, 2018, para. 5). Whether it is someone who has always been impaired or someone who is new to disability, sledge hockey is a way to help athletes, who may not have otherwise had the opportunity, to create and reach goals. For many hockey players in Canada, the dream is often to wear the maple leaf jersey and represent our country, if not to play in the NHL. When the NHL is no longer an option, sledge hockey is a worthwhile choice. I hope that more stories like mine and Straschnitzki's will help the sport grow to be more inclusive of all bodies.

References

Belzil, M., & Block, K. (2017). *The ups and downs of almost dying*. Gatineau, QC: Gauvin.

CTV. (2011, November 23). Kieran Block–CTV Edmonton. *YouTube*. https://www.youtube.com/watch?v=NjB9hlzZpbE

CTV. (2013). Local sledge hockey player's disability denied. https://edmonton.ctvnews.ca/video?clipId=1651771

Dekkers, W. (2015). Pain as a subjective and objective phenomenon. In T. Schramme & S. Edwards (Eds.), *Handbook of the philosophy of medicine* (pp. 1–15). Dordrecht, Netherlands: Springer.

Human Resources and Skills Development Canada. (2013). Definition of disability. *Federal disability reference guide*. https://www.canada.ca/content/dam/esdcedsc/migration/documents/eng/disability/arc/reference_guide.pdf

IPC. (2013). Minimum disability criteria and sport profile. *Ice sledge hockey classification rules and regulations*. https://www.paralympic.org/sites/default/files/document/130801180712197_2013_08_01_IceSledgeHockeyClassification RulesAndRegulations.pdf

IPC. (n.d.a). Classification introduction. https://www.paralympic.org/classification

IPC. (n.d.b). Classification in wheelchair basketball. *Paralympic sports: Wheelchair basketball*. https://www.paralympic.org/wheelchair-basketball/classification

Lough, B. (2018). Humboldt survivor Ryan Straschnitzki on how sledge hockey helps him "stay part of the game." *Global News*. https://globalnews.ca/news/4395055/humboldt-ryan-straschnitzki-sledge-hockey-cowboys-sleds/

The Hockey News. (2014). Sledge hockey ready to become the center of attention after Olympics. https://thehockeynews.com/news/article/sledge-hockey-ready-to-become-the-center-of-attention-after-olympics

United Nations Human Rights Council. (2013). *Report of the special rapporteur on the situation of human rights in the Democratic People's Republic of Korea, Marzuki Darusman*. https://www.ohchr.org/EN/HRBodies/SP/CountriesMandates/KP/Pages/SRDPRKorea.aspx

WHO. (2018). Disability and health. *Fact Sheets*. https://www.who.int/en/news-room/fact-sheets/detail/disability-and-health

WPH. (n.d.). Classification in para ice hockey. https://www.paralympic.org/ice-hockey/classification

8
Skating toward Reconciliation
A Survivance History of Indigenous Peoples in Hockey in Canada

VICKY PARASCHAK

> To cure the settlers from the pathology of colonialism, Indigenous
> people must make public the alternative collective myth that
> comprises our truths, and to heal the wounds that colonialism has
> inflicted on the Indigenous population, we must hear our truths in
> the national collective myth. Without truth there can be no recon-
> ciliation. (Episkenew, 2009, p. 73)

IN THIS CHAPTER, I reflect on and hopefully contribute toward situ-
ating hockey within efforts to address Call to Action #87 of the Truth
and Reconciliation Commission (TRC), which reads: "We call upon all
levels of government, in collaboration with Aboriginal peoples, sports
halls of fame, and other relevant organizations, to provide public education that tells the national story of Aboriginal athletes in history" (TRC,
2015, p. 336). To create this account, I use a *survivance* approach, which
explores Indigenous engagement in hockey in Canada as one part of their
efforts to navigate life successfully. Anishinaabe scholar Gerald Vizenor
(1994/1999) explains that "survivance is an active sense of presence, the

continuance of native stories, not a mere reaction. . .Native survivance stories are renunciations of dominance, tragedy, and victimry" (p. vii). Put another way, this account of Indigenous engagement in hockey in Canada draws on both fictionalized and real-life stories to highlight the agency exercised by Indigenous participants and organizers as they constructed meaningful (real or imagined) opportunities for participation, often but not always within conditions determined by non-Indigenous organizers.

A strengths-and-hope perspective is used; accordingly, I first identify an initial aspiration or "hope" for hockey in Canada that we could all strive to achieve together, which is inclusive of Indigenous players and organizers. I then highlight the strengths that Indigenous individuals have exhibited while striving to achieve their preferred future (which I've assumed is meaningful participation in hockey), and identify resources that helped them to work toward this aspirational goal, as well as ways that Indigenous hockey participants acted as resources to assist others around them, thereby contributing to a hope-enhancing environment (Paraschak, 2013). In this way, I contribute toward a decolonizing account that prioritizes the "truth" of Indigenous strengths at its centre, thereby disrupting and hopefully altering and expanding the existing dominant settler-informed colonial history of hockey in Canada—a bona fide neutral zone trap—that "tends to obfuscate the horrific realities of settler-colonial history and to reify the Canadian nation state" (McKegney & Phillips, 2018, p. 99). Decolonization can be understood as "an expansive collection of activist practices and ideas that works to destabilize the authority of that structure, mute the expressions of its power, and open up possibilities for alternative ways of being in the world that emerge from Indigenous world views" (McKegney & Phillips, 2018, p. 98). By advocating for a shared, Canadian aspiration or hope for hockey that is inclusive of and shaped by Indigenous ways of knowing and playing, I also argue for a possible path toward reconciliation in Canada through hockey.

One objective for this chapter is to have readers reflect more fully on the role of hockey in addressing TRC Call to Action #87. The TRC provided its *Final Report* after the commissioners spent six years listening to Indigenous peoples' accounts of the Indian Residential School system, which had operated for over one hundred years in Canada. In this system, Indigenous children were often forcibly taken from their families and placed in institutions where they were physically, mentally, sexually, and/or culturally abused. In the final report, TRC commissioners provided ninety-four Calls to Action to address these wrongs and to work toward reconciliation between non-Indigenous and Indigenous Peoples in Canada. Five of the Calls to Action specifically addressed sport, and #87 specifically directs Canadians to enhance their knowledge about "the national story of Aboriginal athletes in Canada" (TRC, 2015, p. 336).

As you'll quickly realize in reading this chapter, hockey has been and remains a very important, often culturally confirming activity for Indigenous Peoples. Yet our public knowledge of hockey, which is shaped by both fictional and real-life accounts, is largely a "settler history"—one where Indigenous participants are often invisible. What would a reconciliation history of hockey in Canada look like? What would we need to know, and what would we do once we know? Thomas King, in *The Truth About Stories: A Native Narrative*, finished his book with this final thought, which I offer to you at the start of this chapter:

> Do with [this story] what you will. . .Just don't say in the years to come that you would have lived *your* life differently if only you had heard this story.
>   You've heard it now. (King, 2003, p. 167)

This account has thus been constructed to contribute toward public education about Indigenous athlete engagement in hockey in Canada. To create this history, I had to explore an area of Indigenous participation in sport with which I had limited knowledge, and thereby to enhance my sport history background—and yours, I hope—through an account that places Indigenous participants at its centre. I searched out varieties of stories about the Indigenous experience in hockey in Canada. These sources included autobiographies written by Indigenous hockey players (Leach & Druzin, 2015; Tootoo & Brunt, 2014), books detailing Indigenous hockey players' stories (Ellison & Anderson, 2018; Marks, 2008; Robidoux, 2012; Rondina, 2018), and a fictional account written by an Indigenous author that centred on Indigenous individuals who played hockey (Wagamese, 2012). Wikipedia provided a publicly generated (with the strengths and limitations that produces) source on elite/professional Indigenous hockey players concerning details about their in-career accomplishments/awards and post-career activities and awards/public recognition. I reviewed two television documentaries that addressed Indigenous hockey players in Canada (Marks, 2001; Scherberger, 1991), and two DVDs documenting the careers of specific Indigenous professional hockey players (Malenstyn, 2005, 2007). Academic articles (Forsyth, Giles, & Lodge-Gagne, 2014; McKegney & Phillips, 2018; Pitter, 2006; Robidoux, 2006; Valentine, 2012) rounded out this exploration, along with online sources detailing contemporary experiences of Indigenous hockey players in Canada (Bell, 2018; Douglas, 2018; Little Native Hockey League [Little NHL], 2018; Lu, 2018; Taylor, 2018).

After reading these varied accounts, I focused this chapter around four key themes, in keeping with the strengths-and-hope perspective I currently use in my research. A strengths perspective analysis always begins by identifying personal strengths used by individuals as they navigate through their lives. Theme #1 thus explores the strengths that Indigenous hockey players drew upon during and after their playing career in hockey. A second strengths perspective principle is that there are always resources in the environment that can enhance existing strengths. Theme #2 thus details various human resources that enhanced

Indigenous athletes' ability to play hockey. Theme #3 explores the way(s) that Native hockey tournaments and leagues and Indigenous communities acted as resources for Indigenous hockey players. Theme #4 outlines ways that the mainstream hockey system has presented challenges to Indigenous hockey players, and techniques Indigenous players used to successfully navigate that system. Such methods enabled Indigenous participants to further enhance current strengths or to build new ones, while often concurrently acting as resources for others around them.

In the conclusion, I connect to the hope aspect of the strengths-and-hope perspective. Hope can be understood as an aspiration—a goal—shared among a community of individuals, along with a commitment to work together toward that shared, preferred future (Paraschak, 2013). I'll suggest to you, an individual I assume is committed to all things hockey, a potential goal we could all share: that hockey is a meaningful activity enhancing the lives of all those who reside in Canada, including Indigenous men and women. I also assume in keeping with Call to Action #87 that we all agree to work toward this goal in part by enhancing our limited and/or fragmented knowledge about Indigenous engagement in hockey.

I'd like to introduce this survivance history by outlining the concept of survivance and the way it fits with a strengths-and-hope perspective, using three examples drawn from varied types of Indigenous hockey sources. I then provide a detailed discussion of the four strengths-and-hope perspective themes found in the Indigenous hockey sources I examined.

Survivance Stories: Adopting a Strengths-and-Hope Perspective

If they can get you asking the wrong questions, they don't have to worry about answers. (Pynchon, 1973, p. 251)

The strengths-and-hope perspective (Paraschak, 2013; Paraschak & Thompson, 2014), which frames this account of Indigenous hockey in

Canada, aligns with the concept of survivance. Adopting a strengths-and-hope theoretical perspective is effective for documenting the actions and insights of underserved individuals in society, such as Indigenous Peoples, for whom the "wrong questions" are too often being asked. Information being generated about Indigenous life, such as Indigenous engagement in hockey, is most often framed within a deficit perspective that highlights problems linked to hockey requiring intervention by "outside experts." The strengths perspective instead directs individuals to recognize and focus on already existing Indigenous competencies or strengths tied to hockey, and then to determine how to draw upon available resources to build these strengths further and/or to facilitate the building of additional strengths needed in order to address challenges that arise as, together, we all work toward an agreed upon, preferred aspirational future.

David Heath Justice (2012, paras. 8–9) explains the transformative ability to heal from colonialism made possible by taking a survivance approach:

Colonialism has undeniably assaulted Indigenous communities and wounded untold numbers of individuals for generations. Yet Indigenous people—individually and in community—are not simply passive victims of settler violence, but are instead active respondents to both the troubling and beautiful aspects of their world, respondents who draw on rich cultural, intellectual, spiritual, historical, and aesthetic wellsprings to effect healing of self and society. In telling their own stories, in asserting their own imaginative sovereignty and placing themselves, their communities, and their worldviews at the centre of concern rather than the margins to which Indigenous subjectivities have so long been relegated, Indigenous writers [and histories] affirm their own humanity and dignity, thus countering the "national collective myth" of the settler nation, and helping both Indigenous people and settler descendants "learn that the national collective myth of [Canada], and by extension its societal foundation, is flawed and that its prosperity is built upon the suffering of others." (Episkenew, 2009, p. 73)

Vizenor (2008) explains that survivance stories direct us to focus not on the absences tied to Indigenous Peoples, for example in hockey, but rather on their presence and how they actively carve out responses to their life conditions and challenges in order to create their preferred lives. Within those responses can be found the strengths of each individual. For example, in a DVD documentary, Fred Sasakamoose, the first Indigenous player with treaty status to play in the National Hockey League (NHL) (Saskatchewan Sports Hall of Fame, 2007), outlines how he made intentional choices—a strength he drew upon—tied to hockey in order to create his preferred life, which included addressing challenges as they arose (Malenstyn, 2005). Sasakamoose first learned to skate and play hockey with his family, before he was taken away from them by the RCMP and put into St. Michael's Indian Residential School at Duck Lake for nine years. He spoke of how fear was used by both teachers and coaches as a tactic there, and that it was wrong. He played on a highly successful school hockey team, and when he returned home after nine years, officials from the school came to see if he would try out for the Moosejaw Canucks. He agreed to go, but only for two weeks. While he found it difficult at first to play with the "all-white training camp recruits" (Loyie & Brissenden, 2015, para. 10), he eventually found his teammates respectful of him, even though, as he said, "he was an Indian" (Malenstyn, 2005), and decided to continue playing with the team.

In February 1954, after the conclusion of his fourth season, he received a telegram message telling him to "report immediately to the Chicago Black Hawks" (Loyie & Brissenden, 2015, para. 14). On February 27, he played his debut NHL game at Maple Leaf Gardens, thereby becoming the first Indigenous player with treaty status to play professional hockey in the N H L. He played with affiliated teams the following year, and married his wife in July 1955. He only played two games at the start of the 1955–1956 season, with the Calgary Stampeders of the Western Hockey League; his wife didn't want to leave home on the reserve at Sandy Lake, so he quit and took "a 1,000 km taxi ride from Calgary to be with her" (Loyie & Brissenden, 2015, para. 22). He explained in the documentary that he was opting to prioritize his relationship with his wife over a professional career in hockey (Malenstyn, 2005). He continued to play hockey as an amateur for the Kamloops Chiefs in the Okanagan Senior Hockey League beginning in 1956, living with his wife in Kamloops. He finished his hockey career playing for the North Battleford Beavers (1960–1961) (Loyie & Brissenden, 2015, para. 24). His intentional choices, both to play and where to play, demonstrated his ongoing efforts to work within the conditions he faced to carve out the life he preferred.

In a fictional account that mirrors aspects of the real-life experiences of Fred Sasakamoose, Ojibway author Richard Wagamese writes in *Indian Horse* about the protagonist, Saul Indian Horse, who has also been forcibly taken from his Indigenous family life and placed by Indian Affairs government workers into residential school at a young age, into a set of conditions that destroys all he has known and that devalues all he is. In the "ominous black cloud" that instantly replaces the world he had known (Wagamese, 2012, p. 47), he experiences survivance through hockey. In the beginning, Saul's involvement was just cleaning the outdoor ice surface early each day. Soon he taught himself to skate, the way he saw hockey players do it on televised games he was allowed to watch with Father Leboutilier and other boys. He came to see the mystery embedded in playing hockey, framed within the teachings of his grandmother, and it gave him hope—an ability to imagine and work toward a preferred future (Larsen, 2014)—in an otherwise soul-destroying set of conditions, as he explained:

When I released myself to the mystery of the ice I became a
different creature...For the rest of the day, I'd walk through the
dim hallways of the school warmed by my secret. I no longer felt
the hopeless, chill air around me because I had Father Leboutilier,
the ice, the mornings and the promise of a game that I would soon
be old enough to play. (Wagamese, 2012, pp. 65–66)

His experiences playing hockey also took on meaning because they
connected him to the ways he had learned to understand life, as a
mystery, from his grandmother.

I learned to envision myself making [hockey] moves before I tried
them. If I could see myself doing it, then I could do it. It worked for
any move. There was no explanation for how I could do what I did.
I knew it as a mystery and I honoured it that way.
    My grandmother had always referred to the universe as the
Great Mystery.
    "What does it mean?" I asked her once.
    "It means all things."
    "I don't understand."
    She took my hand and sat me down on a rock at the water's
edge. "We need mystery," she said. "Creator in her wisdom knew
this. Mystery fills us with awe and wonder. They are the foundations of humility, and humility, grandson, is the foundation of all
learning. So we do not seek to unravel this. We honour it by letting
it be that way forever." (Wagamese, 2012, p. 65)

Saul's experience of mystery, outlined in the quote above, became
a personal strength he drew upon as he developed his hockey skills.
This strength is similarly exhibited by those of us who have experienced hockey, or some other sporting activity, in a way that enabled us

to fall in love with it—feeling its gifts, drawing us to learn more from it, feeling humbled by the experience and thus grateful for this knowing. This mystery informed a strength that was then written into our body movements, enriching the ways we could know ourselves and the world around us. Hockey connected Saul to things he loved in a way nothing else did in residential school.

A third example illustrating the use of a strengths-and-hope survivance analysis connects to information in *The Survivors Speak: A Report of the Truth and Reconciliation Commission of Canada*. Former students of residential schools who shared their stories were identified by the commission as "survivors" because they were people "who had taken all that could be thrown at them and remained standing at the end" (*The Survivors Speak*, 2015, p. xiii, cited in Ellison & Anderson, 2018, p. 77). In these TRC accounts there were twelve excerpts mentioning hockey, involving primarily male students from Saskatchewan (4), Ontario (3), Manitoba (2), Alberta (1), Quebec (1), and the Northwest Territories (1); only one of these accounts came from a female survivor of the residential schools.

Personal strengths developed through participation in hockey, and challenges these survivors had to endure associated with hockey and the residential school experience were both evident. In terms of strengths, two individuals (one was female), expressed that hockey was the one positive experience in an otherwise abusive existence at school. Two survivors expressed feeling pride because they were good at playing sports. One said that through hockey he was able to experience winning, while another mentioned the opportunity through hockey to connect to others. Two mentioned that they benefitted by having their coach advocate for them at the school, while the final individual noted that hockey gave him the impetus to do schoolwork. Participation in hockey thus became a positive personal strength for these individuals, in a set of conditions that was otherwise damaging yet had to be endured.

Five other individuals outlined ways that hockey became a negative aspect of their experience while at residential school. One survivor noted that hockey was only used by residential school administrators to try to recruit more students; schools vied for students because they received funding according to their enrolment numbers. In three accounts, hockey sticks were mentioned as being used by principals and teachers to punish students, while the last student noted that the abusive discipline used in the school extended to hockey; it was used by the coach as a strategy to produce success. In these latter accounts, students had to draw upon personal strengths to get past negative associations tied to hockey as part of surviving residential school. Hockey thus played a complicated role in residential schools; in the earlier accounts, participation in hockey aided survivors in making it through their time at school, while in the latter stories hockey was viewed as one of many oppressive activities they had to endure.

Stories of Strengths-and-Hope

In keeping with a strengths-and-hope perspective, I developed four themes to outline the engagement of Indigenous Peoples in hockey in Canada.

Theme #1: Personal Strengths Used by Indigenous Hockey Players

Robidoux (2006) states that "ice hockey is often understood by First Nations people as their own, and part of an Indigenous cultural heritage" (p. 267). This points to the potential for pride as a product of and a personal strength drawn upon by Indigenous hockey players and organizers in relation to their cultural heritage. He also points to a style of play that emphasizes "physical and mental stoicism...[aligning with] the construct of masculinity within First Nations culture" (p. 267). Later, he describes this "stoicism in the face of adversity and their endurance when confronted with hardship, deprivation and pain" (p. 273). He explains that this "physically dominant bush masculinity [versus the gentrified British masculinity was] made popular by the romanticized fur trader, but adopted from First Nations cultures" (p. 279). Indigenous expressions of masculinity thus result in ignoring or laughing off violent acts on the ice, as "enduring injury communicates formidability; the more severe the injury endured, the more formidable the participant" (p. 280).

This description aligns with various personal strengths that Indigenous players have brought to their game, which were identified in the sources I examined. They include 1) love for the game; 2) link to the land; 3) physical prowess or toughness; 4) hard work; 5) importance of family; 6) putting the team first; 7) cultural connection to the community as a role model; and 8) feeling part of the history of hockey within Indigenous (versus non-Indigenous) culture. Some of these strengths are evident, for example, in accounts given about their participation in hockey by Gino Odjick and Jordin Tootoo.

In *All the Way: My Life on Ice* (Tootoo & Brunt, 2014), Jordin Tootoo, an Inuit professional hockey player, discusses his pathway into and through the NHL, from his start in Rankin Inlet, Nunavut. In his account, Tootoo identifies many of the personal strengths, listed above, that he developed and drew upon in his career. He credits the tough upbringing in his family life for generating his interest in playing long games of hockey on the weekends rather than being home. He also notes that his dad fostered his love of participating in traditional activities "on the land" outside of town, a value Tootoo felt was reinforced and drawn upon when he played hockey. Having his older brother, Terrence, lead the way as an outstanding hockey player was a strength Jordin drew upon through their shared careers in hockey. When his brother died by suicide, Jordin's love for his brother kept him going in hockey. He saw hard work and physical toughness as qualities he grew up with in Rankin Inlet, which became personal strengths he could draw upon in his hockey career. And he spoke to the inspiration he drew from being seen as a role model by Indigenous communities, as evident in this quote:

> When I returned to Brandon after the [World Juniors] tournament, it felt like everything had changed. In every arena I played in...people were applauding me, even when I was on the visiting team...But the best reaction came from other First Nations people. I remember going to play in Prince Albert, Saskatchewan, and three-quarters of their fans were Aboriginal people from the reserves around there. They gave me a gift from the reserve; it was one of their traditional blankets with some special designs on it, plus some sweetgrass. When I scored a goal the place erupted, even though I was playing for the Wheat Kings...
>
> I'm very thankful to have a following like that among Aboriginal people...Little do they know that they're what inspires me. I want to be a better professional for them, both on and off the ice. (Tootoo & Brunt, 2014, p. 114)

Gino Odjick, an Algonquian player from Quebec, spoke in a DVD documentary on his career (Malenstyn, 2007) about having and drawing upon many of the personal strengths listed above tied to playing hockey. In his role as one of the top NHL enforcers over an eleven-year career, he pointed to the importance of putting the team first and of bringing physical toughness and hard work to every practice and game. Overuse of alcohol in his social life came to a head in 1994, and he turned to traditional healing practices to get through it. He began to visit First Nations communities and speak to them about staying away from alcohol and drugs and developing good habits that included staying in school. In this way, he continues to use his status as a role model to enhance well-being in Indigenous communities.

Theme #2: Being Helped Out by Others

In accounts by Indigenous hockey players, the support they received
from other people in their lives was evident, including coaches, parents,
extended families and Indigenous spectators. In each case, these individuals served as human resources who helped the player to keep going and
to do his or her best. Jordin Tootoo, as mentioned earlier, felt supported
by spectators but especially by Indigenous fans. He also credited
Predators General Manager David Poile with forcing him to deal with
a substance abuse problem by giving him the ultimatum of going into
a rehabilitative program or being cut from the team (Tootoo & Brunt,
2014). Reggie Leach, an Ojibwe hockey player who received a variety of
awards over his thirteen seasons in the NHL, pointed out the key role
that another player—Bobby Clarke—had on his hockey career, but also
on his life, in *The Riverton Rifle: Straight Shooting on Hockey and On Life*:

> From the moment the puck dropped in the first game, Clarkie
> and I clicked as linemates...Clarkie and I pushed each other,
> competed with each other in a way, and it paid off. We both had
> great seasons...Even when we weren't playing hockey, Clarkie and
> I were inseparable...We spent most of our downtime together and
> even wore some of the same clothes...We finally bought our own
> car together. (Leach & Druzin, 2015, pp. 29–32)

Many of the Indigenous athletes' stories highlighted the key role
their family played in being able to make it to the NHL. Carey Price's
father, for example, bought a plane to fly Carey the 320-kilometre
distance from their home in Anahim Lake, northern British Columbia,
to Williams Lake, the closest community for Carey to continue practising and playing as his career progressed (Rondina, 2018). In the
television documentary, *For the Love of the Game: Hockey, a White
Man's Game?* (Scherberger, 1991), the parents of Gino Odjick spoke
about the moral and financial burden they'd taken on to keep Gino

playing; they cited $175,000 as the cost to get Gino to the point where he could play junior hockey in Laval, Quebec. In the same documentary, when Everett Sanipass, a Mi'kmaq player from New Brunswick, was injured while playing hockey, his father jumped immediately into the car and drove seventeen hours to be with and to support him.

In addition to family support, many of the athletes also mentioned their appreciation for fans who would fill the stands whenever they played, helping them feel supported as an Indigenous athlete. What is clear from all the accounts is that there were numbers of individuals who ensured that Indigenous hockey players could keep going when things got tough, or when they needed to take the next step in their hockey career.

Theme #3: Indigenous Hockey Tournaments, Leagues, Camps, and Communities as Resources

There are numbers of opportunities for Indigenous hockey players to compete in all-Indigenous competitions. Robidoux, in *Stickhandling through the Margins: First Nations Hockey in Canada* (2012), lays out an insightful portrayal of these Indigenous-organized opportunities, both in Indigenous communities and in tournaments with Indigenous participants from across the country. He speaks of "border thinking" wherein meaningful cultural understandings are drawn upon and added to common understandings of the game of hockey, thereby providing positive experiences for Indigenous athletes in these non-mainstream hockey settings.

For example, the Little NHL (or Little Native Hockey League), begun in 1971, has as its vision "to allow our Ontario First Nation children an opportunity to play hockey and represent our Ontario First Nation Communities" (Little NHL, 2018), thereby promoting pride among Indigenous communities through their hockey teams. Participants must be of Indigenous heritage to play; in 2018, approximately three thousand players were involved in the tournament, held in Mississauga, Ontario (Little NHL, 2018, para. 2).

Don Marks, both in his book, *They Call Me Chief: Warriors on Ice* (2008), and in his earlier television documentary on Indigenous hockey (Marks, 2001), outlines how Indigenous scouts, players, and organizers proactively create opportunities for Indigenous youth to hone their playing skills, such as the Aboriginal Role Model Hockey School, co-founded by Kevin Tootoosis and Ron Delorme (Marks, 2001, section 9). A more recent example would be the "3NOLANS First Nation Hockey School, developed in 2013 by Ted Nolan, Brandon Nolan, and Jordan Nolan [as] a hockey school for First Nation youth in First Nation communities across Canada" (3NOLANS, 2020, para. 1). These approaches, along with Indigenous ownership of junior A teams such as the Lebret Eagles (1993–2001) and the Opaskwayak Cree Nation Blizzard (Marks, 2001, 2008) provide a culturally positive environment for Indigenous athletes to excel, to be culturally supported, and to develop skills necessary for continued success in mainstream hockey (Marks, 2001, section 8). These Indigenous-organized events in hockey thus potentially provide participants with opportunities for enhanced pride in their cultural heritage, and positive survivance opportunities as the athletes continue to aspire to be involved in hockey. These leagues and camps, populated by successful Indigenous players, also provide young athletes with role models and insightful advice on how to navigate hockey successfully moving forward. Tournaments open only to Indigenous teams also offer prize money, thus providing an avenue for Indigenous hockey players to make a living outside of mainstream hockey channels (Marks, 2001, sections 7, 9).

Theme #4: Navigating Successfully through Challenges in the Mainstream Hockey System

Numbers of Indigenous athletes from Canada have played in the mainstream hockey system at the elite (e.g., university, international) and/or professional level. I was involved in a sesquicentennial project to address TRC Call to Action #87 by ensuring that Wikipedia entries on elite

Indigenous athletes in Canada were available in an organized fashion to the public, by creating, synthesizing, and/or populating three Wikipedia sites that together outline the accomplishments of First Nations, Métis, and Inuit athletes in Canada in the mainstream sport system (see Paraschak, 2019). Within those categories, hockey stands out as the most popular sport participated in by the 170 identified male and female elite Indigenous athletes in mainstream sport settings. The heritage of Canadian elite/professional hockey players identified on Wikipedia in 2018 included First Nations (51 of 137 total entries, including 4 women [First Nations Sportspeople, 2018]), Métis (21 of 30 total entries, including 1 woman [Métis Sportspeople, 2018]), and Inuit (1 of 3 entries, no women [Canadian Inuit Sportspeople, 2018]).

A total of seventy-three of 170 identified elite Indigenous athletes on Wikipedia in 2018 (43 per cent), therefore, are hockey players. As well, five of the twenty-seven Canadian female Indigenous elite athletes on Wikipedia in these three categories (18.5 per cent) are hockey players. Four of the five Indigenous athletes played for American universities, highlighting their ability to access mainstream education opportunities to play elite hockey provided through universities, in addition to playing on national teams in international sport and in professional leagues. All four women—Kelly Babstock (National Women's Hockey League), Brigette Lacquette (Canadian Women's Hockey League), Jocelyne Larocque (Canadian Women's Hockey League), and Jamie Lee Rattray (Canadian Women's Hockey League)—were playing and being paid for their athletic skills in hockey in 2018. The fifth female player, Beverly Beaver from Six Nations, played on elite competitive teams for over forty years; some of her hockey items, including jerseys and badges, were placed in the 2018 diversity exhibition of the Canadian Hockey Hall of Fame, in honour of her longstanding hockey career (Douglas, 2018).

Indigenous athletes face many challenges when they decide to compete in mainstream hockey. This decision often requires leaving home, with its family, cultural, and community support, as outlined by

Odjick, who commented that when playing junior A hockey, he always wanted to come home (Scherberger, 1991). He explained that reserve life was very different from white society, in that everyone helps each other out, there's more freedom to roam, a slower pace where you can trust others, and lots of caring and sharing. In the same television documentary, Ted Nolan spoke about going to play for the Sault Ste. Marie junior A team as a sixteen-year-old, where he was not supported by teammates; then, when he went home, community members called him an "apple" (red on the outside, white on the inside). Both athletes continued playing despite these challenges, went on to professional hockey careers, and now are active as role models speaking to Indigenous youth about how to survive and succeed in hockey and especially in life.

A second challenge faced by Indigenous hockey players is racism. Marks's (2001) television documentary, *They Call Me Chief*, was given that title because "chief" was a nickname assigned to most every Indigenous athlete who made it in hockey. Rob Pitter (2006) supported that claim, and pointed out that George Armstrong and Jim Neilson, players who did not grow up in Indigenous culture and were of mixed parentage, nevertheless "were each frequently subjected to racial stereotyping, to patronizing remarks and attitudes, and to racist behaviours that made their progress to the N H L more difficult" (p. 130). He then pointed out the institutional racism also embedded in hockey, quoting Ted Nolan as saying, " The way the whole system is set up, even some of our native kids going into A A A programs, they do not [just] have to be as good—they have to be better in order to make teams" (Pitter, 2006, p. 130).

Many athletes, including Fred Sasakamoose, Gino Odjick, and Ted Nolan, spoke of experiencing racism in their professional hockey careers, such as being called names based on a number of racist stereotypes like "wagon burner" (e.g., Gino Odjick), or being subjected to tomahawk chops by jeering spectators (e.g., Ted Nolan). The athletes' survivance strategy (e.g., Reggie Leach, Ted Nolan) was to try to ignore them, and at times to use these hurtful behaviours as motivation to improve and work harder in order to further excel and/or to prove that the stereotypes were not based in fact.

Brigette Lacquette also spoke of facing racist comments while growing up in hockey. She acknowledged her dad, whose support through those tough times helped her to continue playing, which enabled her to compete for University of Minnesota Duluth and eventually for the 2018 Canadian Olympic team. She now sees herself as a role model for other girls, and has had her Olympic stick placed in the diversity exhibit in the Canadian Hockey Hall of Fame (Douglas, 2018).

It would be great to imagine that these racist times are relegated to the past, but in May 2018 racism again raised its ugly head in hockey.

> The First Nation Elites Bantam AAA hockey team played in the spring Challenge Cup in Quebec City from May 25–27, a tournament they say turned ugly almost right away.
>
> Over the course of three days, the Elites say opposing players, coaches and fans taunted them with mock war cries, tomahawk chops and racist slurs, on and off the ice.
>
> "It was awful. It hurt me inside. When it was happening, it felt like I didn't belong there, especially when they were doing the war cries and calling us dirty Indians," said Elites defenceman Carson Shawana. (Lu, 2018, paras. 1–3)

At times, non-Indigenous allies have stepped in to challenge racist behaviour when it emerges in hockey. In the May 2018 case just mentioned, although no action was taken against those being racist at the event, including by referees, the team was "overwhelmed" by the response upon returning home. The team was subsequently invited to a power skating session at the Meredith Centre in Chelsea, Quebec, using ice time donated by a local company. Todd Woodcroft, who was then an assistant coach with the Winnipeg Jets, gave the team an NHL-style prospect camp with some of his team. Students in the Ottawa/Gatineau area sent handwritten cards and messages of support; cards were also received from Ted Nolan and his sons Jordan and Brandon (Bell, 2018). These actions help to show that hockey is a place where there is great support by some members of the public to ensure positive engagement for Indigenous athletes, even as it shows that racism remains integral to hockey.

John Valentine (2012) explored another potential institutionalized discriminatory practice against Indigenous hockey players in the NHL—the idea that they were "stacked" in the enforcer position. He explained that the role of the enforcer is "a player designed to protect the talented players, as well as sell tickets and entertain fans" (Valentine, 2012, p. 117). Valentine demonstrated statistically the overrepresentation of Indigenous hockey players as enforcers, noting "from the mid-1970s until the lockout of 2004–05, Aboriginal players took more penalties, were assessed more major penalties, and were much more likely to fight than non-Aboriginals...[and that] since the disappearance of the enforcer, the number of Aboriginals in the NHL has also declined" (p. 128). Explanations he offered for this "stacking" included:

racism, the role of the coach, discrimination, self-selection, and stereotyping...[it] also coincided with the rise in Aboriginal activism and, more importantly, the negative media coverage Aboriginals were subjected to. This coverage may have contributed to the ongoing stereotyping of Aboriginal peoples as savage. (p. 128)

This overrepresentation of Indigenous players in the enforcer role was potentially constructed through NHL administrators' perceptions of a suitable role for Indigenous players, based on their settler-informed colonial stereotype of the "savage Indian." However, following from Robidoux's (2006) argument that Indigenous hockey players prefer an aggressive, stoic style that aligns with masculine expectations in their culture, and based on explanations provided by Reggie Leach, Jordin Tootoo, Gino Odjick, and others, this overrepresentation in the enforcer role may also be explained in part through a preferred style of play by some Indigenous athletes. As well, the style of play being portrayed by Indigenous role models in hockey may have inspired a comparable approach for up-and-coming Indigenous athletes, thereby aligning with Valentine's self-selection explanation.

Role models who are "making it" in the mainstream sport system are important agents of change for fostering Indigenous athlete engagement in mainstream hockey. Almost every account of Indigenous hockey (e.g., Malenstyn, 2007; Marks, 2001, 2008; Rondina, 2018; Tootoo & Brunt, 2014) noted the lack of Indigenous players—and thus role models— in professional hockey. Two ways that Indigenous youth are exposed to existing role models are through school visitations (e.g., by Gino Odjick) and by attending hockey camps for Indigenous players, often in remote Indigenous communities. Another avenue for role models is the identification of award winners in high-profile sporting and Indigenous celebrations. For example, Brooke Young, a grade ten student from Athabasca, Alberta, played for Team Alberta at the 2018 National Aboriginal Hockey Championships in Membertou, a Mi'kmaq First Nations community located on Nova Scotia's Cape Breton Island. But playing hockey wasn't the only thing she ended up doing in Membertou. She also got to meet former N H L player Reggie Leach. "'Meeting him was very cool,' said Young. 'He is one prime example of somewhere I would like to get to eventually in the sport. He really is an amazing role model'" (Taylor, 2018, paras. 6–7).

Notability (and role models) tied to successful Indigenous hockey players has also been achieved through the annual Indspire Awards, presented to outstanding Indigenous individuals in Canada. The sport category has been part of this award beginning in 1994 (although no sport winner was named in five of the years since its inception); of the twenty-one award winners listed in 2018, nine have been hockey players (Ted Nolan 1994; Brian Trottier 1998; Jordin Tootoo 2002; Reggie Leach 2008; Fred Sasakamoose 2010; Theo Fleury 2013, Gino Odjick 2015; Carey Price 2016; and Heather Kashman 2017 [one of four female winners]). In terms of the other twelve inductees, there are no more than two for any sport, showing the prominence of hockey among the award winners (Indspire Awards, 2018).

Gender expectations provide another potential challenge to Indigenous female hockey players, although there was little evidence available addressing Indigenous female participation, and even less on gender discrimination in the materials reviewed for this chapter. One example given, however, was tied to Beverly Beaver, who pretended to be a boy in order to play hockey on the pond—her chosen method for participating in a sport she loved.

> Nobody else that I knew liked to play hockey. So I just played with the boys and that was fine for everybody…I used to put my hair up under my hat and I used to go down there and they would think I was a boy. They asked me what my name was and I said "Billy"! So that's how I would get to play because they'd think I was a boy. There's another place down the other way but they knew me there. So it didn't matter. I didn't have to disguise myself. Then, when I started getting older I would tape my breasts so they couldn't tell. (Bev Beaver, as quoted in Forsyth, Giles, & Lodge-Gagne, 2013, p. 216)

Conclusion

Hope is a shared belief in a preferred future (Paraschak, 2013). I outlined at the start of this chapter a potential shared hope—that hockey is a meaningful activity enhancing the lives of all those who reside in Canada, including Indigenous men and women. The four themes outlined above have made clear the commitment Indigenous athletes and organizers have brought to their participation in hockey. They have carved out a proud, long, and storied history in hockey. Nevertheless, there remains a "settler history" that makes invisible the engagement of Indigenous athletes in this sport. An expanded and inclusive understanding of hockey will be needed if we are to work toward Call to Action #87 and eventual reconciliation, wherein hockey becomes a safe sporting space that facilitates a positive experience for all. Additional challenges to safe and inclusive hockey practices that were not addressed in this chapter—such as problematic expressions of masculinity, high financial costs for participation, and frequent head injuries—can then be addressed by examining Indigenous as well as non-Indigenous practices, and by drawing upon promising practices for resolving such issues, informed by the experiences of all participants.

In *Indian Horse*, Saul often said that "they" (i.e., non-Indigenous people) think hockey is their game. The captain of the Moose, an Indigenous hockey team Saul played on, explained why some white members of opposing teams wouldn't shake hands or even leave the bench after they'd played: "'White ice, white players,'...[it's] 'Honky Night in Canada'" (Wagamese, 2012, p. 137). It would be nice to be able to explain away this comment as fiction, but recent news articles suggest otherwise. As mentioned earlier, in May 2018 an Indigenous boys' hockey team experienced racist comments from other players, coaches, and spectators while at a tournament, and officials would not intervene to stop those behaviours. Brigette Lacquette, a First Nations athlete on the 2018 Canadian Olympic hockey team, likewise faced racist taunts as she played hockey growing up. Their stories, along with the challenges identified in Theme #4, suggest a "whitestream" structuring of mainstream hockey in Canada, which has "been primarily shaped by individuals of white European heritage in ways that privilege their traditions, practices, meanings, and sport structures" (Paraschak, Golob, Forsyth, & Giles, 2020, p. 101), and thus is more fitted to and comfortable for non-Indigenous players.

Given the many personal strengths and resources identified in this chapter within Indigenous hockey practices in Canada, I would propose adopting an approach for reconciliation that builds upon a double helix model of Indigenous sport in Canada. This model, initially outlined by Alex Nelson, a leading figure in the Indigenous sport movement in Canada, presents the mainstream and Indigenous sport systems as two independent parallel strands of a helix-like structure, each incorporating community to elite levels of sport. At select points, these independent strands are joined by rungs representing specific points of shared inter-action (Forsyth & Paraschak, 2013). In keeping with a strengths-and-hope perspective of reconciliation, once non-Indigenous individuals have a clearer grasp of the national history of hockey inclusive of Indigenous participants and sporting opportunities, we can then incorporate this understanding and a shared commitment to move forward together in a manner that brings to fruition hockey's potential to become a deeply meaningful practice in our shared cultural lives and practices. This could be done in keeping with a double helix understanding that enables Indigenous community hockey to flourish but also to be a basis for the development of elite hockey experiences for all, in both Indigenous and mainstream hockey contexts.

I'd like to return to the shared preferred future we might hold for hockey. We need to honour the mystery of this national sporting expression, as experienced by fictional character Saul Indian Horse and explained by his grandmother: "Mystery fills us with awe and wonder. They are the foundations of humility, and humility, grandson, is the foundation of all learning. So we do not seek to unravel this. We honour it by letting it be that way forever" (Wagamese, 2012, p. 65).

If you, having read this chapter, can more clearly see the privilege you might have exercised through your own experiences in hockey, then our combined hope—a shared preferred vision that all participants in Canada have the same opportunity to love and experience the mystery of hockey in their lives—becomes more attainable. I have identified that Indigenous participants—male and female—have a relatively long and storied history in hockey, both in mainstream and Indigenous sport systems, and that hockey is viewed as an important cultural practice that draws upon and highlights Indigenous strengths in Canada. Non-Indigenous individuals in and outside of hockey have much to learn about the ways that hockey can be organized and played to align with, but also push the boundaries of, the dominant discourse about hockey. That dominant discourse, tied to Canadian national identity, too often assumes as "truth" that "hockey is inevitably a vehicle for intercultural inclusion and social harmony" (McKegney & Phillips, 2018, p. 101). *Indian Horse* presents all those who care about hockey with a challenge—that hockey may be understood as a national practice in Canada wherein everyone belongs. Hopefully, this survivance history, written within a strengths-and-hope perspective, begins to fill in that story, and thus to work toward TRC Call to Action #87.

[History] is good for many things, but none perhaps more precious than to help us imagine otherwise, to help us realize in our lived realities the very best hopes and dreams of our imagined lives, to provide a transformative vision of possibility. Such work is dangerous and difficult, but all liberating transformations are. And if [history] can help us in that struggle, then it is good for very much indeed. (Justice, 2012, para. 24)

References

3NOLANS. (2020). Hockey schools. https://3nolans.com/hockey-schools/

Bell, A. (2018, June 29). Indigenous hockey team that endured racist taunts "overwhelmed" by response to story. CBC *News*. https://www.cbc.ca/news/canada/north/elite-hockey-racism-quebec-1.4727436

Canadian Inuit Sportspeople. (2018). *Wikipedia*. https://en.wikipedia.org/wiki/Category:Canadian_Inuit_sportspeople

Douglas, W. (2018, April 24). Items of unsung First Nations women's hockey star go to Hockey Hall of Fame. *TheColorOfHockey*. https://colorofhockey.com/tag/bev-beaver/

Ellison, J., & Anderson J. (2018). Document 1: Excerpts from *The Survivors Speak*. In J. Ellison & J. Anderson (Eds.), *Hockey: Challenging Canada's game* (pp. 77–82). Ottawa: Canadian Museum of History and University of Ottawa Press.

Episkenew, J. (2009). *Taking back our spirits: Indigenous literature, public policy, and healing*. Winnipeg: University of Manitoba Press.

First Nations Sportspeople. (2018). *Wikipedia*. https://en.wikipedia.org/wiki/Category:First_Nations_sportspeople

Forsyth, J., Giles, A.R., & Lodge-Gagne, V. (2014). Pride and prejudice: How Aboriginal women have experienced Canadian sport. In G. Demers, L. Greaves, S. Kirby, & M. Lay (Eds.), *Playing it forward: 50 years of women and sport in Canada*. Feminist history society series (pp. 210–218). Toronto: Second Story Press.

Forsyth, J., & Paraschak, V. (2013). The double helix: Aboriginal people and sport policy in Canada. In L. Thibault & J. Harvey (Eds.), *Sport policy in Canada* (pp. 267–293). Ottawa: University of Ottawa Press.

Indspire Awards. (2018). *Wikipedia*. https://en.wikipedia.org/wiki/Indspire_Awards

Justice, D.H. (2012). Literature, healing, and the transformational imaginary: Thoughts on Jo-Ann Episkenew's "Taking back our spirits: Indigenous literature, public policy, and healing." *Canadian Literature*, (214), 101–108. https://doi.org/10.14288/cl.v0i214.192773

King, T. (2003). *The truth about stories: A Native narrative*. Toronto: House of Anansi Press.

Larsen, D. (2014, February 7). CBC *Sunday Edition* [Podcast]. https://www.cbc.ca/radio/thesundayedition/cellphone-addiction-socks-for-the-homeless-colm-feore-on-lear-muqtida-mansoor-mail-pete-seeger-loving-the-beatles-mail-traffic-safety-the-science-of-hope-and-optimism-1.2904958

Leach, R., & Druzin, R. (2015). *The Riverton Rifle: Straight shooting on hockey and on life*. Vancouver: Greystone Books.

Little NHL. (2018). Little Native Hockey League hosted by Aamjiwnaang First Nation in the City of Mississauga. http://www.lnhl.ca/about-lnhl.html

Loyie, L., & Brissenden, C. (2015). Fred Sasakamoose. *The Canadian Encyclopedia*. https://www.thecanadianencyclopedia.ca/en/article/fred-sasakamoose

Lu, J. (2018, June 15). #ItsNotoK—First Nations team seeks positives after ugly incident in Quebec. TSN. https://www.tsn.ca/itsnotok-first-nations-team-seeks-positives-after-ugly-incident-in-quebec-1.1114237

Malenstyn, K. (2005). *Fred Sasakamoose: Chiefs and champions* [DVD]. Vancouver: Moving Images Distribution.

Malenstyn, K. (2007). *Gino Odjick: Chiefs and champions* [DVD]. Vancouver: Moving Images Distribution.

Marks, D. (2001). They call me chief ch. 9 of 9. *YouTube.* https://www.youtube.com/watch?v=ZXt6IpBEYlE

Marks, D. (2008). *They call me chief: Warriors on ice, the story of Indians in the NHL.* Winnipeg, MB: J. Gordon Shillingford Publishing.

McKegney, S., & Phillips, T. (2018). Decolonizing the hockey novel: Ambivalence and apotheosis in Richard Wagamese's *Indian horse.* In J. Ellison & J. Anderson (Eds.), *Hockey: Challenging Canada's game* (pp. 97–109). Ottawa: Canadian Museum of History and University of Ottawa Press.

Métis Sportspeople. (2018). *Wikipedia.* https://en.wikipedia.org/wiki/Category:Métis_sportspeople

Paraschak, V. (2013). Hope and strength(s) through physical activity for Canada's Aboriginal peoples. In C. Hallinan & B. Judd (Eds.), *Native games: Indigenous Peoples and sports in the post-colonial world. Research in the sociology of sport, 7* (pp. 229–245). Bingley, UK: Emerald Group Publishing.

Paraschak, V. (2019). # 87: Reconciliation, sport history and Indigenous Peoples in Canada. *Journal of Sport History, 46*(2), 215–230.

Paraschak, V., Golob, M., Forsyth, J., & Giles, A.R. (2020). Physical culture, sport, ethnicity, and race in Canada. In J. Scherer & B. Wilson (Eds.), *Sport and physical culture in Canadian society* (2nd ed.) (pp. 95–120). Toronto: Pearson Canada.

Paraschak, V., & Thompson, K. (2014). Finding strength(s): Insights on Aboriginal physical cultural practices in Canada. *Sport in Society, 17*(8), 1046–1060.

Pitter, R. (2006). Racialization and hockey in Canada: From personal troubles to a Canadian challenge. In D. Whitson & R. Gruneau (Eds.), *Artificial ice: Hockey, culture, and commerce* (pp. 123–139). Peterborough, ON: Broadview Press.

Pynchon, T. (1973). *Gravity's rainbow.* New York: Viking Press.

Robidoux, M. (2006). Historical interpretations of First Nations masculinity and its influence on Canada's sport heritage. *The International Journal of the History of Sport, 23*(2), 267–284.

Robidoux, M. (2012). *Stickhandling through the margins: First Nations hockey in Canada.* Toronto: University of Toronto Press.

Rondina, C. (2018). *Carey Price: How a First Nations kid became a superstar goaltender*. Toronto: James Lorimer & Company.

Saskatchewan Sports Hall of Fame. (2007). Frederick "Fred" Sasakamoose. http://sasksportshalloffame.com/inductees/fred-sasakamoose/

Scherberger, A. (1991). *For the love of the game: Hockey, a white man's game?* [Television documentary]. Collingwood, ON: MapleRock Entertainment.

Taylor, B. (2018, May 21). Local hockey player goes national. *Athabasca Advocate*. https://www.athabascaadvocate.com/article/local-hockey-player-goes-national-20180521

Tootoo, J., & Brunt, S. (2014). *All the way: My life on ice*. Toronto: Penguin Canada.

TRC. (2015). *Final report of the Truth and Reconciliation Commission of Canada volume one: Summary*. Toronto: James Lorimer & Company.

Valentine, J. (2012). New racism and old stereotypes in the National Hockey League: The "stacking" of Aboriginal players into the role of enforcer. In J. Joseph, S. Darnell, & Y. Nakamura (Eds.), *Race and sport in Canada: Intersecting inequalities* (pp. 107–135). Toronto: Canadian Scholars' Press.

Vizenor, G. (1999). *Manifest manners: Narratives on post-Indian survivance*. Lincoln: University of Nebraska Press. (Original work published 1994.)

Vizenor, G. (2008). *Survivance: Narratives of Native presence*. Lincoln: University of Nebraska Press.

Wagamese, R. (2012). *Indian horse*. Vancouver: Douglas & McIntyre.

Masculinity and Sexuality

9

Uncovering the Conspiracy of Silence of Gay Hockey Players in the NHL

ROGER G. LEBLANC

I know there are gay guys in the NHL, because I met one of my
teammate's boyfriend. (Laraque, 2018)

Introduction

Unlike other professional sports organizations, at the time of writing, no
gay player has ever come out "publicly" before, during, or after his hockey
career in the National Hockey League (NHL). In contrast to Ogawa's (2016)
assumption, this is a problem on many psychosocial levels, not just for the
many gay hockey players who exist behind closed doors but also for society
in general. The objective of this chapter is to explain why and how gay
hockey players remain invisible in the NHL—how and why they navigate the proverbial neutral zone trap that silences them. The Conspiracy
of Silence Model (CSM), as well as fictional ethnography, facilitate a
better understanding of this phenomenon through the writings of Davis
and Warren-Findlow (2011); Daynes (2018); Hickey and Roderick
(2017); Holstein and Gubrium (2003); LeBlanc (2004); Merryfeather
and Bruce (2016), as well as Wellard (2014).

Research that seeks to understand the gay NHL player's silence and invisibility is pertinent as gay rights and equality are increasingly manifested within many social institutions, programs, and organizations, including all thirty-one franchises in the NHL (Athlete Ally, 2019; Buzinksi & Zeigler, 2007; Outsports, 2019; You Can Play Project, 2019). The National Hockey League Players' Association (NHLPA) currently works to negotiate fair terms and conditions of employment and assists players with grievances. According to the 2013 collective bargaining agreement (CBA) between the NHL and the NHLPA, a nondiscriminatory clause in Article 7.2 clearly indicates legal protection for gay players:

> 7.2 Neither the NHLPA, the NHL, nor any Club shall discriminate in the interpretation or application of this Agreement against or in favour of any Player because of religion, race, disability, colour, national origin, sex, sexual orientation, age, marital status, or membership or non-membership in or support or non-support of any labour organization. (NHL & NHLPA, 2013, p. 15)

Article 18 focuses on disciplinary measures for on-ice misconducts (NHL & NHLPA, 2013, p. 116), as well as off-ice misconducts (p. 124), adding even more protection and validation for gay players. Hence, the instigators of silence stem from actors other than the gay players, their colleagues from the NHLPA, or from the NHL coaches, owners, and officials. Despite the "pink dollar" (i.e., LGBTQ2+ market) and all the Pride Nights being held in all thirty-one NHL franchise cities, there are still enormous barriers preventing gay NHL players from coming out and being visible and vocal (Ennis, 2019; Jones & LeBlanc, 2005; Pitts, 1989, 2004).

Recently, many authors, such as Anderson, Bullingham, and Magrath (2016), Billings and Moscowitz (2018), Buzinksi and Zeigler (2007), Cavalier (2011), Cronn-Mills (2017), Anderson and Hargraves (2016),

Krane (2019), Lenskyj (2014), Litchfield and Osborne (2017), McGivern and Miller (2018), Mette (2015), Ritchie and Mertens (2015), Roper and Halloran (2007), and Zeigler (2016) have written extensively regarding LGBTQ2+ athletes in general. Emerging authors such as Allain (2008, 2011, 2014), who approaches the topic of masculine identities in ice hockey and MacDonald (2018), who is at the forefront of research on gay hockey players specifically, are noteworthy and will be discussed. However, this chapter limits itself to briefly explaining the CSM in an initial section and then further with fictional ethnography in the second section. Concluding remarks in the last section bring forth recommendations.

Conspiracy of Silence Model

For some men, how they are seen and talked about by their peers may be more important to them than what they do in private. Therefore, some gay NHL players today likely choose to adopt not only masculine behaviours but also hypermasculine behaviours to deter any notion or image of effeminacy that may be associated with their masculine character or hockey persona. Historical lack of acceptance of effeminate gays in society in general and in sport may aggravate the coming-out process of the more archetypical (masculine) hockey players because they feel guilty by association. This aversion to effeminacy that has been termed *homophobia* or *homonegativity* for heterosexuals and *latent homophobia* for gay men was best described by Ryan as early as 1988 as a "toxic, virulent reaction that is fuelled principally by shame, disgust and contempt" (p.7) for behaviours that are deemed unacceptable. Bergling's (2001) term *sissyphobia* describes clearly some gay men's aversion to effeminate behaviour, as do the works of Cavalier (2014), Kennedy and Grainger (2006), Moore (1998), and Pronger (1990). In comparison to MacDonald (2018), the term *homophobia* is better suited for this chapter than *homonegativism*, as fear, oppression, and silence are discussed.

The focus on understanding the experiences of gay players within the NHL organizations from a psychosocial perspective offers an initial explanation of what many earlier authors and academics have referred to as a conspiracy of silence phenomenon (Clarke, 1995; Genasci & Griffin, 1994; Griffin, 1992; Klein, 1989; Krane, 1997; Lenskyj, 1991; Messner & Sabo, 1990, 1994; Nelson, 1991; Pitts, 1989; Pronger, 1990; Rotella & Murray, 1991; and Sparkes, 1994). Henceforth, the phenomenon of presumed silence and invisibility of gay NHL hockey players could be better understood using the CSM to operationalize the phenomenon (LeBlanc, 2004). Its use leads to several important sociological, political, moral, and philosophical questions.

Using the CSM as a framework is one step toward a better understanding of the problem and offers a contribution to the body of knowledge needed for positive social change to occur. Its psychosocial focus is to understand possible forms of injustice caused by discrimination and oppression that exist within the sporting experiences of gay NHL players. Thus, discussing the possible experiences of a gay NHL player and the way he interprets, acts, and gives meaning to his survival in the NHL context is the predominant focus of this chapter.

In addition, it is important to distinguish and define from the onset of this chapter the term *conspiracy* and the term *conspiracy of silence*, as the two differ greatly; they are two separate concepts. A *conspiracy* is an act of working against something or someone, especially in joint secrecy with others for an evil purpose or plot. A *conspiracy of silence* is, thus, a tacit agreement not to discuss something or someone. A tacit agreement is usually an implied but not stated purpose. These terms should not be confused, as this chapter does not seek or expect to uncover an actual conspiracy but endeavours to understand the silence and invisibility of gay NHL players living in fear.

The four tenets of the CSM exposed in this chapter are: 1) hegemonic heterosexuality; 2) spiral of silence theory; 3) identity management; and 4) oppression theory (see Figure 9.1). The combined four perspectives

Figure 9.1: Conspiracy of Silence Model

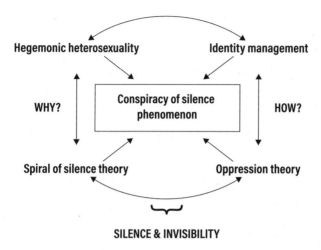

shape the Conspiracy of Silence Model, which represents the organizational politics and policies that subordinate gay players in the NHL. As expressed by Spaaij, Jeanes, and Magee (2014): "A myriad of analytical frameworks have sought to capture and measure, each in its own way, the multidimensional nature of social exclusion" (p. 24). This model, as well as others, is intended to help the reader better understand influential issues surrounding the marked silence of gay hockey players in general and in the NHL specifically. The four tenets of the CSM as defined in the next section help uncover the central questions of how and why gay NHL players remain silent and invisible, using a scholarly and theoretically informed approach.

Hegemonic Heterosexuality

The term *hegemonic heterosexuality* is a feminist concept describing a form of oppression that grounds homophobia and heterosexual privilege within an ideological system of dominant patriarchal values and beliefs. It helps to examine how sport can be a contested terrain that perpetuates society's dominant patriarchal and masculine ideals in the lives of gay NHL players (Coakley, 1990; Genasci & Griffin, 1994; Griffin, 1992; Woods, 1992).

Spiral of Silence Theory

The spiral of silence theory is a framework for understanding the fear of oppression that results from the process of social control by which public opinion influences social behaviour. It is used to examine the effects of the public opinion process on the lives of gay NHL players. Both hegemonic heterosexuality and the spiral of silence theory explain the power of hegemony and its potential ability to silence gay NHL players and render them invisible (Noelle-Neumann, 1992; Steen-Johnsen & Enjolras, 2016).

Identity Management Strategies

Identity management strategies focus on process-oriented issues while exploring and establishing one's sporting, sexual, and social identities during the coming-out process. It is useful for understanding the perceived stages of the coming-out process of gay NHL players and how their behaviour (actions) might be defined and interpreted. These strategies may act as a form of self-imposed control and/or coping mechanism for such athletes (Genasci & Griffin, 1994; Griffin, 1992; Hickey & Roderick, 2017; Oakleaf, 2013).

Oppression Theory

Oppression theory is a framework for understanding how someone feels in an oppressive environment. Both oppression theory and identity management theories are used to understand the processes by which the silence of gay NHL players is actualized. This is to say how gay NHL players may be silenced and how they may be coping, feeling, and managing the contextual issues that render them invisible during their hockey career (Dewar, 1988; Owens, LeBlanc, & Brown, 2016; Tischler & McCaughtry, 2011).

The four previously used tenets of the CSM are equally significant to the understanding of how and why gay NHL players remain silent. In adopting Messner and Sabo's (1990) comparisons to a wheel, the CSM helps to show the relationships between the four tenets and the phenomenon of silence. This permits an illustration and easier comprehension of the mechanisms underpinning the production and manifestation of the gay NHL players' silence. The next section introduces and validates the use of fictional ethnography with the CSM to operationalize the probable experiences of a gay NHL player.

Fictional Ethnography

Fictional ethnography is used to assist in better understanding the probable reasons and ways that gay NHL hockey players remain silent and invisible during their careers. The rationale in utilizing this particular approach is drawn from similar research that seeks to uncover realities and lived experiences of individuals living in fear or isolation and are unable to be heard, seen, or understood by the world that surrounds them (Davis & Warren-Findlow, 2011; Daynes, 2018; Merryfeather & Bruce, 2016; Winskell, Brown, Patterson, Burkot, & Mbakwem, 2013).

The narrative of a fictional player, named Player X, is used to contextualize and highlight his silence in the NHL. In effect, Player X is an apprised representation or "voice" for gay NHL players. In turn, Player X's profile provides a snapshot for the reader to imagine and better appreciate what it means to be gay in the NHL. Player X's profile is intended to complete and reflect the broad range of gay NHL players most probably playing in the league currently.

Although Player X is fictional, the reader should be alert to the likelihood that most gay players in the NHL are possibly very similar to Player X. His situation is certainly believable and plausible when comparing the existence of many other gay professional athletes in other professional team sports, such as David Kopay, Roy Simmons, Esera Tuaolo, and Michael Sam in the National Football League, Jason Collins and John

Amaechi in the National Basketball Association, Ian Roberts in the National Rugby League, Justin Fashanu in soccer's Premier League, and Gareth Thomas in Rugby Union, to mention a few (Amaechi, 1996; Barrett, 2002; Bean & Bull, 2003; Burke & Sherman, 1995; Freeman, 1997; Kopay & Young, 1977; Newman, 1995; Outsports, 2019; Simmons, 2006; Tewksbury, 2006; Tuaolo & Rosengren, 2006; Woog, 1998, 2002). The experience of these professional athletes speaks volumes.

The reality that Player X could not otherwise be heard provides the impetus for his inclusion. Such a narrative is purposefully used in qualitative research studies and well documented (Davis & Warren-Findlow, 2011; Daynes, 2018; Merryfeather & Bruce, 2016; Sparkes, 1994, 1997, 2002; Winskell et al., 2013). Choosing to include Player X gives a voice to the many silenced gay NHL players and illustrates the possibility of his (or their) existence. The narrative given to Player X, the "quotes" presented here, should be judged on their emotive force, their capacity to engage readers emotionally, and their verisimilitude. The intent is to provoke multiple interpretations and responses from the reader. It allows the representation of silenced gay NHL players in a way that acts as a political point of resistance. For Sparkes (2002), "Ethnographic fiction and other kinds of stories by their ability to condense, exemplify, and evoke a world, are as valid a device for transmitting cultural understanding and achieving these goals as any other researcher-produced device" (p. 38).

Player X is the generic player who could be among the seven hundred-plus players within any of the current thirty-one active NHL rosters (teams). He might be an all-star defenseman, centre, winger, or goaltender. He could have had sexual encounters or not. One thing is certain: this player is attracted to the same sex, lives in silence, and is invisible to the public. He is one among many dozens who might fear revealing his attractions to men because the stigma that he perceives may still negatively affect his hockey career. As stated by George Laraque during a 2018 radio interview, "It's impossible for a gay hockey player to come out within the next five or even ten years, the media attention would be too distracting for the whole organization, he'd never survive."

Nevertheless, if Player X was able to share his thoughts, the following quotes in this section are what he'd most likely say. They are written intentionally because it is highly probable that there are current NHL players who are gay, and if there are not, then there were, and if there were not, then there probably will be in the future. Although anecdotal, many sources such as Laraque (2018) strongly suggest that Player X does exist. In fact, ex-Toronto Maple Leafs' general manager and current executive for the Pittsburgh Penguins, Brian Burke, in a statement to the You Can Play organization, said, "If there was any remaining doubt about whether there were gay NHL players, I don't know how anyone could even wonder that," and added that he has spoken to many gay players (LeBrun, 2015). Reflection on such matters respects the traditional objectives of both ethnographic fiction; that of instigating debate on current sociological truths. As an introductory example, Player X would likely describe his hockey career experience as as follows:

> Hockey has left me a bit lonely, really! You know, when I'm sixty years old and still in the closet, I will have never had someone sleep in my bed at night. All I'll be hoping for is that I was thirty or forty years younger and that I could have lived my life all over again more freely. I find that, because of my involvement in hockey and the NHL, I'm missing out on so much of what is important in life. All I wish is that someday I could find someone to love and love me in return, someone to just hug and embrace in my bed all night, someone who would really want to be with me, to love me, and hold me. Just one night, just one entire night!

For clarity, the relationship between Player X's experiences as guided by the model is addressed with quotes in the following order:

1) hegemonic heterosexuality; 2) Noelle-Neumann's spiral of silence theory; 3) identity management strategies; and, finally, 4) oppression theory.

Hegemonic Heterosexuality

Why are gay NHL players silent? For the most part it is because hetero-sexism produces shame for gay hockey players. The hegemonic heterosexuality that prevails in sports such as hockey is isomorphic with power and should be challenged to eradicate the negative influences of such toxic masculinity environments for society in general and players in particular (Taylor & Voorhees, 2018). It is their neutral zone trap. For some players, hockey has not only helped shape their careers, but it has also helped shape how they view others as well as themselves (Bucher, 2014; Coakley, 1990; Eitzen, 1989). The sport of hockey thus serves as a contested terrain between gay and heterosexual athletes, where straight athletes achieve their dominant position in society by a process of power relations through sport. The silence of gay NHL players clearly shows that they cannot be their authentic selves. For Shilling (1991), such a space is no longer seen as just an environment in which interaction takes place but is taken to be deeply implicated in the production of individual identities and social inequalities. Although Rojek (1989) clearly sees sport as a dynamic site for social and sexual emancipation, providing opportunities for resistance and subversion through its ability to desta-bilize gender and power relations, this is not always the case. In the NHL context, heterosexuality is privileged. Heterosexism and homophobia actively limit, control, and regulate expressions of gay sexuality and therefore limit individual emancipation. This is best described by Atkinson (2010): "The hegemonic brand of masculinity establishes, enforces, and legitimates—through complex ideological and discursive frames that produce systems of socialization and matrices of institu-tional support—the ascribed authority of the 'male' figure; as such, it is a privileging cultural status for many men" (p. 20).

Undoubtedly, masculinity in the NHL is represented by strength and heterosexuality. Gay players likely adopt similar stereotypical behaviours to remain invisible within the NHL. As such, hypermasculine vigour among gay NHL players capitalizing upon the violations of traditional gender norms effeminately undergirds the paradoxical nature of being a gay man (Bergling, 2001; Ryan, 1988).

In the absence of any out gay NHL player, NHL fans and players may still have a narrow definition of what it is to be gay. The "limp-wristed" image remains a strong catalyst for the unacceptability of gay hockey players. It is a safe way for heterosexual men to distance themselves from any implication that gays are like them in any way, shape, or form. Although North American society seems to be moving away from restrictive images of men in general, old stereotypes remain strong within the NHL, as well as other sporting codes (Anderson, 2017; Anderson et al., 2016). Obviously, masculine gay NHL players do not stand out in mainstream society; they, in turn, are camouflaged by their behaviour. In this sense, the invisibility of gay NHL players is simply a result of their hypermasculine demeanour.

This aversion to effeminacy for gay NHL players stems from the hegemonic heterosexual belief that all men, gay or heterosexual, must behave in a masculine way. Diversion from such behaviour is considered weak and passive as much for gay NHL players as for heterosexual ones (Bergling, 2001). Gay NHL players who appropriate conventional signifiers of male power would then destabilize the heterosexual monopoly. In this sense, gay NHL players might see other gay NHL players as the problem, rather than seeing mainstream society's intolerance of differences and bigotry as the real quandary. Player X confirms this aversion to effeminacy:

I must admit I'd sooner have a relationship with a guy who seems completely straight. Most of my sexual encounters when I was young were with friends who have since married and had kids.

I still don't know if they were gay or straight, but they were guys who acted like guys. I'm very uncomfortable around guys who act feminine, and I've never been attracted to them or felt like them. Although I have much respect for the courage they must have to be themselves, I still don't feel comfortable around them. They give us a bad rap!

This quote exemplifies the extreme lengths to which some gay NHL players might feel they have to go to avoid being labelled "sissies" (Kennedy & Grainger, 2006; Miller, 2001; Pronger, 1990; Robinson, 1998). The relationship between hegemonic heterosexuality and its influences on the production of silence of gay NHL players has been discussed, bringing forth initial reasons why gay NHL players remain silent.

Spiral of Silence

In this section, the spiral of silence tenets within the CSM are reviewed as illustrated in Figure 9.2. The experience of gay NHL players must be that of constant questioning and self-based feelings of paranoia (Billings & Moscowitz, 2018). They may potentially harbour sentiments of continuous public rejection that are nurtured by the perceived prejudicial opinions of other people in their social and sporting worlds. This phenomenon is best explained using Noelle-Neumann's (1992) spiral of silence theory, where personal opinions are silenced by the perceived public opinion manifested through the media.

As discussed by Holstein and Gubrium (2003), socially organized circumstances provide models of social order through which experience is assimilated and organized; therefore, an opinion is only seen to be the right one if it sustains the institutional thinking that is already in the minds of individuals as they try to decide if it is publicly acceptable or not. In the words of Gramsci, Nowell-Smith, and Hoare (1971), ordinary people give "spontaneous consent" to the "general direction imposed on social life by the dominant fundamental group" (p. 12). In other

Figure 9.2: Spiral of Silence

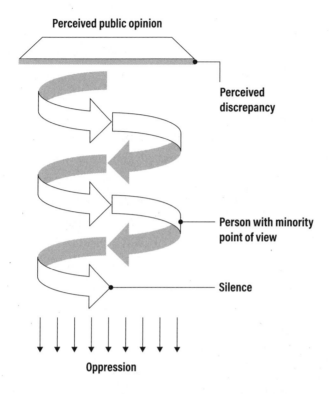

Perceived public opinion

Perceived discrepancy

Person with minority point of view

Silence

Oppression

Source: Adapted from Noelle-Neumann (1992).

words, the public opinion within popular culture legitimizes the socio-political order. Until public opinion manifests itself positively in favour of the inclusion of visible gay players within the NHL, few or no gay NHL players will stand up against homophobia in the NHL. The onus is on influencers within the NHL to recognize the existing injustice and to rectify it (Cavalier & Newhall, 2018; Ensign, Yiamouyiannis, White, & Ridpath, 2011; Gross, 1991; Jones & McCarthy, 2010; Kian, 2015; Kian, Anderson, Vincent, & Murray, 2015; Nylund, 2004).

Player X graphically describes what he believes the existing climate of public opinion is within the NHL today. It is a simple example of the perception gay NHL players have of public opinion and the oppressive nature it has by its ability to silence them. Remaining silent when one does not agree with the action around him is a complicit and subordinate behaviour (Magrath, 2019). Player X best describes this inability to stand up for what is right:

> I don't think I or anyone would speak out against someone during a hockey game who yelled out faggot. Even if they didn't know I was gay, they still wouldn't react negatively to such comments. They wouldn't stand up, cheer and support me, not yet anyway! Especially not the Ryan Getzlafs and Andrew Shaws of the hockey world! Homophobic chirping is still a common strategy to destabilize opponents and win games regardless if there are fines and suspensions currently in place. I hear it all the time, on and off the ice. Being called a fag in the NHL is still not as unacceptable as being called a racist slur! Only racist slurs are officially forbidden in the NHL.

This quote helps describe the powerlessness gay NHL players may feel when wanting to create positive change in a context of acceptance and rejection at the same time. Kielwasser and Wolf (1992) suggest that the symbolic annihilation of gay NHL players exhibited by most media in general contributes to a dysfunctional isolation that is supported by the mutually reinforcing invisibility of gay NHL players in the media and in the real world. However, the media exercises a considerable amount of influence on the degree of isolation some gay NHL players might experience. Obstacles lie with the franchise owners who believe openly gay players will lose them money through diminished sponsorship and TV audiences (Miller, 1998).

According to Walters (2001), "The paradoxes we are witnessing now (the simultaneous embrace and rejection) are reflections of a culture terrified of the potential disruption that full inclusion and integration would provoke" (p. 51). The story of gay visibility is really a story about the long arm of capital and its ability to shape our idea of progress. Within the NHL, the LGBTQ2+ community does not set the agenda— the corporate managers of the mass media do. "We all carry with us," Walters writes, "a belief in a sort of causal connection between cultural visibility and political change, but I am convinced that, often, there is actually a radical disconnection between the two" (p. 51). Dworkin and Wachs (2000) also address the paradoxes that juxtapose public perception of athletes as "positive examples" against media coverage of immorality in athletes. Their work suggests that a newfound media visibility might work against gay NHL players.

Player X would most likely comment on the lack of gay hockey player visibility in the media and the influence the media has on shaping the public's perception and opinion of him. According to Player X, the media coverage or lack thereof may also shape the way gay hockey players think of themselves:

The media has a huge influence. I mean, how many commercials do you see gay NHL players in? I don't care whether they should be representing the society or representing what society is. I mean, the fact that there are no regular car ads that show gay NHL players is a good example. We get pounded and pounded by hetero- sexual content. I feel sorry for younger gay hockey players who are watching TV and just don't see any normalized gay images. The role modelling is so, so critical for young gay hockey players that are coming up and there's just none of it in our mainstream society, sport, and media. You know, I'm lucky because I live in a big city. Where can a gay hockey player from small-town PEI or from the Prairies find people he can identify with? He can't. For me, a lot of what I need to do is to identify with other gay guys in the NHL. And that would help me 'cause I could see that other guys are also gay and then it makes it OK, and I could see how they merge

the different parts of their life, their gay life and their hockey
life. Being silent in the media not only takes its toll on gay NHL
players, but also on gay hockey players period!

Gay NHL players may fear speaking out against anti-gay bias because
of perceived public opinion backlash. The perception of the public backlash
felt by gay NHL players may grow from their fear of exclusion, humilia-
tion, and harassment, even though it is becoming more and more evident
that NHL players are quite happy to provide support for many causes;
they simply don't like speaking about their own personal ones. The way
in which the Hockey Talks initiative has been handled is a great example
(NHL, 2019). Hence, public opinion dictates one's public credibility.
This is largely manifested when one speaks out against public opinion
when one is part of that public. In other words, a heterosexual man
would generate greater support from other heterosexual men toward the
acceptance of gays in sport compared to a gay man or gay NHL players
supporting the same rights. Player X explains this quite clearly in his
own words:

> If you really asked me, I suppose I'd have to say that my whole life
> has been a lie in respect to my sexuality. Now, though, I recognize
> that I should be a good role model for younger gay hockey players,
> but although I've always been supportive of gays and gay rights
> for years, I've never actually had the courage to say, "I'm one." It's
> almost as if you feel you can give gays more support by being a
> "straight" supporter—it gives them more credibility. It's kind of
> like when Jackie Robinson's white manager defended him. Only
> then did he garner credibility in baseball as a Black athlete.

This quote is powerful because he can't even say, "I'm gay," and
instead says, "I'm one." The ideas and concepts drawn from Noelle-
Neumann's (1992) spiral of silence theory in this section were used in

Figure 9.3: Identity Management Strategies (Continuum)

Totally closeted	Passing	Covering	Implicitly out	Explicitly out	Publicly out
	Lying	Censoring	Telling the truth	Affirming identity	
OUT TO NO ONE	I assume you don't know	I assume you don't know	I assume you know	I assume you know	OUT TO COMMUNITY
	You see me as heterosexual	You don't see me as gay	You can see me as gay	You see me as gay	

◄———— Silence ———— Fear ———— Self-integrity ————►

Separation	Personal/Athletic self	Integration

Source: Adapted from Griffin (1992).

the CSM to explore both (a) the role public opinion plays in the lives of silent gay NHL players, and (b) the opinion gay NHL players have of the media's coverage about being gay. For a gay NHL player, silence may mean participation, safety, and acceptance.

Identity Management Strategies

In this section, identity management is discussed in relation to the CSM as shown in Figure 9.3. Strategies used by gay athletes in Cavalier's (2011) and Griffin's (1992) studies explain how gay hockey players possibly survive oppression within hockey organizations by managing their identity. These identity management strategies should be understood as fluid and transient. As stated by Flowers and Buston (2001), "It is the changing matrix of their (gay NHL player) identity categorization that arguably sustains the viability of normative (hegemonic) heterosexuality" (p. 60). Moore (1998) also writes that sexuality, either theoretically, historically, or even politically, is about flux and change, that what we so readily deem as "sexual" is as much a product of language and culture as of "nature." For gay hockey players, gay identity may bring with it both severe costs (fear of exclusion and isolation) and significant benefits (a sense of wholeness and integrity) as shown in Figure 9.3.

To avoid accusations, gay NHL players may remain silent about their sexual orientation, or they may engage in behaviours that lead others to assume they are heterosexual. Accordingly, as the process of self-acceptance increases, gay NHL players may report feelings of wholeness and integrity, and self-esteem may increase outside of the sporting context as they navigate toward self-acceptance and acceptance of others in their coming-out process (Butterworth, 2006; Genasci & Griffin, 1994; Griffin & Butler, 2010; Griffin, 1992; Hickey & Roderick, 2017; Oakleaf, 2013).

Given these difficulties, it may seem impossible for a gay player to ever come out during his hockey career. There are most likely many gay hockey players within the NHL who are still having to "live a lie," who are still experiencing identity management difficulties and conflict. They remain at the frontier of profound isolation. Player X expresses the ways in which one would have to manage one's sexual, social, and sporting identities in life. He also describes the personal toll it takes on one's happiness. These words illustrate the tremendous emotional investments gay NHL players must make as they develop various identity management strategies to hide their sexual orientation.

I've learned to be a very butch sort of man. To behave a certain way, you know, not to cross my legs. I've taught myself not to do certain things as part of my mask, as part of the portrayal of who I am so that I feel that people accept me. I must work so hard to keep that up. I always must be conscious of how I act in order to persuade people, so they cannot penetrate into who I am, and that is how I live.

From this statement one could argue that the human instinct of satisfaction and acceptance is sought and required by the ultimate transgression of boundaries. In other words, Player X negotiates his identity in different situations. At different stages of life, gay NHL players most likely behave differently in different spaces and places. Indeed, the context of sport presents boundaries for gay NHL players to be completely authentic. In this sense, understanding the hesitancy of gay NHL players to claim their space in the league becomes clearer when one acknowledges the intensity of the risks they would have to take. Within the CSM, this tenet shows how gay NHL players remain silent within mainstream hockey and assist in the understanding of their behaviour during their coming-out process. The next section explains further how gay NHL players are silenced by the oppressive nature of their invisibility.

Oppression Theory

Oppression theory is the fourth and last tenet of the CSM. As expressed earlier, the issue of homophobia in sport has little to do with sexuality and everything to do with the power of the dominant culture. Using oppression theory in the CSM facilitates the goal by framing the possible lived experiences of gay NHL players in a broader social context and analysis. The gay NHL players' experiences, when viewed through the lens of oppression, demonstrate the pervasiveness of their stigmatization.

The negative result of oppression on the mental and physical health of gay NHL players is not negligible. Findings from research related to the silence and invisibility of gay male athletes in team sports are governed by ostracism and bullying, feelings of isolation, loneliness, and powerlessness, or the enactment of overachievements and hypermasculinity (LeBlanc, 2004). The invisibility of gay NHL players is arguably due to the level of compatibility these players have with heterosexual men: physically, mentally, and even emotionally. Their sexual orientation could be viewed as the singular difference that divides them.

Figure 9.4: Oppression Theory

Totally closeted	Passing	Covering	Implicitly out	Explicitly out	Publicly out

OUT TO NO ONE

- Ostracism & bullying
- Fear & isolation
- Victims & agents
- Powerlessness
- Alienation
- Loneliness
- Over-achievement
- Hyper masculinity
- Shame & suicide

GREY ZONE

- Enjoyment
- Inclusiveness
- Compatibilities
- Emancipation
- Productivity
- Reconciliation
- Altruism

OUT TO COMMUNITY

SILENCE   VISIBILITY

◄────── Silence ────────── Fear ────────── Self-integrity ──────►

Separation   Personal/Athletic self   Integration

According to Moore (1998), gay stereotypes are inaccurate and inadequate, but they do exist and have some basis in observable behaviour. Although Player X may not use the term "oppression" to describe a personal account specifically, his narrative does reveal the homophobia and heterosexism that envelops his NHL experience as presented in Figure 9.4.

As Player X challenges the underpinnings of his feelings of oppression, he defies stereotypical definitions of masculinity, and, as an athlete, he assumes a role that gay males do not frequently see as accessible. Player X expresses the external pressures and fears of exclusion that exist for gay players in the NHL:

Part of the problem is that we are hockey players first. So, it's a huge, huge step to go from being in the closet or whatever to coming out publicly. You'd have to be a very strong and confident player to come out publicly. We [gay NHL players] harbour the perception that our membership in a [any] team would be in doubt. However, my [our] real hope is that at some point, we'll be able to reconcile or merge our hockey and personal worlds and feel a sense of emancipation fuelled by authenticity.

Consequently, the presence of gay hockey players alone challenges the foundations upon which homophobia and heterosexism are built. Yet, as individuals, they feel powerless to change the institutional and social forces that maintain their status as subordinates in a dominant's world. The negative labelling imposed upon gay men in general, their own internalized homophobia, the harassment and discrimination to which they are subjected, and their perceived socialized roles as subordinates— all serve to maintain and perpetuate an oppressive system. As suggested by Woods (1992), gay athletes such as NHL players may be oppressed in four ways during their coming-out process: 1) they are silenced; 2) they fear being discovered as gay players; 3) they isolate themselves; and 4) they feel powerless (to create change). These outcomes are typical consequences for the subordinates who attempt to survive and live within a successful system of oppression.

The oppression theory tenet of the CSM serves to identify and present the possible consequences of gay players' silence in the NHL and, more specifically, the possible harmful effects it might directly have on all actors within this context. In accordance with Vealey (1997), the silence that exists is detrimental, even devastating, to all athletes, to sports scientists and scholars, and to society at large. Nelson (1991) explained how this silence has extreme negative social psychological consequences for gay athletes, as the silence, designed to protect reputations, deprives those who are hiding (behind it) of a sense of community and history, restricts their cultural and political affiliations, and engenders fear and even paranoia. This is true even today.

Even if other players, fans, and owners feel that the issue of homophobia is no more acceptable in the N H L than racism, Player X still feels that being gay in today's social context remains oppressive:

Some of the real doubts I had about myself when I was young might have been unnecessary if I'd let people know who I really was. But it was so much easier not to let people know. Even now, when it really doesn't matter what other people think and when people are so much more accepting of gays, I'm still not comfortable with letting people know about my sexuality. A lot of my hockey friends might guess, they might even know, but I'm not happy to discuss it with them. I've only talked about it, only come out to a handful of close friends, and most of these friends are also gay.

This comment reflects a contemporary perspective and simultaneously the very real struggle of silence gay N H L players may feel. In extension, the lack of visible gay N H L players needs to be discussed, studied, and debated within the N H L directly. Like all perceptions, the gay stereotype articulated through the media has an impact on the expectations, needs, values, and purposes of the perceiver. Disagreement, argument, and conflict between individuals and groups over the correctness of specific stereotypes are part of the social, political, historical process through which society moves (or tries to move) away from stereotypes, which are valid from the perspective of a whole community (Oakes, Haslam, & Turner, 1994). Findings from LeBlanc's (2004) research state that many gay athletes have experienced common responses to their experiences as victims of oppression. Player X explains more clearly how he would feel as a gay hockey player who has reached the ultimate stage of the coming-out process.

I would have a sense and understanding of diversity, of different people, of things like oppression and all those sorts of things. I could only then understand what that means. Being on the wrong side of it, you know. I think that's one of the key things. It would bring integrity in my life and who I am because then I would be capable [of being honest]. I would begin to understand society and people and all those sorts of things because I would belong to a group that has been a minority group. I think my experience as an out gay man would help me understand the plight of women and other marginalized groups. It's important for me to gain that understanding and then do something about it.

For gay NHL players, oppression comes at a cost to their mental and physical health. Nevertheless, one should sense that none of them would revert to living their lives as heterosexual men should they be able to live their lives openly as gay men. Their ability to recognize oppression and its consequences would profit them greatly as human beings. Common feelings of enjoyment, inclusiveness, sameness, and emancipation for the openly gay NHL players would inspire acts of altruism. A sense of compassion and understanding for other minorities is a consequence of oppression they would see as beneficial to their lives and for others around them.

Clearly, gay NHL players are silenced by the oppression that manifests itself within their lived experiences in hockey organizations. This last section explained how they feel and modify their behaviour as gay NHL players.

Conclusion

From this chapter, readers should understand from the Conspiracy of Silence Model why and how gay NHL players currently remain silent and invisible to the public. At the time of writing, none have ever come out. Using a fictional ethnography approach, the aim was to explore plausible patterned behaviours to uncover how a gay hockey player keeps his sexual orientation silent in his everyday life in the NHL. Correspondingly, many parallels were also drawn between the two tenets of hegemonic heterosexuality and the spiral of silence theory to uncover why silence exists, and the two tenets of oppression theory and identity management, which assist in understanding how silence is felt and produced. As such, linking interpretive practice (how?) and interpretive structures (why?) within the model provided a way of understanding the un-silencing of their experience. As contemporary life, especially that of gay NHL players, is increasingly conducted in a public organizational sphere, such as the NHL, outlining the interrelationships among all four tenets to their overall experiences was essential. Together, all four tenets of the model illustrate the power relations that exist in the lives of gay NHL players to produce the silence and social injustices that construct the social realities of a gay player in the NHL.

As Bill Ryan suggested more than thirty years ago, silence breeds shame every bit as much as shame breeds silence. The two are locked in a self-reinforcing cycle as displayed within the CSM presented in this chapter. Silence first communicates shame because whenever there is a subject that cannot be spoken about openly, we invariably feel shame (Ryan, 1988). Although continuing education is available in Article 29 of the collective bargaining agreement for all involved directly with the NHL, let us be clear that diversity training is essential if the NHL endeavours to move forward. Appropriate training would emphasize that one's sex life is a private matter and non-negotiable in public as much for gay players as it is for non-gay players. In accordance with Article 34.9 of the CBA, the topic of gay players in the NHL is clearly a question for the players' Joint Health and Safety Committee to tackle and remediate (NHL & NHLPA, 2013, p. 184). As the average career lifespan of an NHL player is only five years and the average salary was $3,012,785 USD during the 2016–2017 season and the minimum salary was $650,000

USD for the 2017–2018 season, it is easily understandable that one's sexual identity and orientation is not something one wants to address during their short career (Cohn, 2016; NHL & NHLPA, 2013).

What cannot be spoken of openly must be too shameful to approach, too taboo. Therefore, the silence possibly experienced by most gay men in the NHL may mostly be instigated and driven by the enforced sense of shame experienced within their social and family lives in general and in the context of the NHL. As expressed by many gay athletes from other sports thus far, shame creates silence, and the silence incurred within hockey utilizes shame and fear on a broad scale to keep gay NHL players invisible to the public eye. Nevertheless, to conclude this chapter, it is hoped that this work may save the sporting life of a gay NHL player such as Player X. If not, at the very least, this work has shown a need for positive change in the NHL world of a gay hockey player—before, during, and after his career.

References

Allain, K.A. (2008). "Real fast and tough": The construction of Canadian hockey masculinity. *Sociology of Sport Journal, 25*(4), 462–481.

Allain, K.A. (2011). Kid Crosby or golden boy: Sidney Crosby, Canadian national identity, and the policing of hockey masculinity. *International Review for the Sociology of Sport, 46*(1), 3–22.

Allain, K.A. (2014). "What happens in the room stays in the room": Conducting research with young men in the Canadian Hockey League. *Qualitative Research in Sport, Exercise and Health, 6*(2), 205–219.

Amaechi, J. (1996). *Man in the middle*. New York: ESPN Books.

Anderson, E. (2017). *Sport, masculinities and sexualities*. London, UK: Routledge.

Anderson, E., Bullingham, R., & Magrath, R. (2016). *Out in sport: The experiences of openly gay and lesbian athletes in competitive sport*. New York: Routledge.

Anderson, E., & Hargreaves, J. (2016). *Routledge handbook of sport, gender and sexuality*. New York: Routledge.

Athlete Ally. (2019). Athlete Ally. https://www.athleteally.org

Atkinson, M. (2010). It's still part of the game: Violence and masculinity in Canadian ice hockey. In L.K. Fuller (Ed.), *Sexual sports rhetoric: Historical and media contexts of violence.* (pp. 15–29). New York: Peter Lang.

Barrett, J. (2002). *Hero of Flight 93: Mark Bingham.* Los Angeles: Advocate Books.

Bean, B., & Bull, C. (2003). *Going the other way: Lessons from a life in and out of major-league baseball.* New York: Marlowe & Company.

Bergling, T. (2001). *Sissyphobia: Gay men and effeminate behavior.* New York: Southern Tier Editions.

Billings, A.C., & Moscowitz, L. (2018). *Media and the coming out of gay male athletes in American team sports.* New York: Peter Lang.

Bucher, J. (2014). "But he can't be gay": The relationship between masculinity and homophobia in father-son relationships. *Journal of Men's Studies, 22*(3), 222–237.

Burke, G., & Sherman, E. (1995). *Out at home: The Glenn Burke story.* New York: Excel.

Butterworth, M.L. (2006). Pitchers and catchers: Mike Piazza and the discourse of gay identity in the national pastime. *Journal of Sport & Social Issues, 30*(2), 138–157.

Buzinksi, J., & Zeigler, C. (2007). *The outsports revolution.* Los Angeles: Alyson Books.

Cavalier, E. (2014). I don't "look gay": Different disclosures of sexual identity in men's, women's, and co-ed sport. In J. Hargreaves & E. Anderson (Eds.), *Handbook of sport, gender and sexuality* (pp. 300–308). New York: Routledge.

Cavalier, E.S. (2011). Men at sport: Gay men's experiences in the sport workplace. *Journal of Homosexuality, 58*(5), 626–646.

Cavalier, E.S., & Newhall, K.E. (2018). "Stick to soccer": Fan reaction and inclusion rhetoric on social media. *Sport in Society, 21*(7), 1078–1095.

Clarke, G. (1995). *Homophobia and heterosexism in physical education: Can we move into a new era?* Paper presented at the Physical Education Annual Conference, St Mary's University, Twickenham, UK.

Coakley, J. (1990). *Sport in society: Issues and controversies* (4th ed.). St. Louis, MO: Times Mirror/Mosby College.

Cohn, L. (2016). The ageless Jaromir Jagr. https://www.espn.com

Cronn-Mills, K. (2017). *LGBTQ+ athletes claim the field: Striving for equality.* Minneapolis, MN: Twenty-First Century Books.

Davis, C.S., & Warren-Findlow, J. (2011). Coping with trauma through fictional narrative ethnography: A primer. *Journal of Loss and Trauma, 16*(6), 563–572.

Daynes, S. (2018). *On ethnography.* Cambridge, UK: Polity Press.

Dewar, A.M. (1988). *Sexual oppression in sport: Past, present and future alternatives* (Unpublished conference paper), 1–13.

Dworkin, S.L., & Wachs, F.L. (2000). Masculinity, sport, and the media. In J. McKay, M.A. Messner, & D.F. Sabo (Eds.), *The morality/manhood paradox: Masculinity, sport, and the media* (pp. 47–66). Thousand Oaks, CA: Sage.

Eitzen, D.S. (1989). *Sport in contemporary society: An anthology* (3rd ed.). New York: St. Martin's Press.

Ennis, D. (2019). Every NHL team is celebrating Pride this year. *Outsports.* https://www.outsports.com/2019/6/1/18648240/every-nhl-team-celebrating-pride-nhlpa-hockey

Ensign, K.A., Yiamouyiannis, A., White, K.M., & Ridpath, B.D. (2011). Athletic trainers' attitudes toward lesbian, gay, and bisexual National Collegiate Athletic Association student-athletes. *Journal of Athletic Training, 46*(1), 69–75.

Flowers, P., & Buston, K. (2001). "I was terrified of being different": Exploring gay men's accounts of growing up in a heterosexist society. *Journal of Adolescence, 24*(1), 51–65.

Freeman, P. (1997). *Ian Roberts: Finding out.* Milsons Point, NSW: Random House Australia.

Genasci, J., & Griffin, P. (1994). *Addressing homophobia in sports and athletics.* Paper presented at the 11th Annual Conference on Counselling Athletes: Assisting Today's Athletes toward Peak Performance, Springfield, MA.

Gramsci, A., Nowell-Smith, G., & Hoare, Q. (1971). *Selections from the prison notebooks.* London, UK: New Left Books.

Griffin, L.L., & Butler, J. (2010). *More teaching games for understanding: Moving globally.* Champaign, IL: Human Kinetics.

Griffin, P. (1992). Changing the game: Homophobia, sexism, and lesbians in sport. *Quest, 44*(22), 251–265.

Gross, L. (1991). Out of the mainstream: Sexual minorities and the mass media. In M. Wolf & A. Kielwasser (Eds.), *Gay people, sex and the media* (pp. 19–46). New York: Harrington Park/Hawthorn Press.

Hickey, C., & Roderick, M. (2017). The presentation of possible selves in everyday life: The management of identity among transitioning professional athletes. *Sociology of Sport Journal, 34*(3), 270–280.

Holstein, J.A., & Gubrium, J.F. (2003). Phenomenology, ethnography, and interpretive practice. In K. Denzin & Y. Lincoln (Eds.), *Strategies of qualitative inquiry* (pp. 262–272). Thousand Oaks, CA: Sage.

Jones, L., & McCarthy, M. (2010). Mapping the landscape of gay men's football. *Leisure Studies, 29*(2), 161–173.

Jones, R., & LeBlanc, R.G. (2005). Sport, sexuality and representation in advertising: The political economy of the pink dollar. In S. Jackson & D.L. Andrews (Eds.), *Sport, culture and advertising: Identities, commodities and the politics of representation* (pp. 119–135). New York: Routledge.

Kennedy, S., & Grainger, J. (2006). *Why I didn't say anything: The Sheldon Kennedy story*. Toronto: Insomniac Press.

Kian, E.M. (2015). A case study on message-board and media framing of gay male athletes on a politically liberal web site. *International Journal of Sport Communication, 8*(4), 500–518.

Kian, E.M., Anderson, E., Vincent, J., & Murray, R. (2015). Sport journalists' views on gay men in sport, society and within sport media. *International Review for the Sociology of Sport, 50*(8), 895–911.

Kielwasser, A.P., & Wolf, M.A. (1992). Mainstream television, adolescent homosexuality, and significant silence. *Critical Studies in Mass Communication, 9*(4), 350–373.

Klein, A.M. (1989). Managing deviance: Hustling, homophobia, and the bodybuilding subculture. *Deviant Behavior, 10*(1), 11–27.

Kopay, D., & Young, P.D. (1977). *The David Kopay story: An extraordinary self-revelation*. New York: Arbour House.

Krane, V. (1997). Homonegativism experienced by lesbian collegiate athletes. *Women in Sport and Physical Activity Journal, 6*(2), 141.

Krane, V. (2019). *Sex, gender, and sexuality in sport: Queer inquiries*. London, UK: Routledge.

Laraque, G. (2018, October 26). Homosexualité au hockey: Un tabou [Émission Corde sensible avec Marie-Eve Tremblay]. https://ici.radio-canada.ca/ohdio/balados/5687/corde-sensible-radical-marie-eve-tremblay/418857/homosexualite-hockey-tabou-george-laraque

LeBlanc, R.G. (2004). *The first fifteen: Understanding the conspiracy of silence of gay rugby players in Aotera/New Zealand* (Unpublished doctoral dissertation). University of Otago, Dunedin, New Zealand.

LeBrun, P. (2015, November 4). Patrick Burke: "NHL is ready for a gay player." TSN. https://www.tsn.ca/patrick-burke-nhl-is-ready-for-a-gay-player-1.388059

Lenskyj, H. (1991). Combating homophobia in sport and physical education. *Sociology of Sport Journal, 8*(1), 61–69.

Lenskyj, H. (2014). *Sexual diversity and the Sochi 2014 Olympics: No more rainbows*. Basingstoke, UK: Palgrave Pivot.

Litchfield, C., & Osborne, J. (2017). The gay games, safe spaces and the promotion of sport for all? In R.A. Dionigi & M. Gard (Eds.), *Sport and physical activity across the lifespan: Critical perspectives* (pp. 245–260). London, UK: Palgrave Macmillan.

MacDonald, C.A. (2018). Insert name of openly gay hockey player here: Attitudes towards homosexuality among Canadian male major midget AAA ice hockey players. *Sociology of Sport Journal, 35*(4), 347–357.

Magrath, R. (2019). LGBT *athletes in the sports media.* Cham, Switzerland: Palgrave Macmillan.

McGivern, C.T., & Miller, P.C. (2018). *Queer voices from the locker room.* Charlotte, NC: Information Age Publishing.

Merryfeather, L., & Bruce, A. (2016). Autoethnography: Exploring gender diversity. *Nursing Forum, 51*(1), 13–20.

Messner, M.A., & Sabo, D.F. (1990). *Sport, men, and the gender order: Critical feminist perspectives.* Champaign, IL: Human Kinetics.

Messner, M.A., & Sabo, D.F. (1994). *Sex, violence & power in sports: Rethinking masculinity.* Freedom, CA: Crossing Press.

Mette, A. (2015). *Les homos sortent du vestiaire! La fin du tabou de l'homosexualité dans le sport?* Paris: Lulu.com.

Miller, T. (1998). Commodifying the male body, problematizing "hegemonic masculinity?" *Journal of Sport & Social Issues, 22*(4), 431–446.

Miller, T. (2001). *Sportsex.* Philadelphia, PA: Temple University Press.

Moore, C. (1998). Behaving outrageously: Contemporary gay masculinity. *Journal of Australian Studies, 56*(11), 158–168.

Nelson, M.B. (1991). *Are we winning yet? How women are changing sports and sports are changing women.* New York: Random House.

Newman, S. (1995, February/March). Jumping out of the closet: Former Olympic high jumper Brian Marshall discusses his homosexuality and athletics. *Athletics,* 10–12.

NHL & NHLPA. (2013). *Collective bargaining agreement between National Hockey League and National Hockey League Players' Association.* https://www.nhlpa.com /the-pa/cba

NHL (2019). Hockey talks. https://www.nhl.com/canucks/community/ hockey-talks

Noelle-Neumann, E. (1992). The contribution of spiral of silence theory to an understanding of the mass media. In S. Rothman (Ed.), *The mass media in liberal democratic societies* (pp. 75–83). New York: Paragon House.

Nylund, D. (2004). When in Rome: Heterosexism, homophobia, and sports talk radio. *Journal of Sport & Social Issues, 28*(2), 136–168.

Oakes, P., Haslam, A., and Turner, J.C. (1994). Stereotyping and social reality. London, UK: Blackwell.

Oakleaf, L. (2013). "Having to think about it all the time": Factors affecting the identity management strategies of residential summer camp staff who self-identify as lesbian, gay, bisexual or transgender. *Leisure/Loisir, 37*(3), 251–266.

Ogawa, S. (2016). 100 missing men: Participation, selection, and silence of gay athletes. In J. Hargreaves & E. Anderson (Eds.), *Routledge handbook of sport, gender and sexuality* (pp. 291–299). London, UK: Routledge.

Outsports. (2019). Homepage. https://www.outsports.com/

Owens, R.E., LeBlanc, R.G., & Brown, P.K. (2016). Visual body pedagogies: How anti-oppressive education informs the teaching and learning of sporting bodies. *Sport, Education and Society, 21*(5), 661–676.

Pitts, B.G. (1989). Beyond the bars: The development of leisure-activity management in the lesbian and gay population in America. *Leisure Information Quarterly, 15*(3), 4–7.

Pitts, B.G. (2004). Banking on the pink dollar: Sponsorship awareness and the Gay Games. In *Sharing best practices in sport marketing: The Sport Marketing Association's inaugural book of papers* (pp. 81–97). Morgantown, WV: Fitness Information Technology.

Pronger, B. (1990). *The arena of masculinity: Sports, homosexuality, and the meaning of sex.* London, UK: GMP Publishers.

Ritchie, T., & Mertens, C. (2015). *Rainbow lockers: Queer youth in sports.* Scotts Valley, CA: CreateSpace Independent Publishing Platform.

Robinson, L. (1998). *Crossing the line: Violence and sexual assault in Canada's national sport.* Toronto: McClelland & Stewart.

Rojek, C. (1989). Leisure and "the ruins of bourgeois in the world." In C. Rojek (Ed.), *Leisure for leisure, critical essays* (pp. 92–114). London, UK: Macmillan.

Roper, E.A., & Halloran, E. (2007). Attitudes toward gay men and lesbians among heterosexual male and female student-athletes. *Sex Roles, 57*(11–12), 919–928.

Rotella, R.J., & Murray, M.M. (1991). Homophobia, the world of sport, and sport psychology consulting. *The Sport Psychologist, 5*(4), 355–364.

Ryan, B. (1988). *The elusive rainbow: Gay identity acquisition in the 1980s* (Unpublished master's thesis). Dalhousie University, Halifax, NS.

Shilling, C. (1991). Social space, gender inequalities and educational differentiation. *British Journal of Sociology of Education, 12*(1), 23–44.

Simmons, R. (2006). *Out of bounds: Coming of sexual abuse, addiction, and my life of lies in the* NFL *closet*. New York: Carroll & Graf.

Spaaij, R.F.J., Jeanes, R., & Magee, J. (2014). *Sport and social exclusion in global society*. New York: Routledge.

Sparkes, A.C. (1994). Self, silence and invisibility as a beginning teacher: A life history of lesbian experience. *British Journal of Sociology of Education, 15*(1), 93–118.

Sparkes, A.C. (1997). Ethnographic fiction and representing the absent other. *Sport, Education and Society, 2*(1), 25–40.

Sparkes, A.C. (2002). *Telling tales in sport and physical activity: A qualitative journey*. Champaign, IL: Human Kinetics.

Steen-Johnsen, K., & Enjolras, B. (2016). The fear of offending: Social norms and freedom of expression. *Society, 53*(4),·352–362.

Taylor, N., & Voorhees, G. (2018). *Masculinities in play*. Cham, Switzerland: Springer.

Tewksbury, M. (2006). *Inside out: Straight talk from a gay jock*. Mississauga, ON: Wiley.

Tischler, A., & McCaughtry, N. (2011). PE is not for me: When boys' masculinities are threatened. *Research Quarterly for Exercise & Sport, 82*(1), 37–48.

Tuaolo, E., & Rosengren, J. (2006). *Alone in the trenches: My life as a gay man in the* NFL. Naperville, IL: Sourcebooks.

Vealey, R.S. (1997). Transforming the silence on lesbians in sport: Suggested directions for theory and research in sport psychology. *Women in Sport and Physical Activity Journal, 6*(2), 165–188.

Walters, S.D. (2001). *All the rage: The story of gay visibility in America*. Chicago: University of Chicago Press.

Wellard, I. (2014). Starting points and destinations: Negotiating factual and fictional pathways: A response to Gilbourne, Jones and Jordan. *Sport, Education and Society, 19*(1), 99–104.

Winskell, K., Brown, P.J., Patterson, A.E., Burkot, C., & Mbakwem, B.C. (2013). Making sense of HIV in Southeastern Nigeria: Fictional narratives, cultural meanings, and methodologies in medical anthropology. *Medical Anthropology Quarterly, 27*(2), 193–214.

Woods, S.E. (1992). Describing the experience of lesbian physical educators: A phenomenological study. In A.C. Sparks (Ed.), *Explaining alternative visions*. (pp. 90–117) London, UK: Palmer Press.

Woog, D. (1998). *Jocks: True stories of American's gay male athletes*. Los Angeles: Alyson Books.

Woog, D. (2002). *Jocks 2: Coming out to play*. Los Angeles: Alyson Books.

You Can Play Project. (2019). You can play project. http://youcanplayproject.org/

Zeigler, C. (2016). *Fair play: How LGBT athletes are claiming their rightful place in sports*. New York: Edge of Sports.

10

"I never thought I'd get here, I thought I'd be dead."

An In-Depth Interview with an Openly Gay Former Professional Ice Hockey Player

CHERYL A. MACDONALD & BROCK MCGILLIS

Introduction

Until 2019, Brock Michael Stanley McGillis was the world's only openly gay former professional male ice hockey athlete in the public sphere. A current professional in Denmark and a former professional in Finland both disclosed in 2019 that they are openly gay (Randall, 2019; Villareal, 2019). Brock also played professionally in Europe, which means that, as of 2019, there are not yet any openly gay athletes in the National Hockey League (NHL). Any other former professional hockey athletes who identify as gay may do so publicly in their private social and family circles, but there are no others on a large-scale, media-infused platform. The last time the world knew of an openly gay male professional hockey athlete was in the 1990s when Lars Peter Karlsson of Sweden was stabbed to death, reportedly because of his sexual orientation (Inge, 2015). As such, Brock's story acts as a new point of departure in the history of the participation of openly gay men in hockey culture. A reflection on his story, as other current and former professionals disclose their sexual orientation, presents an opportunity to interrogate present-day forms of hypermasculinity and heterosexism at the most competitive levels of the sport (Allain, 2008; Ingham, Dewar, Coakley, & Donnelly, 1999).

The dearth of openly gay players in the NHL is not necessarily a consequence of virulent homophobia and ignorance on the part of the league. Like the National Football League, National Basketball League, and Major League Baseball, the NHL has signed a partnership with the You Can Play Project, an organization dedicated to the inclusion of LGBTQI2S+ athletes in sport (You Can Play Project, 2013). The NHL also promotes the use of Pride Tape, a rainbow-coloured hockey stick tape created to show solidarity with the queer community. It also featured Brock in its 2019 Pride month programming (NHL, 2019). More broadly, the NHL has revived its Hockey Is for Everyone initiative—a month dedicated to celebrating racial, bodily, gender, and sexual diversity in ice hockey (NHL, 2019). What is it, then, about men's ice hockey that unofficially precludes its most elite athletes from stepping into the spotlight and potentially leading the way for others who may be struggling with their sexuality? The main purpose of this chapter is to provide an extensive and analytical account of Brock's life and his perspective on the role of sexual orientation in hockey.

An in-depth, semi-structured qualitative interview was used to document Brock's experiences and complement the theoretical discussion. The interview was conducted as part of a broader study on gender, sexuality, and ice hockey that captured the opinions and experiences of former NHL players and gay men who competed at lower levels of the game or competed at top levels while posing as heterosexual. Scholarship on masculinity and sport will be used to shore up the discussion. As noted by methodologists Babbie and Benaquisto (2002), an in-depth interview is useful because it "often allows issues and perceptions to emerge that would not emerge in more structured, briefer interviews used for surveys" (p. 335).

Brock Michael Stanley McGillis

Born in 1983, Brock McGillis is a lifetime goaltender from Sudbury, Ontario. Like many Canadians in ice hockey, he played at the levels of competition that were available to him, starting with house league and moving to AA, AAA, major and minor levels, and then junior. In Brock's junior draft year, he was predicted to be a first-round draft pick in the Ontario Hockey League (OHL; a subleague of the Canadian Hockey League [CHL]) until he broke his hand at school. Brock calls this point in his life his "downfall":

> I messed up my season. I was playing ball hockey in class and some kid called me a faggot. I beat the crap out of him and shattered my hand. He also spit on me, kicked me—so he had it coming; it wasn't totally reactionary.

Instead of joining the major junior ranks with the OHL's Windsor Spitfires, he spent that year back in U18, where he recalls feeling "kind of down" because he had begun to "figure [himself] out a bit" in terms of his sexual orientation, which did not seem to fit the mold of a competitive male ice hockey player. He sustained more injuries, this time hockey-related, which lingered into training camp the following year as well. As a result, he found himself playing junior B in Elmira, Ontario, which was not at all where he had originally envisioned his career would take him. He had a favourable season on the ice but struggled emotionally because he felt the need to conceal his true self, and he eventually tore the ligaments in his ankle, which ended his season and saw him return home to Sudbury. Brock described the experience: "I wasn't happy and obviously I was struggling with sexuality issues and everything else. I was just hating my life!"

At the beginning of the 2001–2002 season, Brock had a reasonable chance at being the Spitfires' starting goaltender. His body continued to be disagreeable, however, and he contracted mononucleosis, which caused him to miss a month of play. He rebounded well that year and was predicted to be a high pick in the NHL draft; he felt that his life was "going the way it should go." Less than a month later, his luck changed again as a teammate skated over Brock's finger in a game against the Kitchener Rangers and he was rushed to the hospital. He describes this time as a particularly low point and, coincidentally, the time that he confronted the fact that he was different.

I was two or three weeks removed from mono, so I had lost nearly thirty pounds and I was a mess. I had been suffering from different things like depression for a while. I used to sit at my billets' place and I knew at this point—I was eighteen—one minute I'd be laughing, the next minute I'd break out crying. I was sad and I wanted to die. This is when I started expecting to die and it was a pretty fucked up time. My hormones are out of whack and now I'm not eating and popping painkillers. I was drinking daily. I was a train wreck.

Without any input from his agent or parents, and "in the midst of being depressed, wanting to die, and figuring out [his] sexuality," Brock requested a trade. He wound up in Sault Ste. Marie with the Greyhounds, where he played well when he actually had the opportunity to hit the ice. To his disappointment, those opportunities were limited and he began to isolate himself from others. That same year, Brock tore his meniscus, missing an NHL camp as a result, and went home to wait for another trade.

At twenty years old, after completing his time in the CHL, Brock made his way into the United Hockey League (now the East Coast Hockey League [ECHL]) to play for the Kalamazoo Wings, where, again, he injured his back and was promptly sent home. By the Christmas break that same year, he received a call from the Trenton Golden Hawks, a junior A team in Ontario, and was enticed to join with the promise of the connection to a guaranteed NHL tryout. Having been knocked out of the playoffs in the first round with the Golden Hawks, Brock was conveniently placed for a call from Kalamazoo, who invited him to return to the team. The roller-coaster pattern continued, though: "My first game, I played really well. I'm excited; everything is going well. My second game, I get knocked out cold five minutes in—I hit my head on the post." This incident produced a severe concussion. To make matters worse, Brock's NHL tryout was lost due to the league's lockout that season.

Brock believes that his injuries were psychosomatic because they persisted as he continued to bury his feelings about himself. He notes that the language he heard around him played a key role in shaping his belief that the dressing room was not a safe space in which to be openly gay. Even at the professional ranks, he says, teammates and opponents alike feminize and homosexualize one another as a way to tease or blatantly insult one another. Quite simply, "you're either a fag or a pussy." He remembers hockey players bullying openly gay students in school and says that homosexuality in hockey was simply unheard of because the hockey community is insular and everyone is assumed to be the same—straight.

Brock chooses to linger on the thought that femininity and homosexuality continue to be used interchangeably in the boys' and men's hockey community. He credits portrayals of gay men as dainty or feminine with creating a a stereotype that puts women and gay men in the same category—less than a "real man" (Connell, 1987, 2005). He says,

Historically, in society, men were above women, so if you wanted to put a man down, you called him a woman. The only thing as bad or worse than being a woman was being a homosexual. There was a bit of racism in there too but hockey was really mostly about feminizing and homosexualizing. So, they called each other that and it all meant that you were "less than."

For this reason, he holds that it will only be once sexism and racism are also combatted that the walls of anti-gay attitudes will officially be broken down. He points out that women, gay men, and people of colour can be excellent allies for one another because hockey was built on their collective exclusion (Allain, 2012; Kalman-Lamb, 2018; MacDonald, 2018b). He notes that the Pride movement was borne out of the struggles of the Black queer community (Carter, 2004). He adds that, because heterosexual women can be strong allies for gay men (Levesque, 2019), male hockey players with a vested romantic interest in those women would do well to treat their friends with respect in order to receive the women's approval.

In 2005, the Den Haag Wolves invited twenty-two-year-old Brock to play professionally in Holland. In his words, he "put up a stellar season" that year, even winning goalie of the year. His troubled identity still continued to haunt him and he finally decided that, "enough was enough," that something in his life needed to change or else he would eventually end up attempting suicide. He came home from Holland, went on his first date with a man, realized for certain that he was gay, and began to feel more comfortable in his skin. Unfortunately, this would pose problems for his hockey career. As he recalls,

> I thought, "Okay, my career is getting better and I feel better!" But it actually got worse because I started dating somebody and they wanted to be part of my life. But I knew that if anyone in hockey finds out I'm gay, I'm fucked, so I said "no, no no." So we lived in Toronto and had aliases; his friends [were given] a fake name for me because I was afraid they would look up my name on Google and it would come out that I was a hockey player. We ended up dating for three years. I was elusive and secretive—it was a mess. But I missed hockey. So I go to play at Concordia University in Montreal and I told my partner, three years in, "Listen, I'm going

to have to start dating women to keep up appearances." He was pissed and rightfully so. That ultimately led to our breakup. But I wouldn't even admit to him that I was gay! I tried to say I was bisexual. That's how deep it went—I couldn't even admit it out loud even though I knew.

Brock reports that he often felt the need to overcompensate for his sexual orientation, starting in junior hockey by acting as stereotypically hypermasculine as possible. He compares himself to the hockey players in the Canadian television show, *Letterkenny*, which features hockey players whose characters are constructed similarly to the identity portrayed by Gongshow Hockey Inc., a Canadian hockey apparel company (MacDonald & Lafrance, 2018). He says, "Junior was the most toxic environment I've ever been in, in all my life. I embodied what I thought I had to in order to conform and not be exposed because I hated the idea of being gay." This meant frequently consuming alcohol, having many female sexual partners (he estimates over seventy), using anti-gay language, and carrying an overall sense of entitlement. Essentially, Brock was conforming to the norms that pre-existed within the environment that he was trying to "fit" into. He attributes some of this behaviour to the celebrity status ascribed to junior hockey players in Canada, which affords them privileges that non-athletes may not receive (Adams, 2006).

Girls and women would frequently offer themselves to him sexually. He skipped lineups at bars and received free alcohol underage. He even signed autographs at his own high school. When he says that he isolated himself in Sault Ste. Marie, he means that he discontinued this kind of behaviour. Accompanying that celebrity status is a pressure to conform. Perhaps unsurprisingly, Brock injured himself again—his knee this time—and sat out the remainder of the season at Concordia. Brock describes his behaviour in Montreal that year as "super depressed, partying, eating like shit, and struggling." The following year, some politics over tuition payments accompanied his ongoing injury and he opted to return home at the academic Christmas break.

The pivotal point for Brock occurred in 2009 when he arrived by car at the Canada–United States border on his way to join a hockey team in Texas.

> I turned the car around. I'm serious. The rink had been my safe haven all my life—on the ice I didn't have to think about things. But the locker room and everything else was such a toxic place. I turned the car around and drove to Toronto and I just celebrated my new life.

Perhaps most importantly, at that time, Brock had the text message of a particular friend emblazoned in his memory. Brendan Burke, the son of renowned NHL ice hockey executive Brian Burke, was an openly gay hockey player. (Brendan's death in a car accident in 2010 inspired the creation of the You Can Play Project.) When Brendan's coming out became public, Brock reached out to him and they would text frequently about life and hockey. The last text message Brendan sent Brock before his death read, "I can't wait for the day that you're out to your family like I am to mine." With those words foremost in his mind, Brock returned to Sudbury, Ontario, came out to his family, and enrolled in the sports administration program at Laurentian University.

Brock has since opened a sports training business in Sudbury and also speaks publicly about his life. Early on, a member of the hockey community found out that Brock was gay and disclosed it to others in Sudbury in an attempt to use anti-gay ideologies to threaten Brock's business. Luckily, this did not have much of an effect and Brock was able to move past the incident, embrace his identity, and continue to build his brand. Through his business, he has worked with over one hundred athletes, even sending some of them to the major junior ranks. In November 2016, he opted to go to the media with his story and it spread quickly. He has appeared in print, online, on the radio, and on television, including CTV (Jung, 2018), CBC (Mendelsohn, 2019), Global (Chidley-Hill, 2017), TSN (Clipperton, 2019), *Instinct Magazine* (Keating, 2017), Outsports (Zeigler, 2016), and ET Canada (2019).

Regarding the status of attitudes toward LGBTQI2S+ identities in ice hockey today, Brock sees progress but also sees a long road ahead. In his own life, the young athletes he trains no longer use anti-gay language— at least not in his presence. He also commends the You Can Play Project for its work toward increasing awareness of the LGBTQI2S+ community in fan culture during NHL You Can Play nights. He adds that he was honoured to be invited by the league to march in the parade at WorldPride 2019 in New York City. He comments on the experience:

> I never thought I'd get here, I thought I'd be dead. I think back to all of my pain and struggle and see how it has made me the person I am today. Now I get to walk hand in hand with the man I love, for the NHL in front of the world. This journey was so difficult, but I'm so happy it led me here.

While Brock is impressed with the NHL's efforts at promoting equality, he believes that more work is required to measure the outcomes of these efforts. Put differently, he is pleased that awareness is increasing but is uncertain of the relationship between awareness and acceptance.

The fact that the NHL hosts Pride Nights at all shows progress, but he asks where does it go from here. He feels similarly about Pride Tape and wonders about the extent to which its symbolic use translates into tangible change (King, 2006). He uses this query as an entry point to expand on his thoughts regarding how the NHL could effectively move beyond awareness and into substantial evidence of social change.

> I like the idea behind Pride Tape, but I don't understand why most teams only use it for warm-ups. Warm-ups aren't broadcasted and

fans aren't all in their seats, so I think it loses its effect. I know they talk about superstition and puck visibility, but come on, these guys will play games outdoors in snowstorms, they can play in Europe, and no one other than Kurtis Gabriel can use different stick tape for one game? *Hockey Night in Canada* can be doing more too—create a dialogue instead of just showing solidarity with rainbow tape and some short videos that promote acceptance beyond one's ability to be an athlete. Educate people. Put a flyer on each seat with information. Participate in research. Are you spreading awareness? Yeah. But are you actually creating allies and making athletes feel safe? I don't know. I don't see it yet. I've seen kids who think that if you use Pride Tape, it means you're gay! And that's not the point at all!

Brock also feels that the hockey community does not always understand that it can have a bias toward heterosexuality—and that it is not necessarily intentional. He uses the example of the homosexualization that occurs on kiss cams at hockey games. It is not uncommon for the camera operator to focus in on two members of the opposing team or two male fans of the opposing team as a way to poke fun at them. The undertone of the humour is that the two are romantically involved. The crowd laughs, and likely does not realize that this is understood as anti-gay behaviour. In sum, it appears that for every two steps toward LGBTQI2S+ inclusion in hockey, there is one step back that stems from sexist and anti-gay attitudes.

What else can be done to move from awareness to change, where sexism and anti-gay attitudes and behaviours are concerned in hockey culture? Brock says more organizations must include the LGBTQI2S+ community, not just allies who celebrate their own acceptance of the community. The media also needs to spend more time educating and less time demonizing athletes, and there must be harsher punishment for athletes who do not abide by regulations around proper conduct on and off the ice. Specifically, he points to the Anaheim Ducks' Ryan Getzlaf, who made a comment on the ice that was both sexist and anti-gay. Getzlaf was fined $10,000 as a result (Chidley-Hill, 2017), which Brock found insufficient: "Fining someone a tiny percentage of their income communicates that what he did wasn't all that bad." He adds that, had Getzlaf made the same comment in almost any other profes-sional atmosphere, there is a strong chance that his employment would have been promptly terminated.

Academic Interpretations of Masculinity, Sexual Orientation, and Ice Hockey

Brock's perceptions as an adult working in youth hockey, and his expe-riences as a former athlete competing at some of the highest levels of professional sport while concealing his sexual orientation, are in keeping with some of the scholarly work on masculinity and ice hockey. Specifically, his overall opinion that there has been progress in hockey but more work is required in terms of LGBTQI2S+ inclusion echoes the findings of MacDonald's work (2018a), which concluded that atti-tudes toward sexual orientation were divided, specifically among a study population of approximately one hundred male major U18 AAA ice hockey athletes. Through quantitative surveys and qualitative inter-views, the teenage participants in MacDonald's study expressed varying levels of comfort with the potential of having a gay coach or teammate. This suggests that it may not be completely impossible to function as an openly gay athlete, but not everyone would accept it. For example, 25 per cent of participants would have been uncomfortable having an openly gay coach, and over 50 per cent of participants admitted to frequently making anti-gay jokes; however, the general consensus among inter-viewees was that a gay teammate would eventually be accepted once everyone was comfortable with him (MacDonald, 2018a).

MacDonald's (2018a) work grows primarily out of a body of social scientific literature on masculinity and sport that is divided regarding the status of homophobia in sports. One group of scholars argues that homophobia has decreased over time in male team sporting contexts as a result of a decrease in the expectation of men to be aggressive, competitive, tough, sexually dominant, and anti-feminine (Anderson, 2015; Anderson, Magrath, & Bullingham, 2016; McCormack, 2012; White, Robinson, & Anderson, 2017). Much of this work has resulted from or been informed by American sociologist Eric Anderson's theory of inclusive masculinity (Anderson & McCormack, 2018; Anderson, 2009). Anderson (2009, 2011) postulates that homophobia has decreased in Western society for the following reasons: LGBTQI2S+ activism has increased, the uninformed moral panic over HIV and AIDS has decreased, and homosexuality is increasingly visible in popular culture. As a result, men feel more comfortable expressing themselves and accepting one another.

The opposing group of scholars argues that anti-gay attitudes are either remaining intact or decreasing at a slower pace than the other side of the debate contends. These claims tend to be based on the lived experiences of LGBTQI2S+ athletes or the belief that opposing arguments are biased toward a desire for positive change (Baiocco, Pistella, Salvati, Ioverno, & Lucidi, 2018; Cavalier, 2019; Kimmel, 2013; Messner, 2012; Murray & White, 2017). These arguments are often informed by Australian sociologist R.W. Connell's (1987, 2005) concept of *hegemonic masculinity*, which is often described as hypermasculinity. Connell theorized that the most valued men in Western society are white and hypermasculine: physically and mentally strong, willing to take risks, status-seeking, anti-feminine, and heterosexual. Connell (1990) adds that athletes, in particular, are expected to demonstrate these traits. Given the status ascribed to athletes, and particularly hockey players in Canada, those who embody hegemonic masculinity are part of a process of the normalization of this gender ideology that promulgates the domination of men over women and marginalized men, such as those who identify as gay.

There is less academic debate over the intensity of hypermasculinity and anti-gay attitudes and behaviours where North American ice hockey is concerned; it tends to lean toward the model of hegemonic masculinity when describing athletes. Specifically, literature on gender and sexuality within boys' and men's ice hockey operates from the understanding that male ice hockey athletes are encouraged by their families, peers, opponents, and superiors to demonstrate mental and physical toughness, to embrace competitiveness, to reject emotion aside from that associated with winning and losing, to reject femininity while dominating sexually over girls and women, and to reject homosexuality (Allain, 2008, 2010; Bélanger, 1999; Crawford & Gosling, 2004; Gee, 2009; Ingham et al., 1999; Lucyk, 2011; Robidoux, 2001).

While societal attitudes toward the LGBTQI2S+ community have shifted, and scholarship such as that of MacDonald (2018a) and Denison (see Zeigler, 2019) demonstrates social change in male youth hockey, more research is required on where and how this progressive change is occurring. MacDonald (2018a) found that the U18 A A A athletes all agreed that they were more open and accustomed to having the LGBTQI2S+ community in their lives than their parents were, especially their fathers. This could suggest that older athletes, such as those at the professional ranks, may be part of a generation that is less open-minded where gender and sexuality are concerned, and this could contribute to attitudes toward the idea of openly gay athletes in hockey—whether identifying as one or competing alongside of one. Similarly, from a public health perspective, Denison completed a predominantly quantitative study of all professional male athletes in the Australian Hockey League, where it was discovered that prevalent use of anti-gay language among teammates was more of a function of conformity than virulent homophobia or hatred (Zeigler, 2019). Both MacDonald's (2018a) and Denison's findings are congruent with Brock's argument that, regardless of the intentions behind the language, it must change in order to make the sport safer and more enjoyable for all participants (Zeigler, 2019).

Goals of Future Research

While Brock's case is of utmost socio-historical importance, there is far more information in the hockey community to be collected on the subject. Neither the existing academic literature nor Brock's narrative can produce finite answers regarding the stigma of homosexuality in men's elite-level ice hockey at the moment. Moving forward, there must be more large-scale mixed method studies that get to the root of anti-gay attitudes and homophobia and the nature of their relationship to sexism, heterosexism, and racism at top levels of men's ice hockey. More precisely, it is necessary to move beyond raising awareness and to begin investigating the effectiveness of work being done to shift the culture. Quantitative data collection methods such as structured surveys are beneficial for reaching large populations (Gratton & Jones, 2010). However, qualitative methods such as semi-structured interviews will offer a more robust understanding of the following: why and how anti-gay attitudes and behaviours persist, the reasoning behind the continued use of anti-gay language in men's competitive hockey, and athletes' opinions and personal experiences where masculinity and sexuality are concerned. The main way to facilitate this would be to normalize open conversations about identity and emotions among male ice hockey players, since research shows that the community is insular and tends to operate on a code of silence and gatekeeping (Allain, 2014; MacDonald, 2016). Having access to this kind of data would not only contribute to advancing academic discussions of masculinity and sport, but it could inform policy and programming for inclusion in ice hockey in such a way that prioritizes athletes' well-being and willingness to participate.

References

Adams, M.L. (2006). The game of whose lives? Gender, race, and entitlement in Canada's "national" game. In D. Whitson & R. Gruneau (Eds.), *Artificial ice: Hockey, culture and commerce* (pp. 71–84). Peterborough, ON: Broadview Press.

Allain, K.A. (2008). "Real fast and tough": The construction of Canadian hockey masculinity. *Sociology of Sport Journal, 25*(4), 462–481.

Allain, K.A. (2010). Kid Crosby or golden boy: Sidney Crosby, Canadian national identity, and the policing of hockey masculinity. *International Review for the Sociology of Sport, 46*(1), 3–22.

Allain, K.A. (2012). *The way we play: An examination of men's elite-level hockey, masculinity and Canadian national identity* (Unpublished doctoral dissertation). Trent University, Peterborough, ON.

Allain, K.A. (2014). What happens in the room stays in the room: Conducting research with young men in the Canadian Hockey League. *Qualitative Research in Sport, Exercise and Health, 6*(2), 205–219.

Anderson, E. (2009). *Inclusive masculinity: The changing nature of masculinities.* New York: Routledge.

Anderson, E. (2011). Updating the outcome: Gay athletes, straight teams, and coming out in educationally based sport teams. *Gender & Society, 25*(250), 250–268.

Anderson, E. (2015). Assessing the sociology of sport: On changing masculinities and homophobia. *International Review for the Sociology of Sport, 50*(4–5), 363–367.

Anderson, E., Magrath, R., & Bullingham, R. (2016). *Out in sport: The experiences of openly gay and lesbian athletes in competitve sport.* New York: Routledge.

Anderson, E., & McCormack, M. (2018). Inclusive masculinity theory: Overview, reflection and refinement. *Journal of Gender Studies, 27*(5), 547–561.

Babbie, E., & Benaquisto, L. (2002). *Fundamentals of social research* (2nd ed.). Scarborough, ON: Thomson-Nelson Canada.

Baiocco, R., Pistella, J., Salvati, M., Ioverno, S., & Lucidi, F. (2018). Sports as a risk environment: Homophobia and bullying in a sample of gay and heterosexual men. *Journal of Gay & Lesbian Mental Health, 22*(4), 385–411.

Bélanger, A. (1999). The last game? Hockey and the experience of masculinity in Quebec. In P. White & K. Young (Eds.), *Sport and gender in Canada* (1st ed.) (pp. 298–303). Toronto: Oxford University Press.

Carter, D. (2004). *Stonewall: The riots that sparked the gay revolution.* New York: St. Martin's Press.

Cavalier, E. (2019). Conceptualizing gay men in sport. In V. Krane (Ed.), *Sex, gender, and sexuality in sport: Queer inquiries* (pp. 87–104). New York: Routledge.

Chidley-Hill, J. (2017). Gay hockey player disappointed in Ryan Getzlaf's apology over inappropriate slur. *Global News.* http://globalnews.ca/news/3467773/gay-hockey-player-disappointed-in-ryan-getzlafs-apology-over-inappropriate-slur/

Clipperton, J. (2019). Where does hockey inclusivity conversation go from here? *TSN.* https://www.tsn.ca/nhl-notebook-where-does-hockey-inclusivity-conversation-go-from-here-1.1272682

Connell, R.W. (1987). *Gender and power: Society, the person, and sexual politics.* Palo Alto, CA: Stanford University Press.

Connell, R.W. (1990). An iron man: The body and some contradictions of hegemonic masculinity. In M. Messner & D. Sabo (Eds.), *Sport, men, and the gender order: Critical feminist perspectives* (pp. 83–95). Champaign, IL: Human Kinetics.

Connell, R.W. (2005). *Masculinities* (2nd ed.). Los Angeles: University of California Press.

Crawford, G., & Gosling, V. (2004). The myth of the "puck bunny" female fans and men's ice hockey. *Sociology, 38*(3), 477–493.

ET Canada. (2019). Brock McGillis talks use of homophobic slurs in NHL. *YouTube.* https://www.youtube.com/watch?v=GuA3WP8vTcc

Gee, S. (2009). Mediating sport, myth, and masculinity: The National Hockey League's "inside the warrior" advertising campaign. *The Journal of the British Sociological Association, 26,* 578–598.

Gratton, C., & Jones, I. (2010). *Research methods for sports studies* (2nd ed.). New York: Routledge.

Inge, S. (2015). Swedish ice hockey club launches LGBT appeal. *The Local.* https://www.thelocal.se/20150728/swedish-ice-hockey-club-launches-lgbt-appeal

Ingham, A., Dewar, A., Coakley, J., & Donnelly, P. (1999). Through the eyes of youth: "Deep play" in peewee ice hockey. In J. Coakley & P. Donnelly (Eds.), *Inside sports* (pp. 17–27). New York: Routledge.

Jung, A. (2018). "You can play sports and be gay": Former hockey player speaks out. *CTV News.* https://edmonton.ctvnews.ca/you-can-play-sports-and-be-gay-former-hockey-player-speaks-out-1.4003735

Kalman-Lamb, N. (2018). Whiteness and hockey in Canada: Lessons from semi-structured interviews with retired professional players. In J. Anderson & J. Ellison (Eds.), *Hockey: Challenging Canada's game* (pp. 287–300). Ottawa: Canadian Museum of History and University of Ottawa Press.

Keating, M. (2017). Hockey heartthrob, Brock McGillis. *Instinct Magazine.* https://instinctmagazine.com/instinct-exclusive-hockey-heartthrob-brock-mcgillis/

Kimmel, M. (2013). *Angry white men: American masculinity at the end of an era*. New York: Nation Books.

King, S. (2006). *Pink ribbons, inc: Breast cancer and the politics of philanthropy*. Minneapolis: University of Minnesota Press.

Levesque, A. (2019). "I've always wanted a gay family member!": Straight ally girls and gender inequality in a high school gay-straight alliance. *Qualitative Sociology, 42*(2), 205–225.

Lucyk, K. (2011). Don't be gay, dude: How the institution of sport reinforces homophobia. *Constellations, 2*(2), 66–80.

MacDonald, C. (2016). *"Yo! You can't say that!": Understandings of gender and sexuality and attitudes towards homosexuality among male major midget AAA ice hockey players in Canada* (Unpublished doctoral dissertation). Concordia University, Montreal, QC.

MacDonald, C.A. (2018a). Insert name of openly gay hockey player here: Attitudes towards homosexuality among Canadian male major midget AAA ice hockey players. *Sociology of Sport Journal, 35*(4), 347–357.

MacDonald, C.A. (2018b). Tweeting sexism and homophobia: Gender and sexuality in the digital lives of male major midget AAA hockey players in Canada. In J. Ellison & J. Anderson (Eds.), *Hockey: Challenging Canada's game* (pp. 231–242). Ottawa: Canadian Museum of History and University of Ottawa Press.

MacDonald, C., & Lafrance, M.E. (2018). "Girls love me, guys wanna be me": Representations of men, masculinity, and junior ice hockey in *Gongshow* magazine. *The International Journal of Sport and Society, 10*(1), 1–19.

McCormack, M. (2012). *The declining significance of homophobia: How teenage boys are redefining masculinity and heterosexuality*. New York: Oxford University Press.

Mendelsohn, P. (2019). "Kids are hurting. Adults are hurting": Brock McGillis fights homophobia in hockey. *CBC Sports*. https://www.cbc.ca/sports/hockey/brock-mcgillis-fights-homophobia-1.4982708

Messner, M. (2012). Reflections on communication and sport: On men and masculinities. *Communication & Sport, 1*, 113–124.

Murray, A., & White, A. (2017). Twelve not so angry men: Inclusive masculinities in Australian contact sports. *International Review for the Sociology of Sport, 52*(5), 536–550.

NHL. (2019). Hockey is for everyone. https://www.nhl.com/community/hockey-is-for-everyone

Randall, D. (2019). Danish ice hockey goalie Jon Lee-Olsen came out. *Instinct Magazine*. https://instinctmagazine.com/danish-ice-hockey-goalie-jon-lee-olsen-came-out/

Robidoux, M.A. (2001). *Men at play: A working understanding of professional hockey*. Montreal: McGill-Queen's University Press.

Villareal, D. (2019). Former pro hockey player Janne Puhakka is the first in Finland to come out as gay. *Outsports*. https://www.outsports.com/2019/10/29/20937333/hockey-finland-janne-puhakka-gay-pro-sports-player-coming-out

White, A., Robinson, S., & Anderson, E. (2017). Inclusive masculinity: Sport's role in the liberation of the male gender. In D. Kilvington & J. Price (Eds.), *Sport and discrimination* (pp. 796–808). New York: Routledge.

You Can Play Project. (2013). Our Mission. http://youcanplayproject.org/pages/mission-statement

Zeigler, C. (2016). Former semi-pro hockey player Brock McGillis comes out as gay. *Outsports*. https://www.outsports.com/2016/11/3/13510626/brock-mcgillis-gay-hockey-player

Zeigler, C. (2019). Study shows homophobic language doesn't mean rejection of gay athletes. *Outsports*. https://www.outsports.com/2019/6/20/18692467/gay-hockey-slurs-study-australia-monash-university

11

"What do you mean you don't play hockey... you a queer or somethin'?"

Reflections on Life as a Non-Hockey Playing Canadian Boy

WILLIAM BRIDEL

1977

I am five years old and have my first pair of figure skates. They have these things on the blades that are completely foreign to me: toe picks. My first time wearing them, I slam face first into the ice. It would seem that toe picks are not only foreign but also entirely dangerous. I am not deterred, however, and I slowly start to get better, more adept. I am assigned by a figure skating coach to the advanced learn-to-skate sessions that take place two times per week, typically ending at 5:45 PM. Boys, in their CCM or Bauer hockey skates (which are without toe picks), who are waiting to practise or play a game after the ice resurfacing, make fun of me. They make fun of me because these skates, which belonged to my sister before me, are white. The problem, it seems, is that white skates are for girls. *Everyone knows that.*

I have no choice but to wear my sister's hand-me-down skates, primarily because there is nowhere to buy "boys" figure skates in the town where I live. It is, however, remarkably easy to buy hockey skates, which are not designated as "boys" because girls do not play hockey. *Everyone knows that.* In an effort to help, my mother dyes a pair of white skate covers black. They turn out dishwater grey. This is less than ideal, to be sure, but I wear them because I will not stop skating. The music playing in the rink makes me move my body in ways I do not get to do elsewhere. The ice allows me to seemingly float over it, which just feels right, especially now that I can make better use of those troublesome toe picks. I learn more advanced jumps and spins. My growing love of the sport allows me to be (mostly and somewhat blissfully) unaware that I am doing something I am not supposed to be doing. This is not just about wearing white skates. The hockey-playing boys also make fun of me because I am figure skating. In Canada, boys play hockey. *Everyone knows that.*

On the Power and Potential of Stories

For as long as I can remember, I have loved stories. I loved having them read to me and then reading them myself. I loved writing them, producing "novels" as a child that my grandmother was always kind enough to read and praise. And, eventually, as a competitive figure skater, I loved telling stories through music and performance. In an introduction to sociological research methods during my undergraduate degree, I was thrilled to learn that people's stories could be an important and valued way to learn about social life, to acquire knowledge, and to challenge dominant ways of thinking. In graduate school, I was curious to learn—but admittedly not initially wholly convinced—that my story could be a part of the research spectrum in the form of autoethnography (Ellis, 2004; Ellis & Bochner, 2000; Markula & Silk, 2011). This evocative form of research posited that my experiences had some saliency and that sharing my stories, with critical reflections on them, could contribute to academic knowledge and, quite possibly, social change.

It was timely that, as I was writing the vignettes that form the basis for this chapter, a friend and colleague brought a meme on social media to my attention. It was an excerpt from an interview with author Arundhati Roy: "People spend so much time mocking [Donald] Trump or waiting for him to be impeached. And the danger with that kind of obsession with a single person is that you don't see the system that produced him" (Flanders, 2018, para. 3). It served as a poignant reminder of what I am meant to do as a sport sociologist, as someone who has been trained to use their sociological imagination to connect (auto)biography with history and social structure (Mills, 1959).

Thus, in this chapter I share a series of stories from my life that I have come to make sense of through engagement with academic literature on (broadly) sport, gender, and sexuality, with a critical lens turned inward. While I have shared elsewhere some of my experiences in relation to figure skating vis-à-vis gender and sexual diversity (Bridel, 2018), my more specific objective in this chapter is to speak from the margins in order to augment critical conversations about "hockey culture" and masculinity in Canada through my (paradoxically) non-hockey story. More specifically, I share often painful stories from my life in order to expose understandings of masculinity in Canada and the role that hockey has played in creating and maintaining limited and problematic ideas of what it means to be a boy, to be a man, in the Canadian context. That the personal stories I share in this chapter largely took place in an Ontario town in the 1970s and '80s could make it easy to conceptualize my experiences as an unfortunate reality of "days gone by." It would be easy to suggest my stories are remnants of a (sporting) history that are no longer relevant in a contemporary and so-called progressive Canada, and so I also incorporate the stories of others. It is through storytelling and critical reflection that we can move toward the sort of social change that we need, the sort of social change that will benefit the lives of all Canadians, regardless of gender identity and/or sexuality.

1983

I am eleven years old. I have endured six years of being called "queer, sissy, faggot" on a more-or-less daily basis. I am frequently shoved around, punched, and on occasion kicked. This mostly happens during recess at school, but the boys who bully me are hockey players so it is pretty much guaranteed that if they miss me at school, they will find me at the rink. One day they do catch me at school out of view of the teachers on yard duty. They grab me by the wrists and ankles, spread my legs, and ram me crotch-first over and over into a tetherball pole calling me "faggot figure skater" as they do. I do not really understand why this is happening. Just because I figure skate, I should be treated this way?

I do my best to ignore it. I do not tell anyone it is happening. I am ashamed. I am scared. I try to become as invisible as possible at school, especially during recess. But I am evolving into a decently good figure skater and I love everything about the sport. I do everything to not be invisible on the ice. I want to be a star like Toller Cranston. I want to be Brian Pockar. I emulate Robin Cousins. I do not know that I can ever be as good as Brian Orser, but I really want to try. I live and breathe figure skating. When I am not actually on the ice, I am thinking about it. When I am not actually on the ice, I still practise jumps, spins, and some "sassy" creative movements in my socks on the carpet. The ice, the music, the movement, the sparkles, and (admittedly) the trophies and medals are my passions and my rewards. I cannot fathom stopping.

I continue to be centered out, picked on, bullied for being different. It is mostly older boys at my school who play hockey but also older hockey players at the rink who do not go to my school. They shout over the boards while I train. They whisper in my ears as I leave the ice and head to the locker room: "queer, sissy, faggot." The whispering is worse than the shouting. But it has become so normal to me that I just assume that this will be part of my life for, well, the rest of my life. I do not know any different and so I expect nothing different.

At a skating seminar for talented youth where I am one of a handful of boys from different parts of Ontario, someone tells us that to counter being made fun of, we should challenge hockey players to a skating race: they would go forwards, we would go backwards. We are told we are the better skaters and that we will win these races; that this approach will shut them—the hockey players—up. What we are not told is that this behaviour should be unacceptable, that we are not "less than" because of our choice of sport.

On Hockey, Maleness, and Canadian Identity

In the Canadian context, it has been normalized over time that *ice* hockey is somehow the appropriate sport for boys, a way to learn and to prove one's masculinity. This is not new. Robidoux (2018) has argued, for example, that hockey has functioned as a male preserve, "making it a popular site for males to define their worth as men, drawing on notions of masculinity that date back to seventeenth-century Canada" (p. 75). This discursively constructed relationship between hockey, maleness, masculinity, and Canadian identity is maintained or upheld by individuals, institutions, and social processes, even in contemporary times. Critical sport scholars have produced an important body of work elucidating how a particular form of masculinity, often referred to as *hypermasculinity*, perpetuated by and expected in hockey, remains troubling, in particular given its connections to notions of "Canadianness" (Adams, 2006; Allain, 2008, 2010, 2014; Bridel & Clark, 2012; MacDonald, 2014, 2018a, 2018b; Robidoux, 2001, 2012, 2018).

When you are a Canadian boy and do not participate in hockey, it is seen to be odd. When you do not participate in hockey and, in fact, figure skate—constructed as a "girl's sport" in North American culture—you are thought to be "queer," ergo the cause for much speculation about one's sexuality and one's masculinity (Adams, 2007, 2011). This oft-unquestioned norm certainly impacted my experiences growing up as one of the few male figure skaters in the small Ontario town where I lived; frequently, I was the *only* male figure skater as other boys and young men switched to ice hockey or left sport altogether. My choice was made that much harder in the beginning because I had to wear white skates, which within the sport and the larger cultural context have come to be constructed as the appropriate colour of skates for girls and women; "male" skates are black (Adams, 2011; Rand, 2012). Despite all this, I persevered and learned all about the sport of figure skating by being the best student of it that I could be. I learned about gender and sexuality, however, because I failed to adhere to socially acceptable performances of maleness and masculinity within the Canadian context. Importantly, limited and problematic ideas about masculinity not only impact those of us who did not/do not play hockey but also boys and men who did/do.

1984

I am twelve and my only hockey-playing friend invites me to a sleepover at his house. I have never been invited to such an event before and I'm entirely excited. Actually, it is more than that: I have a secret, impossible crush on this friend and spending the night at his house seems other-worldly. I arrive only to find that there are, in fact, ten boys sleeping over. I am the only one who does not play hockey. I am the only one who figure skates. I want to leave right away, to escape. But I am frozen. I endure what seems like hours of having pop thrown on me. Two or three boys hold me down while the others take turns shoving their fingers, popcorn kernels, and other objects into my anus. "You like this don't you." Said more as an assertion than a question. I fake being asleep the whole time. I somehow hold back tears, but they are there, lingering dangerously just behind my eyelids. I know ultimately that is what they want. And I know that it will only make it worse, that it will allow them to think (or say), "The queer can't take it; look at the sissy crying." I pour all my hurt and anger into figure skating. I feel like it is all I have. I vow to never tell anyone what has happened.

On Hockey, Maleness, and Violence

In their powerful and highly disturbing autobiographies, former NHL players Theo Fleury and Sheldon Kennedy (without wanting to over-simplify their messages) expose how the hypermasculine culture of hockey forced them to remain silent about terrible atrocities done to them by Graham James; they also expose the system that failed them over and over (Fleury & McLellan Day, 2009; Kennedy & Grainger, 2011). In 2018, two-time Stanley Cup champion Daniel Carcillo published a Twitter thread in which he highlighted the brutal locker-room hazing he witnessed and experienced during his time on a major junior hockey team. And then statements of denial from current and former NHL players were published on social media and in the main-stream press, statements that asserted that Carcillo's experiences did not reflect the current state of the game (CBC, 2018; Strashin, 2018).

At the 2018 Hockey Conference held in Edmonton, Alberta, I was fortunate to hear a talk by one of hockey's "agents of change," Brock McGillis. I knew in advance of the conference that McGillis was the only living professional hockey player to come out publicly as gay, some-thing he did after leaving the sport. And no wonder he waited. I listened to him speak openly about the toxic culture of the sport that he expe-rienced as a closeted gay man, a culture that led to substance abuse and thoughts of suicide. I was moved to tears during his presentation because it is this same toxic culture that contributed to my own experi-ences at the hands of hockey players back in that small Ontario town.

It is tempting (read: easier) to think about "bad behaviour" in a singular, reductive way. It is tempting (read: easier) to think that it was just badly behaved individuals who bullied me and others, individ-uals who assaulted me and others, individuals who themselves were not products of a system. The stories from those within hockey suggest otherwise; the stories from those within hockey necessitate thinking about a system that encourages and rewards such rigid and toxic notions about what it is to be a boy, to be a man. In her research focused on experiences of non-Canadian players in the Canadian Hockey League (CHL), for example, Allain (2008) notes that the "hegemonically desirable Canadian hockey masculinity [is] predicated on a hard-hitting, physically aggressive game" (p. 478). In more recent empirical work, MacDonald (2018b) has extended the conceptualization of Canadian hockey masculinity to include male players' use of misogyny, sexism, and (perhaps to a lesser extent) homophobia vis-à-vis "fag discourse" (see Pascoe, 2005) in interpersonal relationships and on social media as a way to fit in, to succeed—at the expense or peril of others.

That said, there is evidence of greater acceptance of gender and sexual diversity in the Canadian context, for some. Examples include the introduction of same-sex marriage in 2005, recognition of gender identity and gender expression as protected identities in federal law in 2017, and greater numbers of gay-straight alliances in schools. Within sport, we have witnessed the creation of so-called ally organizations such as the You Can Play Project, which are meant to provide athletes—including hockey players—with education on the problems of using misogynistic and homophobic language (MacDonald, 2018b), and to encourage empathy, respect, and compassion for others. The potentiality of a shift within the culture of sport—and hockey in particular—is an important one, taking the focus from individual behaviour to structural and systemic issues that fail to be addressed when accepted as "the norm."

1988

I am fifteen and things are going extremely well. I have qualified to compete at my first national figure skating championships. In conjunction with the 1988 Olympic Winter Games torch relay, I am named "Male Athlete of the Year" for the town of Aurora, beating out a male skier who is actually competing in the Calgary Olympics. I also beat out all of the local hockey players! I have to wonder how many times my mother voted to make that happen. Regardless, the local junior hockey team approaches the skating club where I train: they want me to perform an exhibition between the first and second periods of a hockey game. I vomit when I am told. I cannot imagine anything I would rather do less. Then I am told they will pay me a performance fee and the idea does not seem so bad anymore: figure skating is expensive, and my family has made sacrifices so I can continue to pursue my dreams.

I perform at the game on a Saturday night—my competitive program set to music from the ballet *El amor brujo*. When the music begins, my apprehension fades and I become the character my coach has choreographed for me. I perform all technical elements to the best of my ability. When I am finished, however, I am reminded of where I am, who I have just performed in front of. I exit the ice as quickly as possible, scarcely taking time to bow.

The following Monday, one of the players from the local team approaches me at school. I know he was there at the game, that he saw me skate. I prepare myself for the usual. But this time the hand extended is not a fist. He is asking to shake my hand. He tells me that I am an amazing skater and that he is sorry he has not stood up for me before. I resist pointing out that he was more than an onlooker. He appoints himself my protector and, although I hate the idea of violence, I really do not mind when he says he will "pound the shit out of anyone who picks on you." I realize that maybe I will not be alone in this now. What I fail to recognize, however, is how brave he is really being, how hard it must be to break from the others, how, unlike my aforementioned sleepover "friend," this young man decided that my humanity was more valuable than the cultural capital earned by abusing someone different, someone fey.

As far as I know, his protection was never required, but I do know that I finished my last two years of high school feeling, if not fully included, far safer than I ever had. I also finished my last two years of high school thinking that my non-hockey story was complete, that the sport that I had never played would no longer be the powerful absent presence it had been from the time I was five years old. I perhaps believed that my passion for figure skating had been more powerful than every social force that told me I was wrong for being a non-hockey playing Canadian boy. This was all rather naive.

On Canadian Sport "Beyond" Hockey and Figure Skating

The connection between hockey, masculinity, and Canadianness is a powerful one. During my doctoral studies, a friend and I were asked to contribute a sport-focused chapter to a book on Canadian masculinities (Bridel & Clark, 2012). We agreed, with one condition: that we could write about something other than men's ice hockey. Over coffee (and a pint or two), we both felt we could learn something interesting and expand conversations about Canadian sporting masculinity by turning to athletes other than hockey players. The timing could not have been more perfect. The 2010 Olympic Winter Games had just taken place with all the media that traditionally comes along with the Games, but even more so since it was hosted in Canada. What might mediated representations of Canadian male Olympians tell us about masculinity and Canadian identity ten years into the new millennium?

While striving to think critically about how "lesser-known" sports contribute meaning to Canada and to masculinities, we discovered that ice hockey nevertheless featured in these athletes' stories (Bridel & Clark, 2012). The roots of hockey were even deeper than we had imagined. As just one example, multiple media stories about free-style skier Alexandre Bilodeau—who became an instant Canadian sport celebrity by winning the first-ever Olympic gold medal on home soil—emphasized that his father had been a successful hockey player and that Bilodeau himself had sacrificed a "successful" career in hockey to dedicate himself to freestyle skiing. Moreover, it was made clear that Bilodeau's "huge sacrifice" was mostly encouraged by Bilodeau's mother so he could spend more time with his brother, who is disabled (Coyne, 2010; MacQueen, 2010). It is important to note that in our research not once did we find reference to Bilodeau himself constructing his departure from hockey as a "sacrifice"; this became part of his story through the words of others.

It seemed to us that Canadian journalists did not know how to talk about male athletes without relying on well-worn narratives of hockey and Canadianness. And, yet, this idea remains poignant. Allain and Marshall (2018) have argued, for example, that even curling, a sport in which masculinity was once connected to "maturity and sportsmanship," has shifted to representations of muscularity, strength, power, and performance. Put another way, acceptable masculinity in Canadian curling is becoming predicated on hockey masculinity, which as Robidoux (2018) has asserted is based on attributes "valued in patriarchal relations: stoicism, courage, perseverance, and proficiency" (p. 75). The more things change...

2014 to 2019

On December 4, 2014, I am ecstatic to learn that (now World and Olympic) champion pair skater Eric Radford has come out publicly as gay in an article on Outsports.com. He is the first Canadian male figure skater still actively competing at the most elite level of the sport to come out publicly. I cry in my campus office. I think about how powerful this could be for young Canadian boys who figure skate and who may be questioning their own sexuality. When reading the story, I note that Radford commented that "he was teased mercilessly by other boys for his lisp and mannerisms that screamed 'gay'" and that "the other kids used it against him, pounding him verbally with gay epithets" (Zeigler, 2014, para. 23). I cannot help but note the consistency in our stories, although they took place ten years apart—mine in the 1970s and '80s, his in the 1980s and '90s.

In the years following Radford's announcement, I am conducting research with Canadian athletes, including figure skaters, who identify as LGBTQI2S+ (lesbian, gay, bisexual, trans, queer, intersex, two-spirit). Regardless of sport, many athletes speak about being bullied in relation to their sexuality and their perceived failure to perform gender "appropriately." Some of the figure skaters comment specifically about their experiences in school. One, only recently retired from competitive sport, notes that the verbal abuse directed toward him was almost constant: "fag, queer, that's so gay." He said that he ignored it the best that he could. I cannot help but be transported back to my own experiences growing up; I feel sick to my stomach. He has experienced the same things I did, that Radford did, but post-new millennium. Our stories span more than thirty years. Thirty years.

On Pink Shirt Day in 2017, I decide it is time to share more publicly my experiences of being bullied growing up. I choose this day because I believe fundamentally in the mission of the Canadian initiative, which two Nova Scotia teenagers began ten years earlier. These two young men wanted to show support for a schoolmate who was being bullied for wearing a pink shirt (https://www.pinkshirtday.ca/about/). The morning of February 22, I upload a five-minute Pink Shirt Day video to Facebook, telling my story while also incorporating my now "academic knowledge" that positions bullying as a learned behaviour, identifying cultural ideologies such as sexism, racism, ableism, and homophobia as the root causes (Short, 2013). I expect maybe my mother and a few friends will watch the video I have created at my desk. I think that maybe those friends will share it with a handful of their friends. Emphasis on *maybe*.

Throughout the day and the days following I am amazed, however, as my hastily produced, one-take video message hits 52,000 views and is shared over five hundred times. I watch the "like" tally escalate on the post. I receive notes and messages from people via email, Facebook, and Messenger; this includes people active in my life, people I have not heard from in years, and people I do not know. Many of these people—boys and men mostly—tell me that my story was their story. Some of the men I hear from, skaters from "back in the day," tell me that they wished we had known each other was gay when we were competing against each other, suggesting how much easier things might have been had we been able to talk about our experiences—and our sexuality—openly. Male figure skaters who identify as heterosexual confess that they have been too ashamed to tell people that they had also been called "queer, sissy, faggot," that they were also threatened and sometimes beaten up when they were younger. Skaters-turned-coaches tell me that they still lose male athletes with whom they have been working, sometimes for years—boys and young men who leave the sport because of the abuse they receive, regardless of how good they are or how much they love figure skating. Many of us talk, for the first time, about the fact that no one really talked about any of this.

On Hockey, Maleness, and Canadian Identity: Revisited

I know that it was hockey players who bullied and assaulted me. I do not know that it was hockey players who took part in the abuse that Radford and the other young male skater experienced. I also do not know that it was hockey players who were central to the experiences of all the other men I heard from in response to my Pink Shirt Day video. What I do know, however, is that all our experiences took place in cultural and temporal contexts that have promoted (and promote) very limited ideas about what it means to be a boy, to be a man. The same cultural context that allowed the abuse of hockey players such as Fleury and Kennedy and that ignored hazing as described by Carcillo. As many scholars before me have argued, sport scholars, sport professionals, sport media, sport enthusiasts, and the broader sporting community must continue to think critically about the ways that hockey produces and maintains such limited ideas about what it means to be a boy, to be a man, in contemporary times. There can be no question that it is imperative to have these critical conversations for the sake of boys and men in hockey. But we must remember to also consider as equally important the need for critical, intersectional conversations for the sake of Canadians who just do not want to be part of "Canada's game," but who experience its scope and its influence, nevertheless.

"What do you mean you don't play hockey…you a queer or somethin'?" I hear those words as clearly in my head now as I did the first time they were spat at me when I was five years old. I am now forty-seven. No, I did not play hockey. I have never played hockey. I have never watched a complete hockey game at any level. In her essay on ice hockey, race, and gender, Adams (2006) stated, "If hockey ceased to exist tomorrow, my life would not really change" (p. 71). I could have written those words myself. I had absolutely no connection to Sidney Crosby's gold medal goal at the 2010 Olympics in Vancouver. I was, in fact, teaching a yoga class at the time, one filled with other Canadians who also did not seem to care about the outcome of that game, as it happened. Perhaps there is some irony in the fact that the class took place in Kingston, Ontario—one of the Canadian cities that lays claim to inventing the sport (Holman, 2018).

I really had no connection to the stories of national pride that followed Crosby's goal and the Canadian team's win, except to be reminded that of all the gold medals won at the 2010 Olympic Winter Games—and there were many, fourteen gold in total, the most of any nation—this one counted more, meant the most. And it meant the most because it was men's ice hockey. As Adams (2006) has argued, that story never really changes. That Canadian national identity is so intricately tied to hockey, hockey to masculinity, and that hockey is intertwined in the stories we tell about ourselves and others could be shrugged off as harmless nostalgia, a point of pride for an otherwise humble, overly apologetic nation. This non-hockey playing Canadian boy sees and has experienced it far differently.

References

Adams, M.L. (2006). The game of whose lives? Gender, race, and entitlement in Canada's "national" game. In D. Whitson & R. Gruneau (Eds.), *Artificial ice: Hockey, culture, and commerce* (pp. 71–84). Peterborough, ON: Broadview Press.

Adams, M.L. (2007). The manly history of a "girls' sport": Gender, class and the development of nineteenth-century figure skating. *The International Journal of the History of Sport, 24*(7), 872–893.

Adams, M.L. (2011). *Artistic impressions: Figure skating, masculinity and the limits of sport.* Toronto: University of Toronto Press.

Allain, K.A. (2008). "Real fast and tough": The construction of Canadian hockey masculinity. *Sociology of Sport Journal, 25*(4), 462–481.

Allain, K.A. (2010). Kid Crosby or golden boy: Sidney Crosby, Canadian national identity, and the policing of hockey masculinity. *International Review for the Sociology of Sport, 46*(1), 3–22.

Allain, K.A. (2014). "What happens in the room": Conducting research with young men in the Canadian Hockey League. *Qualitative Research in Sport, Exercise, and Health, 6*(2), 205–219.

Allain, K.A., & Marshall, B. (2018). "Buff boys" with brooms: Shifting representations of masculinity in Canadian men's curling. *NORMA, 13*(2), 119–135.

Bridel, W. (2018). It was a good day if I wasn't called a queer, a faggot, or a sissy: Reflections of a male figure skater turned scholar. In C.T. McGivern & P.C. Miller (Eds.), *Queer voices from the locker room* (pp. 27–33). Charlotte, NC: Information Age Publishing.

Bridel, W., & Clark, M. (2012). If Canada is a "team," do we all get playing time? Considering sport, sporting masculinity, and Canadian national identity. In J.A. Laker (Ed.), *Canadian perspectives on men and masculinities: An interdisciplinary reader* (pp. 185–200). Toronto: Oxford University Press.

CBC. (2018, November 29). "I don't care if it's hockey tradition": Sens players speak out about hazing. *CBC Sports.* https://www.cbc.ca/news/canada/ottawa/daniel-carcillo-hazing-matt-duchene-mark-borowiecki-1.4925879

Coyne, A. (2010, March 15). Canada reborn. *Maclean's Magazine.* https://www.macleans.ca/general/canada-reborn/

Ellis, C. (2004). The call of autoethnographic stories. In C. Ellis (Ed.), *The ethnographic I: A methodological novel about autoethnography* (pp. 24–57). Walnut Creek, CA: Altamira Press.

Ellis, C., & Bochner, A. (2000). Autoethnography, personal narrative, reflexivity: Researcher as subject. In N. Denzin & Y. Lincoln (Eds.), *Handbook of qualitative research* (pp. 733–768). Thousand Oaks, CA: Sage.

Flanders, L. (2018, December 31). Arundhati Roy on fiction in the face of rising fascism. *Truthout.* https://truthout.org/video/arundhati-roy-on-fiction-in-the-face-of-rising-fascism/

Fleury, T., & McLellan Day, K. (2009). *Playing with fire.* Toronto: HarperCollins.

Holman, A.C. (2018). A flag of tendons: Hockey and Canadian history. In J. Ellison & J. Anderson (Eds.), *Hockey: Challenging Canada's game* (pp. 25–44). Ottawa: Canadian Museum of History and University of Ottawa Press.

Kennedy, S., & Grainger, J. (2011). *Why I didn't say anything.* London, ON: Insomniac Press.

MacDonald, C.A. (2014). Masculinity and sport revisited: A review of literature on hegemonic masculinity and men's ice hockey in Canada. *Canadian Graduate Journal of Sociology and Criminology, 3*(1), 95–112.

MacDonald, C.A. (2018a). Insert name of openly gay hockey player here: Attitudes towards homosexuality among Canadian male major midget AAA ice hockey players. *Sociology of Sport Journal, 35*(4), 347–357.

MacDonald, C.A. (2018b). Tweeting sexism and homophobia: Gender and sexuality in the digital lives of male major midget AAA hockey players in Canada. In J. Ellison & J. Anderson (Eds.), *Hockey: Challenging Canada's game* (pp. 231–242). Ottawa: Canadian Museum of History and University of Ottawa Press.

MacQueen, K. (2010, March 1). An inspiration. *Maclean's Magazine,* 32–34.

Markula, P., & Silk, M. (2011). *Qualitative research for physical culture.* London, UK: Palgrave Macmillan.

Mills, C.W. (1959). *The sociological imagination.* Oxford, UK: Oxford University Press.

Pascoe, C.J. (2005). "Dude, you're a fag": Adolescent masculinity and the fag discourse. *Sexualities, 8*(3), 329–346.

Rand, E. (2012). *Red nails, black skates: Gender, cash, and pleasure on and off the ice.* Durham, NC: Duke University Press.

Robidoux, M. (2001). *Men at play: A working understanding of professional hockey.* Montreal: McGill-Queen's University Press.

Robidoux, M. (2012). Male hegemony or male mythology? Uncovering distinctions through some of Canada's leading men: The Coureurs de Bois and professional hockey players. In J.A. Laker (Ed.), *Canadian perspectives on men and masculinities: An interdisciplinary reader* (pp. 114–125). Toronto: Oxford University Press.

Robidoux, M. (2018). Imagining a Canadian identity through sport: An historical interpretation of lacrosse and hockey. In J. Ellison & J. Anderson (Eds.), *Hockey: Challenging Canada's game* (pp. 61–76). Ottawa: Canadian Museum of History and University of Ottawa Press.

Short, D. (2013). *"Don't be so gay!": Queers, bullying, and making schools safe.* Vancouver: UBC Press.

Strashin, J. (2018, November 29). "It's toxic": Former NHLer Carcillo says he won't be silent about hockey's hazing culture. CBC *Sports.* https://www.cbc.ca/sports/hockey/nhl/carcillo-hazing-hockey-culture-ohl-abuse-1.4922623

Zeigler, C. (2014, December 4). Eric Radford: Olympic figure skater, medal-winning family man. And gay. *Outsports.* http://www.outsports.com/2014/12/4/7321931/eric-radford-gay-figure-skater

12

The Tragedy of the Enforcer in Lynn Coady's The Antagonist *and Jeff Lemire's* Roughneck

FRED MASON

IN 2011, the role of the "enforcer" in hockey and the impact that playing such a role can have on players' lives came to attention far outside of the culture of hockey fans.[1] In March, scientists discovered that Bob Probert, a former enforcer who had died of a heart attack, had suffered from chronic traumatic encephalopathy (CTE), a progressive brain disease caused by repetitive trauma to the brain (National Hockey League [NHL], 2011). During the off-season, three active or just retired enforcers passed away. In May, Derek Boogaard died of a drug overdose. Boogaard's family donated his brain to science, and it was discovered that, despite being only twenty-eight years old, he also suffered from CTE (Branch, 2011). In August, Rick Rypien and Wade Belak both died by suicide after long battles with depression (The Canadian Press, 2011; Harrison, 2011). Later that year, the film *The Last Gladiators* premiered at the Toronto International Film Festival (Gibney, 2011). This film featured several retired enforcers speaking on their careers, with a particular focus on Chris Nilan, who played in the NHL from 1979 to 1992, and who has battled drug and alcohol dependency since he retired (Gibney, 2011).

In December 2011, retired enforcer Georges Laraque published a memoir that received a fair amount of critical press, because, unlike most athlete memoirs, Laraque's book (*Georges Laraque: The Story of the* CBC's *Unlikeliest Tough Guy* in English, and *La force d'y croire* in French) had a number of critical things to say about his sport and his life experiences. While the book might have been less successful at showing Laraque "as he really is," or in resolving contradictions in using violence to prevent further violence (Martin, 2017), Laraque did open up about the mutual respect among fighters, the importance of establishing a reputation, and his regular fear and anxiety at performing his job.

Enforcers are a disappearing breed in the NHL. With new salary caps, roster spots are at a premium and even fourth line players are expected to contribute to team scoring (Campbell, 2014; Del Mundo, 2016). Most enforcers are expected to be skilled at fighting and intimidation rather than other facets of the game, so the jobs are drying up. At the same time, enforcers have become culturally relevant in public discourse around concussions, injuries, and player retirement. In the last decade or so, efforts to understand enforcers and their place in hockey have produced much cultural work. Since the success of Laraque's (2011) book, several memoirs and autobiographies of former enforcers have come out, some more celebratory (Domi, 2015), some more explanatory (James & Gallagher, 2015; Scott, 2016), and some with a focus on life outside hockey (McCarty, 2013; Nilan, 2013). Critical biographies of deceased enforcers question the culture that produces this role, and the impact it has on players' lives (Branch, 2014; Dryden, 2017).

Serious journalistic inquiries have sought to understand the place of fighting in hockey and explain the "code" of masculinity that dictates behaviours in the sport (Bernstein, 2006; Proteau, 2011). Even comedic films have ventured into the territory of enforcers, with the 2011 film *Goon* (Dowse, 2011) featuring a Laraque cameo, and achieving enough popularity to produce a sequel (Baruchel, 2017). While these films can be criticized for a "depiction of hockey as hyper violent, homophobic and the enforcer as an extreme simpleton with little regard for his own health" (Boyle, 2014, p. 328), they did explore the idea of the enforcer's code of behaviour, and their presence speaks to the cultural importance of the enforcer in this time frame.

This chapter is focused on two fictional narratives that feature former enforcers as the main character. These works constitute important literary contributions to the cultural discussion occurring around hockey enforcers since they offer musings on the development of someone into the enforcer role, the internal psychology of enforcers, and the impact on their later lives, in novel-length studies. While there are many popular reviews on each, little academic attention has yet been paid to either. Lynn Coady's 2011 novel, *The Antagonist*, features former university hockey and real-world enforcer Gordon Rankin, Jr., more commonly known as "Rank," whose sheer size drew him into an enforcer role in many facets of his life. Jeff Lemire's 2017 graphic novel, *Roughneck*, centres on fictional former NHL enforcer Derek Ouelette, living out the shambles of his life in his small Northern Ontario home town in an alcoholic and violent haze.

Before getting into these novels, it is worth mentioning other fictional works that focus on hockey enforcers. Enforcers are often among the most popular players, as fans see them as "working-class heroes" and "real men" who are willing to sacrifice themselves for the team (Gruneau & Whitson, 1993). Despite this, enforcers rarely take the role of main character in fiction, even though hockey fiction regularly focuses on and critiques violence and fighting (Blake, 2010). In their exhaustive approaches to hockey literature, Blake (2010) and Buma (2012) only mention a handful of short stories and two novels that really focus on enforcers. The novels are Roy MacGregor's *The Last Season* (1983) and Mark Anthony Jarman's *Salvage King, Ya! A Herky-Jerky Picaresque* (1997).

The Last Season is important for truly inaugurating the genre of the hockey novel (Blake, 2010). It focuses on the aptly named Felix

Batterinski, a fictional enforcer who ended up playing for the 1970s goon-era Philadelphia Flyers. The novel follows his rise through the ranks, and how "Batterinski's coaches and supporters shape his identity by encouraging him to fight and play violently" (Buma, 2012, p. 193). In the late years of his career, he ends up as a player-coach in Finland but cannot conceptualize a way of playing hockey that does not involve fighting, aggression, and violence. The novel was meant to be a criticism of hockey violence but might be so linked to the 1970s and its excesses that its critique seems quaintly historical (Buma, 2012).

Novels that took a thoughtful stance on hockey were more common by the time Mark Anthony Jarman released his 1997 work, *Salvage King, Ya!* (Buma, 2012). In this, the narrator Drinkwater is a journeyman hockey player near the end of his career who has become an enforcer out of necessity to keep his career going. Drinkwater is a thoughtful anti-hero, musing on the place of masculinity and violence in hockey frequently, but, unfortunately for him, he is not a very good fighter. He sometimes wakes up in the locker room after fights but knows he cannot deny a fight, or he will lose his job and be traded. Drinkwater knows the "Tough Guy" code and uses it the best he can for his own purposes; his insight "makes his complicity in the culture of violence all the more acute" (Blake, 2010, p. 111).

A more recent novel, *The Good Body* (2000) by Bill Gaston, also focuses on a character who is winding up a minor league career that saw him turn into a fighter in the later stages. Bob Bonaduce's role as a fighter played a part in the dissolution of his marriage, as it turned off his wife, Leah (Dopp, 2018). However, the novel is concerned with Bonaduce's relationships, his negotiation of his aging body, and dealing with the onset of multiple sclerosis—the fact that he was a fighter seems mostly irrelevant to all of that. This likely links to Blake's (2010) notion that violence in hockey literature is in part linked to a player having less talent and skill; portraying the retiring Bonaduce as a tough guy puts him in that situation.

The novels discussed above all portray and critique violence in hockey by having enforcers and tough guys as their narrators. However, they all focus on players still involved in their playing careers, even if it is in the twilight near retirement. The two novels analyzed here, *The Antagonist* and *Roughneck*, involve long-retired enforcers exploring the impact that the role had on them and where they ended up later in life. These two main characters share a similar backstory as to how they ended up becoming enforcers, with an abusive father and a mother who died young. The novels also mostly cast them in the role of tragic hero, being swept along by circumstance but having created their own issues through bad choices. With this, treating them together makes sense, even though Lemire's work is different with its graphic medium.

Lynn Coady and *The Antagonist*

Lynn Coady is a well-known Canadian literary figure whose novels, typically set in the Maritimes, frequently deal with issues of social class, small-town ennui, and regional stereotypes. As she put it in an interview, she tries to "stay true to my experience of Cape Breton without being stereotypical and reductive" (Berry, 2002, pp. 82–83). Coady's work has been shortlisted for the Governor General's Award (*Strange Heaven*, 1998), and several of her books were named *Globe and Mail* Best Books for their respective years—(*Play the Monster Blind*, 2000; *Saints of Big Harbour*, 2002; and *Mean Boy*, 2006). *The Antagonist* (2011) was shortlisted for the Scotiabank Giller Prize.

Coady previously used hockey as part of the background context for a novel, in *Saints of Big Harbour*. The violence and hypermasculinity in hockey is an analogy for the same things in broader small-town life for the protagonists of the novel, Acadian teenager and narrator Guy Boucher, and his gigantic, alcoholic, violent uncle, Isadore Aucoin. Aggression and violence are things to which one is socialized, both on and off the ice. When Isadore finds out that Guy is playing hockey, he appoints himself Guy's mentor and unofficial coach. When Guy is slow to respond to an attack on a teammate, Isadore gives him a lesson in the unwritten codes of retribution, hollering, "Fuck the penalty! This is hockey!" (Coady, 2002, p. 59). Isadore sets up a punching bag in the shed and tries to train Guy to fight. As Blake (2010) notes, Guy comes to understand violence and abuse in hockey as reasonable and acceptable. Guy rejects hockey and its violence, quitting in the playoffs, which is his first step toward rejecting the overpowering masculinity of his unpredictably violent uncle (Buma, 2012). Ironically, suggesting that lessons on "justifiable" violence transfer out from hockey, this rejection of his uncle culminates in Guy whacking Isadore with a snow shovel.

The Antagonist is written as an epistolary novel, where protagonist Rank is writing emails to former college buddy Adam, and, occasionally, an ex-girlfriend, Kristen. Adam has written a novel where Rank's story is told, portraying him as a violent and completely unsympathetic character, one whose life problems come out of his "innate criminality." Rank retells his own story in a set of outraged, beer-fuelled emails, filling in parts of his life that were not in Adam's novel, and setting the record straight from his perspective.

Rank grew up as a large young man who was thrust into adult roles by nature of being so big. He says, "I was a thug from the moment I popped from the womb, or so rumour has it. Ten pounds, bruiser hand and feet" (Coady, 2011, p. 9). By the time he was fourteen, he was 6'4" and a hairy, hulking giant, with a voice that had "plummeted into Darth Vader, Luke-I-am-your-father territory" (p. 60). While he wanted to stay a kid, people treated him differently, since he already had the body of a grown man. This intimidated people. As well,

> the problem with being my size is that I can't get away with displays of aggression in mixed company. I can't shout around women no matter how angry or frustrated I get because it scares the living shit out of them. They start cowering, and then I feel like a monster. (p. 30)

The preceding quote relates to Rank's limited perspective on women, as well. Rank grew up with a saint of a mother, Sylvie, which he admits has given him a Freudian Madonna complex for almost all women, meaning he sees them all as saintly Madonnas regardless of reality. In direct counterpoint, his father Gord was abusive and domineering. As Rank puts it, "Gord is not a hitter of ladies, he is at heart a courtly little bugger...But he sneers...He berates. He insults" (p. 48).

Gord's abuse was verbal, and through manipulation he set his son up in violent situations. Gord used Rank as a bouncer of local "punks" at his Icy Dream Restaurant, young men who came in drunk at the end of the night looking for "sport"—essentially, to annoy Gord to the point of him attempting to climb over the counter while Rank held him back. The parking lot fights after Rank ejected the punks became spectator sport for men from the Legion next door, who would come out to watch, and the local police even referred to it as "dog-fighting." Unfortunately, Rank pummelled one victim, the local drug dealer, giving him brain damage in a fight. He never got over this, living with guilt and grief— "even as I was doing it, I was regretting it" (p. 115)—and describing how he was haunted by the sound of head hitting pavement. Rank was sent to juvenile corrections for this, and readers only learn late in the novel that his mother died in a car crash while driving him to the detention centre. So the Rank of the main part of the story was a young man who earned an athletic scholarship as a gigantic hockey player presumed to be an enforcer, who is drunken, foolish, and violent as a result of his grief.

Hockey was a means for Rank to get away from his dad, and the only thing in his life that he felt was his own. Rank describes hockey as "the only thing that shut out all the noise, all those desperate voices" (p. 118), as his church and escape. While his high school coach and social worker tried to help Rank keep hockey as a safe place, Rank had the enforcer role thrust upon him because of his size and reputation, especially when he got to university. There, his coach wanted the team to toughen up, and attempted to needle and shame them, with a particular focus on Rank, into playing aggressively and fighting the other team to intimidate them. He delivers an ultimatum: "Anyone who's afraid to get their knuckles bloody this evening can leave right now. And I have never been more serious in my life, gentlemen. There's the door" (p. 171). Rank, who has crushed people both on the ice and in parking lots, and worries about his potential for destruction, performs the incredibly moral act of walking away from hockey, leaving the coach speechless, and sacrificing his athletic scholarship.

In his epistolary dialogue, several times Rank suggests that the gods mess with him, that his destiny is to impact people's lives in negative ways. Unfortunately, he may be the tragic figure that he suspects. After dropping out of university, Rank worked as a bouncer at the local dive bar, Goldfinger's. One night, while there with friends, he got into a fight over how one of those friends treats women. The other bouncer, Ivor, who had been sober but was clearly back on drugs, went after this friend and died while Rank was holding him down. Rank goes through a life of further guilt and grief from this, and only later finds redemption through telling his own story through his email harangues and thereby re-experiencing it, while giving the nuance and reasons behind his actions.

Readers familiar with the culture and rules of university hockey have probably already put their finger on a fundamental error with the novel's premise—there really is no fighting in university hockey in Canada, or in the National Collegiate Athletic Association for that matter, and these rules have been in place as far back as the 1960s (Gruneau & Whitson, 1993). With strict penalties and extra game suspensions, fighting has a particularly negative impact on teams, so someone like Rank would not exist in college hockey, let alone be on a scholarship. Some would find this annoying and that it detracts from the novel, but, realistically, Rank does not have to be a hockey enforcer for the novel to work. He is so similar to Chuck Slaughter, a football player from Coady's earlier novel *Mean Boy* (2006)—gargantuan, with an air of violence and unpredictability around him, who drinks far too much, partly in reaction to the recent death of his mother—that you could call Rank "Slaughter 2.0." Meanwhile, by bringing Rank into the world of hockey, Coady places him in a space where the violence and destruction in his wake is naturalized, expected, and understood, and she places him in a context more innately comprehended by many readers. In addition, Coady does well to get the relationship styles of young men correct, namely through showing the banter between them, the need for connection, and the occasional heartlessness that comes out of the performance of traditional versions of masculinity.

Jeff Lemire, Hockey, and *Roughneck*

Jeff Lemire is one of Canada's best-known cartoonists and writers in the medium of comics and graphic novels. Writing for industry giants, Lemire's work includes such mainstays as *Justice League* and *Green Arrow* for DC, and *Hawkeye* for Marvel (CBC Books, 2017). He is widely known for his independent work and his more alternative creations under DC's Vertigo imprint. His independent release, *The Underwater Welder* (2012), focused on the coming to terms with adulthood and parenthood of the title character, suffused with supernatural elements related to his deceased father. Lemire collaborated with Gord Downie on *Secret Path*, a multimedia product that told the story of Chanie "Charlie" Wenjack, a young Indigenous boy who froze to death attempting to escape from a residential school in Northern Ontario in 1966 (Downie & Lemire, 2016). Lemire's most famous independent work, *Essex County*, won several awards, including an Alex Award from the American Library Association. *Essex County Collected* (2009) was a 2011 CBC Canada Reads selection, with the theme for that year of the program being "essential novels of the decade," demonstrating its place as "serious literature" (Reid, 2016). Lemire won an Eisner Award in 2017 after several nominations, considered one of the comics industry's highest honours.

Hockey appears in Lemire's independent work in several significant ways. Hockey seems to "haunt" many of the people and events in *Essex County*. Split into three volumes, *Essex County* tells a set of interlinked stories centring on residents of a small Ontario farming community. In the first volume, "Tales from the Farm," the main characters include a young boy named Lester, and his friend Jimmy Lebeuf, who was a hockey player who played one game for the Maple Leafs, scoring a goal and taking a hit that makes him "different now...kinda slow" (Lemire, 2009, pp. 35–36). The second volume, "Ghost Tales," features Jimmy's uncles Lou and Vinnie Lebeuf, who were semi-pro hockey players in their early days. In his old age, physical cues and dreams set Lou off on reminiscences of the past (Mullins, 2014), on how hockey linked him and his brother, and was something he could turn back to after love interests and family issues drove them apart. In their analysis, Jacob and Paziuk (2016) note that Lemire deploys hockey throughout *Essex County* as a means of showing people coming together, playing shinny on a creek, with locker room banter, or in shared spectatorship. It is also deployed to show when people are alone and lonely, such as Lester and his uncle watching the same hockey broadcast but in separate rooms, or Lou and Vinnie watching *Hockey Night in Canada*, Vinnie with his family on the farm, and Lou alone and drinking in Toronto.

Hockey also appears in a unique way in Lemire's post-apocalyptic work, *Sweet Tooth* (2016, first appearing in a comics serial over forty issues), in that a couple of the main characters are former hockey tough guys. The premise is that a plague is wiping out humanity. At the same time, children are being born immune but as animal-human hybrids. One of the main characters, "the Big Man" Tommy Jeppard, is portrayed in flashback as a former professional player who transitioned from star player to tough guy late in his career. As the plague begins to spread, Jeppard is handed a suspension for a hockey fight that went too far. He muses that his past was good preparation for the end times, saying, "I've always been good at fighting. It's the rest of it I ain't worth a damn at. But fighting…fighting I can do" (pp. 124–125). Jeppard travels with and protects the primary character, a boy named Gus, and later, a whole group of hybrid children. Because of the violent and ominously dangerous way that Jeppard is portrayed, and some of the extremely violent actions he undertakes, readers cannot really tell that he is a hero, rather than a villain, until well into the second volume of *Sweet Tooth*. The question of hero or villain might also be asked about many real-life hockey enforcers.

Another minor character in the third and final volume is also a former hockey tough guy. When he figures out who Jeppard is, Jimmy "Fat Man" Jacobs is joyous to remind him that their teams played a championship series against each other, and that he and Jeppard fought in game 6. Near the end of the narrative, Jeppard and Jacobs contemplate a last stand to protect the kids from a militia group that has been hunting them to experiment on them. When Jeppard asks if Jacobs has a last fight in him, Jacobs responds, "One more fight? Hell, we didn't grow these playoff beards for nothing, Jeppard" (Lemire, 2016). Both Jacobs and Jeppard end up sacrificing themselves to save the children, much like enforcers do to protect teammates.

In *Roughneck* (Lemire, 2017), fictional former NHL enforcer Derek Ouelette lives in his small Northern Ontario town of Pimitamon (the Cree word for "crossroads"). He drinks constantly and brawls with random men in the local bar, and wherever else he takes offense. In the opening scene of the novel, a snowmobiling tourist asks if he is the "Derek Ouelette who used to play for the Rangers?" (p. 5) then gets insulted when Derek wants to be left alone. The snowmobiler aggressively and unwisely insinuates that Ouelette is stuck up, and has taken too many punches, at which point Derek breaks his nose with a head-butt and beats him down with his fists. This scene suggests the beating is a common occurrence, reinforced immediately afterward with the local Ontario Provincial Police officer and childhood teammate Ray, saying, "I'm pretty much the last guy in the Pit you ain't beat up yet" (p. 15). The state of Derek's life is indicated by his living arrangements—he sleeps in a janitorial room in the local rink managed by an Indigenous man named Al who tries to look after him. The night of the opening scene, Derek forgets his keys and passes out on the ice, which a subsequent conversation with Al indicates is not that unusual. Al becomes a key figure in the narrative, and readers learn that he grew up with Derek's mother, and went to school with her at the Fort Albany Residential School.

Visually, the art is rough and basic like much of Lemire's independent work, which is intentionally drawn more simply than his superhero comics. Meanwhile, there is deeper detail in *Roughneck* than in previous books like *Essex County*. With some exceptions, scenes play out mostly in black and white, with shades of blue and grey providing context of nighttime and winter. Throughout the book, Lemire features long shots of characters walking—in town, along the highway, in the woods while hunting—with their feet crunching snow underfoot. Colour is reserved to stress a point, with flashback scenes rendered in soft colours, and blood splashing red among the blacks and greys in fight scenes.

The first third of the novel sets up the context of Derek's life, his drinking, his repetitive and banal job as a fry cook, and his few functioning relationships. Derek is haunted by a skinny, stray dog in many scenes throughout the book, which seems to represent aspects of his past and, occasionally, the underlying rage in his personality. Approximately one-third of the way through the book, Derek's sister Bethy shows up, drug-addicted, pregnant, and on the run from her abusive boyfriend Wade. It is notable that Wade's plaid shirt is always rendered in red in otherwise black-and-white scenes, establishing a link between the danger Wade represents and blood.

While Derek is working his job (at the same restaurant that their mother worked when they were kids), Bethy gets a fix from the local drug dealers and overdoses. Derek goes out and beats them up. Police officer Ray works out a deal that, rather than prosecution, which would be bad with Derek's lengthy record, Derek and Bethy will lay low at Al's camp. Flashback scenes from conversation and memory fill in details of the siblings' lives while there. We learn that Derek's father was abusive, and it was he who pushed Derek to be a tough guy in hockey. Another scene portrays how Derek's mother died in a car crash on the night she attempted to take her children and leave her husband. Young Derek, Bethy, and the dog are left sitting beside the overturned car. A flashback also relates the episode that got Derek kicked out of hockey, a vicious stick attack that went well beyond the acceptable violence of the game, leaving his opponent on a stretcher.

At the camp, Derek begins a path of redemption through starting to sober up (if against his will), and through connecting to his Indigenous roots on his mother's side by trapping and hunting with Al. As Derek and Bethy seem to turn a corner, individually and in their relationship, a call comes in that Bethy's boyfriend Wade is in town. Derek goes off, joined by the stray dog, to confront him. Rather than giving rein to the violence as he has throughout the story, he allows Wade to beat him up, which gets Wade arrested and brings the main tension to a resolution. Derek hits his head on the pavement in the process of accepting his beating, and it is possible that he dies from it. Bethy and Al arrive in time for her to take Derek in her arms. She asks him, "What did you do?" and he responds, "I let it go, Bethy" (pp. 239–240), perhaps meaning the lifetime of rage and suffering.

Lemire leaves it intentionally questionable at the end of the story whether Derek died in the process. During the fight scene, readers see visual parallels to the death of a moose shot by Al and Derek earlier. As the moose died with Al and Derek by its side, it had a life flashback portrayed in their collective breaths in the cold air. Derek experiences a similar vision of his family during his childhood while hitting his head on the ground, so the parallel is suggestive. The last scene featuring Derek in the book shows him and the dog walking quietly in the woods, not crunching snow underfoot as was the case in every other instance. Whether this is because he has achieved some peace and connection in the world, or is a ghost, is left to the reader.

Throughout *Roughneck*, Lemire alludes to issues related to Ouelette's Indigenous heritage (likely a Cree heritage with Derek's mother coming from the Fort Albany First Nation). Lemire travelled in the north during research for *Secret Path*, but questions of cultural appropriation need to be considered here, given the debates that have raged within Canadian literary circles in the last few years. The author himself is aware of the potential for appropriation. In an interview with the *Globe and Mail* (Medley, 2017) he said,

> I've never claimed to be anything other than what I am, and I've never claimed to be a spokesperson for Indigenous rights, or anything like that. I'm just a white guy. If anything, these projects were a way for me to learn more about something I'm very igno-rant about. That's what art is. For any artist, you're trying to learn something. For me, this was a big part of Canada and a big part of our history that I didn't know enough about, and I still don't know enough about. By going up there and doing these books I know more than I did, and maybe if I can share what I learned with people who otherwise wouldn't read about this stuff, then it's worth doing.

Rather than being heavy-handed, Lemire subtly raises concerns and leaves the reader to ponder them.

Lemire raises the possibility of racial stereotypes about Indigenous players in a scene involving two teenaged hockey players outside the rink (whom Derek later beats up). One asks Derek why he got kicked out of hockey and the other says, "Dude. Don't you know? He chopped some guy right across the face! Like a fucking tomahawk, right?" (Lemire, 2017, p. 60). Perhaps this is just off-hand dialogue, but this could be taken as pointing to the racial stereotypes many Indigenous players face, as it is clear that Derek's action had been framed that way by at least this young player. Looking at the life stories of First Nations players in the NHL collected by Don Marks (2008) and Will Cardinal (2008), racial slurs and stereotypes dogged them almost universally. Marks makes the point that, based on his interviews, every player has been called "Chief" in their career, as a mark of respect among many teammates, and as a jibe by many opponents and opposing fans. Indigenous players who played as tough guys or enforcers are vastly overrepresented among those who have made the NHL, suggesting that systemic position stacking is occurring, or at least that stereotypes of the "savage" or the "warrior" are so prevalent that they affect style of play (Marks, 2008).

Issues of intergenerational trauma and resilience within Indigenous communities could also be read from the pages of *Roughneck*.[2] Social scientists and Indigenous leaders seeking to explain the dispropor-tionate social problems among Indigenous communities have turned to the concept of *intergenerational trauma*, whereby numerous and sustained attacks on a group through public policy can have a cumulative affect over generations, and can interact with more proximal stressors to undermine collective and individual well-being (Bombay, Matheson, & Anisman, 2009, 2014). As a prime factor, the experiences of residential school for generations of Indigenous people, with removal of children from their communities and physical and sexual abuse, can have nega-tive consequences for subsequent generations because of such things as diminished transmission of family values and parenting knowledge, and substance abuse (Menzies, 2010).[3]

In *Roughneck*, readers know that the Ouelettes' mother attended resi-dential school with Al. Suggesting a removal from her culture, Derek at one point tells Al, "She never really talked about Indian stuff," which makes Al harrumph (Lemire, 2017, p. 115). She married and put up with an abusive husband for a long time, and both of her children ended up with substance abuse problems. Lemire does not point directly to any of these things as intergenerational trauma, but it seems plausible.

Al represents the figure where Indigenous resilience comes through. *Resilience*, in a broad sense, is looking at the strengths of individuals and communities, despite challenges (Fleming & Ledogar, 2008). Indigenous resilience is a positive concept, with a collective aspect combining such things as spirituality, family strength, Elders, ceremonial rituals, oral tradition, identity, and support networks (HeavyRunner & Marshall, 2003). Al is the figure of strength and support for the Ouelettes and he helps Derek begin to connect to his heritage while out trapping and hunting. The novel ends with Al taking a very pregnant Bethy on a trip to visit family in the Fort Albany First Nation, something he suggested earlier in the book, showing the persistence of family and communal ties.

Personal Issues and Hockey Issues

In *Roughneck*, Lemire implies that injustices such as systemic racism and intergenerational trauma influence Derek, but much of the story centres on Derek's family relationships. In this, he possesses a similar background to Coady's Rank. The similarities in the characters suggest that either Lemire was familiar with Coady's work, or that there is some sort of clichéd fictional enforcer who gets lost in their own trauma. Much of the backstory is the same—there is the abusive father who drove the son into being an enforcer, the mother who died in a car crash, and the former enforcer riddled with guilt who drinks as a coping mechanism. The root of both characters becoming enforcers lies in relationships with abusive fathers. In *The Antagonist*, Rank serves as a conduit for his father Gord's rage, maybe outrage, at the world. He feels obligated to serve as bouncer at the Icy Dream Restaurant to prevent Gord from getting into trouble, and he develops a reputation that follows him going forward. Hockey is an escape from his father, and Rank feels guilty about that, but he cannot escape the enforcer role. His father explicitly pushes Rank into being a tough guy, an enforcer. In *Roughneck*, Derek's rage about his father's abuse and the loss of his mother gets channelled into his job with catastrophic consequences for him and others, with Derek ultimately being kicked out of hockey for a retaliatory stick attack. Both Coady and Lemire seem to see the violence of the enforcer as reactive to a troubled personal past, which is a narrow vision of enforcers and what drives someone to become one. It also mostly ignores systemic issues within hockey related to such things as violent masculinities and the perception of the need for players to police themselves.

Coady gives a nod to systemic issues within hockey by having the coach bully his players and demand violence, and Lemire suggests the potentiality of racism within the sport, but most of what drives the characters is internalized trauma and raw emotion. The novels, in part, tap into and feed the "catharsis theory" of violence in hockey, where fighting comes out of emotions that boil over in a fast-paced, already violent game (Gruneau & Whitson, 1993). While supporters of fighting in hockey often advocate for this theory, it is clear that much more is happening to explain its presence in the game. As MacDonald (2014) writes in her review of the literature on fighting in hockey, the fist fight is a legitimate act in hockey (if penalized): "the fist-fight has symbolic significance as a way to settle battles of dominance, restore order, release aggression, and show respect for opponents (i.e., a just way to settle disputes)" (p. 104). As opposed to an act of rage or the blowing off of aggression, fighting in hockey has many strategic and ritualistic purposes. Intimidation of opponents and attempting to swing the momentum of the game comprise one set of tasks for enforcers (Weinstein, Smith, & Wiesenthal, 1995). There are notions that the enforcer serves as a "policeman," keeping stickwork and other nastiness at bay with the threat of retribution, and that the fight is the manly, "proper" way to settle a dispute (Coburn, 1985; Kennedy, 2014). Fights are far more calculated than impulsive most times (Goldschmeid & Espindola, 2013), which contradicts the catharsis theory. There is even

some indication that fighters served economic purposes for professional teams (Burdekin & Grindon Mortin, 2015; Lavoie, 2000), with
employing enforcers as a draw for fans.

Memoirs from enforcers speak to the rational and workmanlike ways
in which they approach their jobs. Rage sometimes enters into fights in
the moment, but most enforcers assert that it is a role they play and just
a job they have to do. Many former enforcers note they did not intend
to become one, but it was something expected of them by coaches and
organizations and they embraced it as a way they could have a professional career (see, for example, Laraque, 2011; Scott, 2016). In sum,
systemic and ideological influences within hockey go a long way to
explaining the presence of enforcers. All of this clearly contradicts the
catharsis theory, or notions that enforcers are an aberrance. Yet these
novels, in constructing the enforcer as a person responding to individual
and personal traumas, rather than systemic issues, tend to exonerate
hockey for many of its more problematic elements.

Despite such criticism, it is perhaps unfair to make demands of novels
for what they are not; the focus should instead be on what they offer to
the cultural conversation around enforcers. Both *The Antagonist* and
Roughneck give strong psychological studies of the enforcer, and the
impact that the role can have on players' lives. Both Rank and Derek feel
guilt and pain from the roles they have had to play. Rank wallows in
grief and self-guilt, both in the younger version of himself that he tells
about, and the older version doing the telling, often under the influence
of several beers. Derek is broken, coping through constant drinking and
random acts of violence. While the retired athlete who struggles in later
life is a trope of sport literature (Oriard, 1982), Derek is at an extreme
that is rarely seen. This, sadly, matches up with the experience of some
real-world enforcers. Georges Laraque (2011), for example, talked about
the psychological pain and the constant stress of having to psych himself
up for a job where he knows the biggest guy on the other team was going
to try to punch him out, on a daily basis. Moreover, there have been

several examples of former enforcers with substance abuse issues whose abuse dated back to their careers but who worsened post-retirement—for example, see the memoirs of Dave Semenko (1989), Bob Probert (2010), Chris Nilan (2013), and Darren McCarty (2013). While it is difficult to say whether enforcers are more susceptible to substance abuse problems than other former players, there is a high prevalence among the few enforcers who have written memoirs, and, unfortunately, among those who have died young.

Both Rank and Derek are tragic figures because, while they have character flaws that lead to their own undoing, they are thrust into roles they are unsure of or explicitly do not want, with negative outcomes for themselves and others. However, both characters ultimately receive a form of redemption. In telling his own story, Rank humanizes himself and explains all the things that were going on that drove him to be who he was. In the end, it seems he is finally finding a way to forgive himself for the damage in his wake, but he still seems to have a long way to go in liking himself, past or present. Derek receives his redemption in connecting to some of his Indigenous roots in hunting and trapping with Al, and ultimately in sacrificing himself for Bethy, and learning to not fight back. His redemption allows him to become a tragic hero, pushed by circumstance, but acting nobly in the face of it. Perhaps there is life after hockey, even for those badly damaged by it.

These novels fit into a context where people are trying to understand the hockey enforcer more deeply, as the consequences of being an enforcer—the stress, injuries, trauma, and CTE, in many cases—are coming into the public eye. There is nostalgia for enforcers past as they disappear from hockey, but also an amount of collective guilt, since enforcers and hockey fights have always been popular. This overall context has brought the enforcer to the fore as a cultural issue to be understood. Now that the silence over the impact that the enforcer role can have on players has been broken, in media and memoir, a space has been opened where creative representations of enforcers seem more possible, and where such narratives might contribute useful perspectives. More stories by and about enforcers are likely forthcoming, in fiction, film, and nonfiction, as part of the broader "working through" that is occurring.

Notes

1. The author acknowledges the Social Sciences and Humanities Research Council (SSHRC) for funding a larger project on LGBTQI2S+ inclusion in sport, which contributed to the creation of this chapter.

2. The author wants to acknowledge Vicky Paraschak for pushing him to think about these issues, both from her presentation at the Hockey Conference 2018, and in subsequent conversation.

3. An important work on hockey and the residential school experience is Richard Wagamese's 2012 novel *Indian Horse*. The main character, Saul Indian Horse, plays hockey and suffers all sorts of abuse (including sexual) at a residential school. The novel follows how this trauma affects Saul throughout his life, while also focusing on societal racism and racism in hockey. For an appreciative yet critical analysis of *Indian Horse*, see McKegney and Phillips (2018), "Decolonizing the Hockey Novel."

References

Baruchel, J. (Director). (2017). *Goon: Last of the enforcers* [Motion picture]. Canada: No Trace Camping/Caramel Films.

Bernstein, R. (2006). *The code: The unwritten rules of fighting and retaliation in the NHL*. Chicago: Triumph Books.

Berry, M. (2002). Interview with Lynn Coady. In M. Berry & N. Caple (Eds.), *The notebooks* (pp. 73–89). Toronto: Anchor Canada.

Blake, J. (2010). *Canadian hockey literature: A thematic study*. Toronto: University of Toronto Press.

Bombay, A., Matheson, K., & Anisman, H. (2009). Intergenerational trauma: Convergence of multiple processes across First Nations people in Canada. *Journal of Aboriginal Health, 5*(3), 6–47.

Bombay, A., Matheson, K., & Anisman, H. (2014). The intergenerational effects of Indian Residential Schools: Implications for the concept of historical trauma. *Transcultural Psychiatry, 51*, 320–338.

Boyle, E. (2014). Requiem for a "tough guy": Representing hockey labor, violence and masculinity in *Goon. Sociology of Sport Journal, 31*, 327–348.

Branch, J. (2011, December 5). Derek Boogaard: A brain "going bad." *The New York Times.* http://www.nytimes.com/2011/12/06/sports/hockey/derek-boogaard-a-brain-going-bad.html?pagewanted=all&_r=0

Branch, J. (2014). *Boy on ice: The life and death of Derek Boogaard.* Toronto: HarperCollins.

Buma, M. (2012). *Refereeing identity: The cultural work of Canadian hockey novels.* Montreal: McGill-Queen's University Press.

Burdekin, R.C.K., & Grindon Morton, M. (2015). Blood money: Violence for hire in the National Hockey League. *International Journal of Sport Finance, 10*, 328–356.

Campbell, K. (2014, December 8). Fighting for a job. *The Hockey News, 68*(10–11), 36–39.

Canadian Press. (2011, August 16). NHLer Rick Rypien found dead. *CBC Sports.* http://www.cbc.ca/sports/hockey/nhler-rick-rypien-found-dead-1.1086034.

Cardinal, W. (2008). *First Nations hockey players.* Stony Plain, AB: Eschia Books.

CBC Books. (2017, July 25). Jeff Lemire. https://www.cbc.ca/books/jeff-lemire-1.4723264

Coady, L. (1998). *Strange heaven.* Fredericton, NB: Goose Lane Editions.

Coady, L. (2000). *Play the monster blind.* Toronto: Doubleday Canada.

Coady, L. (2002). *Saints of Big Harbour.* Toronto: Anchor Canada.

Coady, L. (2006). *Mean boy.* Toronto: Doubleday Canada.

Coady, L. (2011). *The antagonist.* Toronto: House of Anansi Press.

Coburn, K. (1985). Honour, ritual and violence in ice hockey. *Canadian Journal of Sociology, 10*, 153–170.

Del Mundo, R. (2016). *Hockey's enforcers: A dying breed.* Toronto: Moydart Press.

Domi, T., with Lang, J. (2015). *Shift work.* Toronto: Simon & Schuster.

Dopp, J. (2018). Hockey, Zen, and the art of Bill Gaston's *The Good Body.* In A. Abdou & J. Dopp (Eds.), *Writing the body in motion: A critical anthology on Canadian sport literature* (pp. 43–56). Edmonton, AB: Athabasca University Press.

Downie, G., & Lemire, J. (2016). *Secret path.* Toronto: Simon & Schuster.

Dowse, M. (Director). (2011). *Goon* [Motion picture]. United States: Myriad Pictures.

Dryden, K. (2017). *Game change: The life and death of Steve Montador and the future of hockey.* Toronto: Signal/McClelland & Stewart.

Fleming, J., & Ledogar, R.J. (2008). Resilience, an evolving concept: A review of literature relevant to Aboriginal research. *Pimatisiwin: A Journal of Aboriginal and Indigenous Community Health, 6*(2), 7–23.

Gaston, B. (2000). *The good body*. Dunvegan, ON: Cormorant Books.

Gibney, A. (Producer & Director). (2011). *The Last Gladiators* [Motion picture]. United States: Locomotion Pictures.

Goldschmeid, N., & Espindola, S. (2013). "I went to a fight the other night and a hockey game broke out": Is professional hockey fighting calculated or impulsive? *Sports Health: A Multidisciplinary Approach, 5*, 458–462.

Gruneau, R., & Whitson, D. (1993). *Hockey Night in Canada: Sport, identities and cultural politics*. Toronto: Garamond.

Harrison, D. (2011, September 1). Ex-NHLer Belak committed suicide: Sources. CBC *Sports*. http://www.cbc.ca/sports/hockey/ex-nhler-belak-committed-suicide-sources-1.1011307

HeavyRunner, I., & Marshall, K. (2003). "Miracle survivors": Promoting resilience in Indian students. *Tribal College Journal, 14*(4), 15–18.

Jacob, D., & Paziuk, G. (2016). The chance of a life: Jeff Lemire's *Essex County* trilogy, Canadian identity, and the mythos of hockey. *Canadian Review of Comparative Literature/Revue canadienne de littérature comparée, 43*(1), 75–56.

James, V., & Gallagher, J. (2015). *Black ice: The Val James story*. Toronto: ECW Press.

Jarman, M.A. (1997). *Salvage king, ya! A herky-jerky picaresque*. Vancouver: Anvil Press.

Kennedy, R. (2014, December 8). Fighting in the NHL. *The Hockey News, 68*(10–11), 30–35.

Laraque, G. (2011). *Georges Laraque: The story of the NHL's unlikeliest tough guy*. Toronto: Viking Press.

Lavoie, M. (2000). Economics and sport. In J. Coakley & E. Dunning (Eds.), *Handbook of sport studies* (pp.157–170). London, UK: Sage.

Lemire, J. (2009). *Essex County collected*. Atlanta, GA: Top Shelf Productions.

Lemire, J. (2012). *The underwater welder*. Atlanta, GA: Top Shelf Productions.

Lemire, J. (2016). *Sweet tooth: The deluxe edition* (Vols. 1–3). Burbank, CA: DC Vertigo. Originally published in serial 2009–2013.

Lemire, J. (2017). *Roughneck*. New York: Gallery 13.

MacDonald, C.A. (2014). Masculinity and sport revisited: A review of literature on hegemonic masculinity and men's ice hockey in Canada. *Canadian Graduate Journal of Sociology and Criminology, 3*(1), 95–112.

MacGregor, R. (1983). *The last season*. Markham, ON: Penguin.

Marks, D. (2008). *They call me chief: Warriors on ice, the story of Indians in the NHL*. Winnipeg, MB: J. Gordon Shillingford Publishing.

Martin, P. (2017). *La force d'y croire*: The literary battles of Georges Laraque. In A.C. Holman & J. Blake (Eds.), *The same but different: Hockey in Quebec* (pp. 209–236). Montreal: McGill-Queen's University Press.

McCarty, D., with Allen, K. (2013). *My last fight: The true story of a hockey rock star.* Chicago: Triumph Books.

McKegney, S., & Phillips, T.J. (2018). Decolonizing the hockey novel: Ambivalence and apotheosis in Richard Wagamese's *Indian horse*. In A. Abdou & J. Dopp (Eds.), *Writing the body in motion: A critical anthology on Canadian sport literature* (pp. 167–184). Edmonton, AB: Athabasca University Press.

Medley, M. (2017, April 21). The all-star (interview with Jeff Lemire). *The Globe and Mail.* https://www.theglobeandmail.com/arts/books-and-media/the-all-star-with-roughneck-jeff-lemire-shows-why-hes-one-of-canadas-beststorytellers/article34773902/

Menzies, P. (2010). Intergenerational trauma from a mental health perspective. *Native Social Work Journal, 7*, 63–85.

Mullins, K. (2014). Embodiment, time and the life review in Jeff Lemire's *Ghost Stories*. *English Studies in Canada, 40*(4), 29–54.

NHL. (2011, March 3). CTE found in Probert's brain tissue. https://www.nhl.com/news/cte-found-in-proberts-brain-tissue/c-554909

Nilan, C. (2013). *Fighting back: The Chris Nilan story.* Toronto: HarperCollins.

Oriard, M.V. (1982). *Dreaming of heroes: American sports fiction, 1868–1980.* Chicago: Nelson-Hall.

Probert, B., with McLellan Day, K. (2010). *Tough guy: My life on the edge.* Toronto: HarperCollins.

Proteau, A. (2011). *Fighting the good fight: Why on-ice violence is killing hockey.* Mississauga, ON: Wiley.

Reid, S. (2016). Meet Jeff Lemire: The next big thing. *Maclean's Magazine.* https://www.macleans.ca/culture/books/jeff-lemire-is-the-next-big-thing-in-comics/

Scott, J., with Cazaneuve, B. (2016). *A guy like me: Fighting to make the cut.* New York: Howard Books.

Semenko, D., with Tucker, L. (1989). *Looking out for number one.* Toronto: Stoddart.

Wagamese, R. (2012). *Indian horse.* Vancouver: Douglas & McIntyre.

Weinstein, M.D., Smith, D.S., & Wiesenthal, D.L. (1995). Masculinity and hockey violence. *Sex Roles, 33*, 831–847.

Afterword

COLIN D. HOWELL

IN VIRTUALLY EVERY ASPECT OF LIFE there are neutral zone traps, hegemonic structures built upon taken-for-granted assumptions of "normal practice" that regulate the process of change and limit the imagining of what might be. In short, the central issue is that of power—where social authority resides and who shapes processes of inclusion and accessibility. Each of the chapters in this volume address control, resistance, agency, and change within hockey, which is appropriate given that it is on the ice where the term *neutral zone trap* originated. Intended as more than just an academic exercise, this volume extends beyond both the academy and the rink and talks to the broader processes of social change occurring in our contemporary world. Divided into three sections: Challenging Hockey's Norms, Access and Support, and Masculinity and Sexuality, the chapters offer numerous examples of "agents of change" who have fought to make hockey more inclusive. Their experiences—rising "from the ice up," so to speak—extend our appreciation of how sport often connects to broader emancipatory and democratic impulses.

Many of the contributors to this volume have connected through the international Hockey Conferences, a series I established at Saint Mary's University in 2001. From the outset, these conferences were intended to connect the scholarly study of sport to those who involve themselves in the game as participants, practitioners, and organizers in the broader community. Indeed, as an indication of this marriage of theory and practice, what other event would urge academic participants to lace up their skates and take to the ice in a friendly game of shinny like the Hockey Conference does? Although advancing age and wobbly ankles make my participation more demanding every time, I have always appreciated the symbolic importance of these games in underscoring the intent to bring scholars together with other members of the community in a broader discourse about hockey's social meanings and value.

Of course, there have always been those—many of whom consider themselves progressives—who denigrate sport, dismissing it as frivolous at best and reactionary at worst. I have always considered this a naive and elitist assumption. Even a cursory investigation reveals that virtually any sport, hockey included, is deeply implicated in the social struggles of its time, and the chapters in this volume reinforce this conclusion. Whether we are speaking of the importance of the game to Indigenous Peoples in their struggle for respect, misconceptions about the value of U SPORTS hockey, or the struggles of members of the LGBTQI2S+ community in sport, the issue of empowerment and resistance comes through loud and clear. If volumes like this one achieve nothing more, giving a platform to those battling the neutral zone trap is an important contribution to the struggle for a more inclusive and accessible sporting culture. Thanks to the editors and all the contributors for being part of such a worthy cause.

Contributors

ANGIE ABDOU has published seven books and co-edited *Writing the Body in Motion*, a collection of essays on Canadian sport literature. *Booklist* declared her memoir, *Home Ice: Reflections of a Reluctant Hockey Mom*, "a must-read for parents with youngsters who play organized sports." Angie Abdou is an associate professor of creative writing at Athabasca University.

KIERAN BLOCK is a teacher, a former Paralympic sledge hockey (para hockey) player, a graduate of the Western Hockey League, and a former University of Alberta Golden Bear. He also survived a near-fatal cliff diving accident and wrote a book about it titled *The Ups and Downs of Almost Dying*.

CAMERON BRAES has a master's degree in sport and recreation studies. He successfully defended his thesis using a case study to explore the legitimacy of U SPORTS men's hockey member schools as a pathway to professional hockey. While completing his undergraduate and master's degrees, he played collegiate hockey at the University of New Brunswick, winning three national championships. Since graduating, he has continued to play hockey and is currently in his third season playing professionally in Europe.

WILLIAM BRIDEL is an associate professor in the Faculty of Kinesiology at the University of Calgary. His research includes work on LGBTQI2S+ inclusion in Canadian sport (funded by the Social Science and Humanities Research Council of Canada), bullying in the context of sport and recreation, and sport-related concussion. He is a member of the LGBTQI2S+ Sport Inclusion Task Force Coordinating Committee.

JUDY DAVIDSON is an associate professor in the Faculty of Kinesiology, Sport, and Recreation at the University of Alberta. Her research interests include queer and feminist approaches to sport and leisure phenomena. She has published on homonationalism, the international LGBT sport movement, and arena gentrification projects as forms of settler colonialism.

JONATHON R.J. EDWARDS is an associate professor in the Faculty of Kinesiology at the University of New Brunswick in Fredericton. He uses applied qualitative research methodologies to explore sport delivery systems through institutional theory, and has published in a variety of sport management journals, has spoken at a number of conferences, and has conducted research on behalf of national sport organizations. In 2016, he was the host of the Hockey Conference, which was held in Fredericton at UNB. He has a passion for studying the sport management side of the hockey industry.

CATHERINE HOUSTON is a PHD candidate in the Faculty of Kinesiology and Physical Education at the University of Toronto. Her research focuses on sport for development and peace, international relations, and the emergence of international sporting organizations within international development and humanitarian intervention.

COLIN D. HOWELL is Professor Emeritus in History and the recently retired academic director of the Centre for the Study of Sport and Health at Saint Mary's University in Halifax, Nova Scotia. One of Canada's foremost historians, his work focuses on the history of sport, medicine, and health in Canada.

CHELSEY LEAHY recently completed her MHK in sport management at the University of Windsor. She completed a BA in sociology with honours at St. Thomas University, where she focused her research on gender issues in university ice hockey. Her current research focuses on transgender-related policies in U SPORTS and the Canadian Collegiate Athletic Association.

ROGER G. LEBLANC is a French-speaking Acadian and father of a beautiful thirty-five-year-old daughter. He earned his doctorate degree from University of Otago, New Zealand, a master's degree from the Université de Montpellier, France, and his undergraduate degree from the Université de Moncton, New Brunswick. Currently, he is an associate professor at the Université de Moncton.

CHERYL A. MACDONALD is the associate director of outreach at the Saint Mary's University Centre for the Study of Sport & Health in Halifax, Nova Scotia. The Social Science and Humanities Research Council of Canada has funded her predominantly qualitative research. Her research has been informed by theories of masculinity and sport as they pertain to ice hockey. She has been a two-time host of the Hockey Conference, is a former contributor to the blog *Hockey in Society*, and has been featured on Sportsnet's *In Conversation* with Ron MacLean.

FRED MASON teaches sport sociology and the history of sport and recreation in kinesiology at the University of New Brunswick. His research varies across sport in literature, film, and various types of media. He was named University Teaching Scholar in 2018 at UNB, an honorary designation focused on the scholarship of teaching and learning.

BROCK MCGILLIS is an openly gay former professional hockey player. His career has brought him to the Ontario Hockey League, East Coast Hockey League, U SPORTS, and the Holland Premier League. He holds a communications degree from Laurentian University and now works as a public speaker. His story has been featured in mainstream media sources such as CBC's *The National*, CTV's *Your Morning*, and Sportsnet's *In Conversation* with Ron MacLean.

VICKY PARASCHAK is a professor in kinesiology at the University of Windsor. Drawing upon a strengths-and-hope perspective, her research focuses on Indigenous Peoples' engagement in physical activity broadly understood. As a non-Indigenous ally, she values the opportunity to be co-transformed while documenting individual- and community-based Indigenous strengths.

BRETT PARDY is a PHD candidate at McGill University and an instructor at the University of the Fraser Valley. When he is not waiting for the Vancouver Canucks to be good, he is interested in the intersection of critical theories of media with sport and both popular and transnational cinemas.

ANN PEGORARO is the Lang Chair in Sport Management at the University of Guelph and co-director of E-Alliance, the National Research Network for Gender Equity in Sport. Her research focuses on digital media, gender, and diversity in sport.

KYLE RICH is an assistant professor in the Department of Recreation and Leisure Studies at Brock University. His research focuses on community sport and recreation policy, rural community development, and social inclusion in the context of sport and recreation.

TAVIS SMITH is a PHD candidate in the Faculty of Kinesiology and Physical Education at the University of Toronto. He focuses his research and teaching on questions of social change, relationships, and sustainability, specifically in hockey and informal/lifestyle sport.

NOAH UNDERWOOD is a graduate student at the University of Alberta in the Faculty of Kinesiology, Sport, and Recreation. His research interests include examining social and political resistance(s) prevalent within online sporting communities.

Other Titles from University of Alberta Press

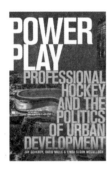

Power Play
Professional Hockey and the Politics of Urban Development
JAY SCHERER, DAVID MILLS & LINDA SLOAN MCCULLOCH

Big money and municipal politics collide in the story of Edmonton's Rogers Place hockey arena.

Game Plan
A Social History of Sport in Alberta
KAREN L. WALL

Patterns and layers of sport history emerge as almost-forgotten stories of Alberta's marginalized populations surface.

Taking the Lead
Strategies and Solutions from Female Coaches
Edited by SHEILA ROBERTSON

A deep look at female coaching—its values and tribulations—by leaders in the field.

More information at uap.ualberta.ca